JEWISH
PHILOSOPHERS

JEWISH PHILOSOPHERS

Edited by STEVEN T. KATZ

BLOCH PUBLISHING COMPANY
New York

Published in the Western Hemisphere by
BLOCH PUBLISHING COMPANY
915 Broadway, New York, N.Y. 10010

SBN 0–8197–0010–X
Library of Congress Catalog Card Number 75–7590

Set, printed and bound by Keterpress Enterprises, Jerusalem
Printed in Israel

CONTENTS

GENERAL INTRODUCTION

In this work an attempt has been made to supply the reader with a broad, intelligible, yet reasonably detailed conspectus of the results of the dialectic between Judaism and philosophy which has produced the hybrid known as Jewish Philosophy. We have supplied a survey of Jewish philosophy from the time of its initial encounter with external philosophical thought in the Hellenistic world, which produced the remarkable figure of Philo, through the early and later medieval period when Judaism re-encountered philosophy in Islamic and Christian forms, and up through the modern period when Jewish thought was liberated along with western thought generally from the limits of the medieval world-view and shared in the consequences of this emancipation. The work finishes in the contemporary period with a survey of the most significant issues in Jewish philosophy since World War II. If one follows the evolution of Jewish thought one will see how each generation builds upon and develops the thought of its predecessors, and how the Jews of today are the heirs of a rich and important intellectual tradition. Furthermore, this philosophical tradition helps us, whatever our own theological and philosophical commitments, to understand Judaism in its various modern guises.

The specific issues and personalities which play the dominant role in the development of this subject are dealt with in the main body of this work. Three general issues, however, need to be appreciated in order to gain an accurate understanding of Jewish philosophy as a whole. The first is its authentic Jewishness; the second is the nature of its encounter and fundamental relation with non-Jewish thought; and the third is the essential character of medieval and modern thought respectively and the differences between them.

(1) Although, with the exception perhaps of Philo, Jews were not the originators of any philosophical movements, Jewish philosophers,

in their treatment and adaptation of conceptual problems suggested by non-Jews, teach a great deal about Judaism and Jewish self-understanding. In their disagreements over the exact boundaries of faith and reason, in their evaluation of the authority of the Greek and German philosophical giants, in the faith commitments which effect one's whole systematic program, in the seemingly minor but all-important differences in their understanding of the idea and activity of God, they help us to see deep into the recesses of the Judaic spirit. For example, Maimonides' preference for the biblical account of creation rather than the theory advanced in Aristotle's metaphysics tells us something very important about the character of Maimonides' religion and its God. The biblical account of creation depicts a loving God possessed of a moral personality who cares for His creatures and would enter into relation with them. The biblical account suggests a God who possesses and exercises a loving will. This conception of God is the essential factor in Jewish life and Maimonides' discussion helps us to understand how and why this is, and what it really means.

Another example is found in the general optimism and activism of Buber's philosophy of dialogue which, drawn as it is from Jewish sources, stands in opposition to the passivity and negativism of his fellow existentialists. His account gives an insight into the biblical anthropology which sees man as a majestic being created by God to be his partner (shuttaf) in the work of creation. It helps us to fill out the meaning of human existence and to understand better the Jewish insistence on seeing man as God's co-worker. This anthropological view distinguishes Judaism from both Christianity and Islam and must be appreciated if Judaism is to be rightly understood.

Within the tradition of Jewish thought the most important thing has always been halakhic (religious law) activity. This legal tradition however is enriched by philosophy as it is by poetry, for these products of the Hebraic spirit, different as they are from one another, emerge from a common ground and reflect in their diversity the multi-faceted variety of Judaism. Authentic Jewish spiritual creativity is not limited to one or the other category but finds expression in all these different ways. Thus it is the rule rather than the exception that the major contributors to the philosophic tradition have also been major contributors to the halakhic tradition, and very often the poetic tradition as well.

Saadyah Gaon, Maimonides and Crescas are paradigms of the former; Ibn Gabirol and Judah Halevi of the latter.

(2) With regard to Jewish philosophy's relation with non-Jewish thought, it must be remembered that throughout its long history Judaism has never existed in either a socio-political or intellectual vacuum. In both Eretz Israel (the Land of Israel) and the diaspora Judaism has found itself involved in a successive series of cultural relations (for example, with Hellenistic and Roman civilization, Islamic and Christian societies, and today's largely secular and technological era) in the midst of which it has had to define and defend itself. Judaism has had to develop and maintain its identity as a religious civilization centering around a Divinely revealed religious law and tradition (the Torah and Halakhah) against a background of alternative cultures, different religious communities, and alien forms of life. During this process of self-definition Judaism has not been hermetically insulated. This cultural inter-action has produced myriad effects, not least of which has been the emergence and sustainment of an identifiable and unique Jewish philosophical tradition.

As part of the dialogue between Judaism and its environment Judaism twice encountered and was challenged by Greek philosophy. The first meeting was during the Hellenistic and Rabbinic period (3rd century B.C.E. to 5th century C.E.). With the exception of Philo no major crossfertilization resulted in this initial encounter. The Rabbis purposefully, and largely with success, rejected Greek philosophical speculation as "foreign wisdom." Given the threat of a vibrant Hellenism to Jewish life in Palestine and the Roman diaspora, this was prudent counsel. Within the boundaries of Islamic civilization (8th century onward) there was a second confrontation. This time however Greek thought was no longer part of a dynamic and imperialistic culture which threatened to overwhelm Judaism; instead, it lived on only in passive texts. Furthermore, it had already been at least partially domesticated by Christian and Islamic thinkers who showed that some rapprochement between religious faith and philosophy was not only possible but in many ways desirable. As a result of the different nature of this second meeting and the new social conditions which surrounded it, Jewish thinkers began to feel the need to engage in philosophical activity even though it was not *necessarily* part of Judaic self-consciousness. Initially, Jews began to philosophize as a result of the polemical requirement to defend Judaism against various charges levelled against it by philosophically trained Islamic and Christian thinkers. For example, Islamic thinkers argued that the richness of biblical language about God was anthropomorphic and hence improper in respect of a true monotheistic expression of faith. Jews had to develop philosophical arguments about biblical language (e.g., that biblical language was only allegorical) in order to reject the charge of anthromorphism. Later, Jews began to creatively develop philosophical arguments as a way of giving expression to Judaism's deepest convictions and as a means of articulating the profoundest elements of Judaism's own self-consciousness. Philosophy was transformed from a threatening "foreign wisdom" to the "handmaiden of theology," as the famous medieval phrase describes it. In the modern period the relationship between philosophy and theology has changed radically but the inseparability of philosophy and theology remains. Modern Jewish man enriches his philosophical awareness through his faith and enriches and clarifies his faith through his philosophical concerns.

As a result of its cultural involvement Jewish philosophy has naturally shared many of the broad intellectual and religious values, metaphysical assumptions, and logical notions present in a given time and environment. In addition to this shared conceptual scheme, Jews also shared in the medieval economic and political structures and the general social milieu of their Christian and Islamic neighbors in the same way as they share in the very different common socio-economic and political structures of modern life. In both periods Jewish thought cannot help but reflect these non-philosophical influences. The strength of Jewish philosophy lies in its ability meaningfully to absorb and where necessary re-fashion the common elements which it shares with non-Jewish thought.

(3) The medieval synthesis was based on the assumption that God was the source of all truth and therefore philosophy and theology could not differ in the truth they taught, only the form and presentation of the truth could differ. Moreover, the understanding of the nature of this truth was generated from theological values. Theology suggested the issues and the limits of medieval thought. It dictated what conclusions could not be reached. Theological criteria were the most important criteria and the standard against which all conclusions had to be measured. Jewish, Christian, and Islamic thinkers, with few exceptions, shared these views. Furthermore, Jews shared with their neighbors the

basic conception of "rationality" operative in the medieval period, i.e., that it was "rational" to accept "valid tradition" as a source of authentic knowledge. Both in philosophy and religion, authority was a main factor in ascertaining truth. Though major strides were made in the medieval period, especially in the study of logic, there was no dissenting from the agreed premise that the foundation of all wisdom came from tradition, i.e., the Bible and religious tradition on the one hand, and the Greek philosophers, especially Plato and Aristotle, on the other.

In the modern period the basic structure of the medieval synthesis came apart—indeed "modernity" is made possible only by its dissolution. The idea of God as the author of all truth, with its corollary that philosophy and religion were similar in content if not in form, was rejected. In its place a new inquisitiveness sought to define the precise nature and function of religion and philosophy. The assumption of parallelism and complementariness between the two was rejected and replaced by the very different pre-supposition that religion and philosophy were different in both their methods and their subject matter. Even more significant was the re-appraisal of the value of religion. Whereas in the medieval period it was the supreme science to which all other studies were ancilliary and supportive, in the modern period the scientific re-appraisal of the world undermined religion's place in the hierarchy, and science became both independent of and if not superior at least equal to religion. Logical and scientific criteria replaced theological ones as the source of value and correctness. The conception of "rationality" itself was revolutionized. No longer was it "rational" to accept claims based on authority—it mattered not whether the tradition cited was philosophical, scientific, or religious. Now to be "rational" meant to question authority. An aggressive empiricism and experimentalism was let loose whose implications still govern our conceptual schema and to which we are all heirs. Modern Jewish thought participates in this new way of looking at the world.

The medieval Jewish philosophers were fond of arguing that the revelation at Sinai was an undeniable historical fact. The Bible tells us that it was witnessed by 600,000 Israelites and therefore what could be more certain than this biblical tradition. These thinkers never realized that such biblical testimony was no evidence at all to the uncommitted for its acceptance was based on a prior belief in Scripture and thus the argument was circular: "Why do you believe in the Biblical revelation at

Sinai?" "Because 600,000 Israelites witnessed it!" "How do you know 600,000 Israelites witnessed it?" "Because the Bible tells me so!"

Alternatively, the modern Jewish thinker accepts very little on the basis of tradition. Instead, he seeks justification of his belief, struggling to show its rationality, or he rejects all justification in a "leap of faith" which overcomes tradition and philosophy together. In both situations, the modern Jewish thinker starts by questioning the normativeness of *halakhah* and biblical revelation. The tension of modern thought emerges just here: the modern Jew wants to believe in the God of Abraham—not only because Abraham did but because he has found a way to make this belief meaningful to himself. The whole question of the Torah's legitimacy and authority is an issue. The final decision of the issue is to be judged by those same canons and criteria that govern other areas of modern concern. The religious life is not isolated and sacrosanct; it must come into the open marketplace of ideas and prove its worth in the full exposure of critical investigation. It may well be, as Hermann Cohen reminded us and the majority of Jewish thinkers since have echoed, that the methods of philosophy and human conceptual enterprises generally do not appropriately apply to religion. If, however, they do not, then this too must be argued for on the generally accepted criterion of modern rationality. No return to a pre-modern synthesis based on Scripture and the unquestioned testimony of religious worthies is seen to be legitimate.

The present work is divided chronologically into several sections. Part One, Two and Three are primarily drawn from articles prepared for the *Encyclopaedia Judaica* (Jerusalem, 1972), whose Philosophy section was edited by Prof. Arthur Hyman. Many articles have been substantially revised to accord with the scope of the present work. The names of the authors of the original articles will be found after this Introduction. Part Four was written specifically for this volume. A special effort has been made to explain the underlying concepts and major implications of ideas, as well as to indicate the significance of particular philosophers and schools of philosophy.

The major philosophers of the Jewish tradition are discussed individually in depth. It is hoped that these individual studies are sufficiently detailed to allow the reader to gain a full grasp of the thinkers' major ideas and philosophical importance. These individual studies presented a problem as to what to include in each. For medieval thinkers, though it is almost equally true of "moderns" like Mendelssohn, Krochmal, and Buber, philosophy meant almost the whole range of human knowledge. Thus they showed an interest not only in philosophy narrowly defined but also in mathematics, astronomy, poetry, biblical studies, halakhic codification, liturgical creations, grammatical investigations, and the list continues. Therefore, in order to understand the philosophical essence of a thinker's work it was felt necessary that his whole intellectual concern be represented. For example, in the case of Solomon Ibn Gabirol and Judah Halevi we have included an analysis and review of their poetry as no full appreciation of their thought can be gained without some understanding of their poems. In the case of Maimonides his philosophical work is only fully understood and appreciated in relation to his work as a great student of the *halakhah*. Mendelssohn's *Jerusalem* is intelligible only against the background of his role in the struggle for Jewish emancipation in late 18th century German, while Buber's thought makes sense only if we appreciate the malaise of Jewish intellectuals in the early part of the 20th century and Buber's escape from it through Zionism and then Ḥasidism.

Part Four gives a general survey of contemporary Jewish thought since 1945. The Nazi Holocaust and the re-establishment of a Jewish state have presented Jewish thinkers with two enormous issues of revolutionary import. Various responses to these two events, as well as some related topics, are considered. In order to give the reader a synoptic over-view of the significant developments in recent Jewish thought it was felt that the most effective way of presenting this material would be to organize it around major themes rather than individual thinkers. Philosophers, however, do not always fit into convenient niches and therefore in a number of instances the topical approach has had to give way to individual studies of particular thinkers.

It is hoped that this book will serve, among other purposes, as an introductory work for those seeking to learn the history of Jewish philosophy. With this audience in mind special care has been taken in the preparation of the Glossary, Biographical Index, and Bibliography. The Glossary contains religious and philosophical terms in Hebrew and English, as well as a few terms in other languages, which it was felt would be unknown to readers at an introductory and intermediate level. The Biographical Index which is found at the end of this work lists the majority of the thinkers discussed in this volume so that the reader can easily gain some basic idea of who someone is, to what historical period he belongs, and the philosophical and theological tradition from which he emerges. The bibliography has been prepared to provide the reader with a starting point for future research.

* * *

The material in this book is based for the most part on entries that appeared in the *Encyclopaedia Judaica*. These include the general entry Jewish Philosophy by Prof. Arthur Hyman; Philo, by Dr. Yehoshua Amir; Saadiah Gaon, by Prof. A.S. Halkin; Neoplatonism, by Prof. Joel Kraemer; Solomon ibn Gabirol, by Prof. Shlomo Pines and editorial staff; Baḥya ibn Paquda, by Prof. Georges Vajda; Judah Halevi, by editorial staff; Aristotelianism, by Prof. Alexander Altmann; Isaac Israeli, by editorial staff; Maimonides, by Prof. L.I. Rabinowitz, Prof. J.I. Dienstag and Prof. Arthur Hyman; Levi ben Gershom, by Prof. B.R. Goldstein; Ḥasdai Crescas, by Prof. Warren Zev Harvey; Joseph Albo, by Prof. Alexander Altmann; Spinoza, by Prof. R.H. Popkin and Prof. R. Smend; Moses Mendelssohn, by Dr. Alfred Jospe and Dr. Leni Yahil; Nachman Krochmal, by Prof. Moshe Schwartz; Hermann Cohen, by Prof. S.H. Bergman; Leo Baeck, by Prof. A.E. Simon; Abraham Isaac Kook, by Zvi Yaron; Franz Rosenzweig, by Prof. S.S. Schwarzschild; Martin Buber, by Prof. S.H. Bergman and Prof. M. Friedman; Mordecai Menahem Kaplan, by Dr. J.J. Cohen. The introduction and last section of this book have been specially written by Prof. Steven T. Katz.

Part One

ANCIENT PERIOD

INTRODUCTION

Jewish philosophy may be described as the explication of Jewish beliefs and practices by means of general philosophic concepts and norms. Hence it must be seen as an outgrowth of the biblical and rabbinic traditions on which Judaism rests as well as part of the history of philosophy at large. This description must, however, be expanded to include the general philosophic literature in Hebrew produced by Jews in the latter part of the Middle Ages and the various secular philosophies of Jewish existence formulated by modern Jewish thinkers. General philosophers who happened to be Jews or of Jewish extraction are not considered part of the tradition of Jewish philosophy. Whereas the biblical and rabbinic traditions were indigenous products of the Jewish community, Jewish philosophy arose and flourished as Jews participated in the philosophic speculations of the external culture.

Significant religious and philosophical differences distinguish ancient and medieval from much of modern Jewish thought; nevertheless, the subject matter of Jewish philosophy may be divided into three parts. First, as interpretation of unique aspects of Jewish tradition, Jewish philosophy deals with such topics as the election of Israel; the revelation, content, and eternity of the Torah; the special character of the prophecy of Moses; and Jewish conceptions of the Messiah and the afterlife. Second, as philosophy of religion, it investigates issues common to Judaism, Christianity, and Islam (as well as to certain kinds of metaphysics), such as the existence of God, divine attributes, the creation of the world, the phenomenon of prophecy, the human soul, and general principles of human conduct. Third, as philosophy proper, it studies topics of general philosophic interest, such as the logical categories, the structure of logical arguments, the division of being, and the nature and composition of the universe. Historically, Jewish philosophy may be divided into three periods: (1) its early development in the Diaspora community of the Hellenistic world, from the second century B.C.E. until the middle of the first century C.E.; (2) its flourishing in Islamic and Christian countries during the Middle Ages from the tenth until the early 16th century; and (3) its modern phase beginning in the 18th century and continuing to the present. Its prehistory, however, begins with the Bible.

BIBLICAL AND RABBINIC
ANTECEDENTS

Although the Bible and the rabbinic literature contain definite views about God, man, and the world, these views are presented unsystematically, without a technical vocabulary, and without formal arguments in their support. Hence, it is more appropriate to speak of biblical and rabbinic theology rather than philosophy. Nevertheless, Jewish philosophers of all periods held that their opinions were rooted in the Bible and the rabbinic writings, and they quote these literatures extensively in support of their views. Interestingly, quotations from the Bible far outnumber those from the rabbinic writings, so that one may speak of a certain "Bible-centeredness" of Jewish philosophy. In quoting the Bible, Jewish philosophers often imposed a philosophic rigor on its vocabulary and thought that is not immediately apparent from the literal reading of the text. However, besides quoting the Bible, certain philosophers also had a theory concerning the nature of this document. Aware that the world view of the Bible is rather simple and unphilosophical, they found it difficult to accept that the Bible lacked philosophical sophistication. If God created man with reason, the discoveries of the human mind must be related in some fashion to the content of divine revelation. Hence, they viewed the Bible as twofold: on its literal level it was addressed to philosophers and non-philosophers alike, and thus it had to speak in a manner intelligible to all; but behind its rather simple exterior it contained a more profound meaning, which philosophers could discover by proper interpretation. This esoteric content is identical, fully or in part, with the teachings of philosophy. In assuming this methodological principle, Jewish philosophers resembled Jewish mystics, who discovered secret mystical teachings behind the literal biblical text. We may now examine some representative biblical passages which Jewish philosophers cited to support their views.[1]

5

BIBLE

Of verses concerning God that were cited by Jewish philosophers, perhaps the central one was "Hear, O Israel: the Lord our God, the Lord is one" (Deut. 6:4), which was held to refer to God's uniqueness as well as to His simplicity. The opening of the Decalogue—"I am the Lord thy God" (Ex. 20:2, Deut. 5:6)—was understood as a declaration of God's existence, and, by some, even as a positive commandment requiring the affirmation of the existence of God. God's omnipotence was indicated by the verse: "I know that Thou canst do all things, and that no purpose of Thine can be thwarted" (Job 42:2), and His omniscience, by the verse: "His discernment is past searching out" (Isa. 40:28). That God is incorporeal was derived from the verses: ".. for ye saw no manner of form" (Deut. 4:15) and "To whom then will ye liken Me, that I should be equal?" (Isa. 40:25), and that His essence is identical with His existence, from the verse: "I am that I am" (Ex. 3:14). How God can be known was derived from a story concerning Moses. Moses had asked God to show him His ways and then he had requested that He show him His glory. God granted Moses the first of these requests, but denied him the second (Ex. 33:12ff.). This story was interpreted to mean that God's glory, that is, His essence, cannot be known by man, but His ways, that is, His actions, can be known.

Of passages and verses concerning the universe, the creation chapters (Gen. 1–2) were interpreted as stating that the world was created out of nothing and in time. The creation of the universe was also derived from the verses: "I have made the earth, and created man upon it; I, even My hands, have stretched out the heavens, and all their hosts have I commanded" (Isa. 45:12) and "It is He that hath made us, and we are His" (Ps. 100:3). That the celestial spheres are animate and rational was deduced from the verse: "The heavens declare the glory of God" (Ps. 19:2), and the verse: "The sun also arises, and the sun goes down, and hastens to his place where he arises" (Eccles. 1:5) was seen as a description of the daily motion of the uppermost celestial sphere, which produces day and night. That the heavens and the earth are finite was derived from the verses: " ... from the one end of the earth even unto the other end of the earth" (Deut. 13:8) and " . . . from the one end of heaven unto the other . . . " (Deut. 4:32).

From four terms appearing in Genesis 1:2 it was deduced that the sublunar world consists of the four elements: earth *(erez)*, air *(ru'ah)*, water *(mayim)*, and fire *(hoshekh*—ordinarily darkness, but here interpreted as fire). Reference to the composition of these four elements of matter and form and to the succession of forms in matter was seen in the verses: "Then I went down to the potter's house, and, behold, he was at his work on the wheels. And whensoever the vessel that he made of clay was marred in the hand of the potter, he made it again another vessel, as seemed good to the potter to make it" (Jer. 18:3–4). Somewhat more fancifully, Abraham and Sarah, respectively, were identified with form and matter.

Other verses provided a description of human nature. The verses: "See, I have set before thee this day life and good, and death and evil . . . therefore choose life, that thou mayest live . . . " (Deut. 30: 15–19) were frequently quoted in support of the notion that man possesses freedom of choice. That man's essential nature is his reason was derived from the verse: "Let us make man in our image . . . " (Gen. 1:26), and that wisdom distinguishes him from other creatures, from the verse: "He that teaches man knowledge" (Ps. 94:10). That man has five senses is indicated by the verses "They have mouths, but they speak not; Eyes have they, but they see not: They have ears, but they hear not; Noses have they, but they smell not; They have hands, but they handle not . . . " (Ps. 115:5–7). "For the life of the flesh is in the blood . . . " (Lev. 17:11) refers to the nutritive faculty of the human soul, and "Notwithstanding thou mayest kill and eat flesh within all thy gates, after all the desire of thy soul . . ." (Deut. 12:15), to the appetitive.

Some interpreted that man's ultimate goal in life is to understand God from the verses: "Know this day, and lay it to thy heart, that the Lord, He is God in heaven above and upon the earth beneath . . . " (Deut. 4:39) and "Know ye that the Lord He is God" (Ps. 100:3); but others invoked the verse "And thou shalt love the Lord thy God . . ." (Deut. 6:5) to show that man's final goal is the love of God. That man should be modest in his conduct is indicated by the verse: "The righteous eateth to the satisfying of his desire . . ." (Prov. 13:25), and that the middle way is the best is shown by the verse: ". . . and thou shalt walk in His ways" (Deut. 28:9). While many other verses and passages were cited in support of these and other teachings, Jewish philosophers were also interested in whole chapters and complete biblical books. The theophany in Isaiah 6 and the account of the divine chariot in Ezekiel 1 and 10 were used as descriptions of God and the angelic realm. Of special interest were the more philosophical books of the Bible, including Proverbs, Job, Song of Songs, and Ecclesiastes, on which numerous philosophical commentaries were written, especially in the late Middle Ages.

RABBINIC LITERATURE

Since the Greek philosophers had appeared by the time the rabbis of the Talmud formulated their teachings, it may be asked whether the rabbinic literature reveals any Greek philosophical influence. While the rabbis had some acquaintance with Greek philosophical ideas, particularly with those of the Stoics (in popular versions), it has now been shown that the rabbis were not familiar with formal philosophy.[2] The names of the major philosophers are absent from the rabbinic writings, and the only philosophers mentioned by name are Epicurus and the obscure, second-century cynic Oenomaus of Gadara. In the tannaitic literature the term "Epicurean" (apikoros) is used, but it seems to refer to a heretic in general rather than someone who embraces Epicurus' doctrines.

H. A. Wolfson, the modern historian of philosophy, stated that he was unable to discover a single Greek philosophic term in rabbinic literature.[3] Jewish philosophers cited rabbinic sayings, as they did biblical quotations, for support of their views, once again imposing a philosophic rigor that the sources, on literal reading, lacked. To indicate that attributes describing God in human terms must be interpreted allegorically, philosophers invoked the saying: "The Torah speaks in the language of man" (Yev. 71a; BM 31b). How circumspect one must be in describing God is shown in the following story:

> Someone reading prayers in the presence of Rabbi Ḥanina said "God, the great, the valiant and the tremendous, the power-ful, the strong, and the mighty." Rabbi Ḥanina said to him, "Have

you finished all the praises of your Master? The three epithets 'the great, the valiant, and the tremendous,' we should not have applied to God, had Moses not mentioned them in the Law, and had not the men of the Great Synagogue followed and established their use in prayer; and you say all this. Let this be illustrated by a parable. There once was an earthly king who possessed millions of gold coins; but he was praised for owning millions of silver coins. Was this not really an insult to him?" (Ber. 33b).

To show that the substance of the heavens differs from that of sublunar beings the philosophers cited R. Eliezer's saying: "The things in the heavens have been created of the heavens, the things on earth of the earth" (Gen. R. 12:11). Similarly, that the heavens are animate beings was derived from a passage in *Genesis Rabbah* (2:2) which states in part " ... the earth mourned and cried on account of her evil lot saying, 'I and the heavens were created together, and yet the beings above live forever, and we are mortal.'" The saying "The world follows its customary order" (Av. Zar. 54b) was taken as confirmation that a natural order exists in the world.

Other rabbinic sayings deal with human nature. The saying: "All is in the hands of heaven except the fear of heaven" (Ber. 33b; Nid. 16b) is interpreted to mean that while certain natural dispositions are fixed in man, his actions are free. That there is a correlation between what man does and the fate he suffers is supported by the sayings: "There is no death without sin, and no sufferings without transgression" (Shab. 55a) and "A man is measured with the measure he uses himself" (Sot. 1:7). The spiritual nature of the afterlife is taught in the saying of Rav: "In the World to Come, there is no eating, no drinking, no washing, no anointing, no sexual relations, but the righteous sit, their crowns on their heads, and enjoy the radiance of the *Shekhinah*" (Ber. 17a). Many other citations could be added to this list.

Of special interest are two esoteric rabbinic doctrines known respectively as "the account of creation" *(ma'aseh bereshit)* and "the account of the divine chariot" *(ma'aseh merkavah)*. While it is clear that, historically speaking, these two doctrines were forms of Jewish gnosticism,[4] philosophers saw in them philosophical truths. Maimonides goes so far as to identify *ma'aseh bereshit* with physics and *ma'aseh merkavah* with metaphysics, holding that the rabbis were conversant with philosophic doctrines but presented them enigmatically.

HELLENISTIC JEWISH PHILOSOPHY

Jewish philosophy began, as has been noted, in the Diaspora community of the Hellenistic world during the second century B.C.E. and continued there until the middle of the first century C.E. It arose out of the confrontation between the Jewish religion and Greek philosophy (particularly the Stoic-Platonic tradition) and had as its aim the philosophic interpretation of Judaism. It also had an apologetic purpose: to show that Judaism is a kind of philosophy, whose conception of God is spiritual and whose ethics is rational. Jewish philosophers polemicized against the polytheism of other religions and against pagan practices. In spite of their philosophic interests they maintained that Judaism is superior to philosophy.[5] Philo of Alexandria is the only Jewish Hellenistic philosopher from whom a body of works has survived; all the other materials are either fragmentary or only allude to philosophic or theological topics. The dating of these other materials also presents considerable difficulties. The language of Hellenistic Jewish philosophy was Greek. Jewish Hellenistic culture may be said to have begun with the Septuagint, the Greek translation of the Bible. The translation of the Pentateuch[6] dates from the third century B.C.E. Some scholars have held that this translation already manifests philosophic influences.

The first Jewish philosopher appears to have been Aristobulus of Paneas (middle of second century B.C.E.), who wrote a commentary on the Pentateuch, fragments of which have been preserved by Christian Church Fathers. He argues that Greek philosophers and poets derived their teachings from the wisdom of Moses, and he interpreted the Bible allegorically. He held, for example, that the expression "hand of God" refers to God's power. He maintained that wisdom (the Torah) existed prior to heaven and earth and that God's power extends through all things. He gives a symbolic interpretation of the Sabbath

10

and comments on the symbolic character of the number "seven." The Letter of Aristeas,[7] a pseudepigraphic account of the history of the Greek translation of the Bible, which incidentally polemicizes against paganism, states that God's power is manifested throughout the world, praises the mean as the best course of action, holds that the help of God is necessary for the performance of good deeds, and advocates the control of passions. The author also presents moral interpretations of the ritual laws, holding that such laws are designed to teach man righteousness, holiness, and perfection of character.

II Maccabees[8] mentions cryptically resurrection and creation out of nothing. IV Maccabees, evidently written by someone familiar with Greek philosophy, particularly with the teachings of the first-century B.C.E. Stoic Posidonius, maintains that reason can control the passions, illustrating this theme through examples from Jewish history. The author cites the Stoic definition of wisdom and identifies wisdom with the Law. The Sibylline Oracles (in their extant form a combination of Jewish and Christian teachings) denounce paganism and mention the resurrection and the messianic age. The Wisdom of Solomon, which is patterned after Hebrew Wisdom Literature, contains occasional philosophic terms and arguments. The work polemicizes against idolatry, holding that it is a source of immoral practices. H.A. Wolfson[9] maintains that the author's conception of wisdom is the same as Philo's conception of the logos (see below), although others have argued that the two conceptions are different. According to this work, wisdom first existed as an attribute of God, then as an independent being created by God prior to the creation of the world, and, finally, as immanent in the world. God created the world out of formless matter. Man can love righteousness, God, and wisdom, and the love of wisdom is manifested in the observance of the Law. The attainment of wisdom also requires the help of God. The righteous are rewarded with immortality, while the wicked shall perish.

PHILO JUDAEUS

Philo is the most important figure in Jewish Hellenism and has been credited with being the father of what was to become the medieval philosophical tradition. The only known date of Philo's life is 40 C.E., when as an elderly man he headed a delegation of the Jewish community of Alexandria to the Roman emperor Gaius Caligula. He belonged to the noblest family of Alexandrian Jewry, which had connections with the Herodian dynasty and the Roman court. Whereas his brother, the high official and rich banker Alexander, is known through Josephus, and his nephew, Alexander's son, Tiberius Julius Alexander, is a well-known historical personality, there is only scanty information about Philo's life. His works are written in an exceedingly rich Greek, and show great erudition in classical literature and both classical and contemporary philosophy, a thorough training in the art of rhetoric, and a broad knowledge of general science. Philo must have obtained this education in Greek schools. Everything that has been inferred as to the sources of his Jewish knowledge remains highly hypothetical. It is very doubtful that he had any knowledge of Hebrew,[10] there being certain indications that he drew his Hebrew etymologies, which he used in his allegorical interpretations, from onomastica (lists of Hebrew names with Greek translations). It is clear that he grew up in a house devoted to Jewish faith and tradition. He may have acquired his very intimate familiarity with the Septuagint (Greek) text of the Pentateuch (and, to a much lesser extent, his knowledge of the other parts of the Bible) through participating in Sabbath synagogue services with their ample exegetic sermons. He relates that he sometimes consulted the elders of the community about aggadic traditions. At least once in his life he undertook a pilgrimage to Jerusalem, and on that occasion he may have gathered from the priests his information about the Temple cult. His acquaintance with earlier Jewish allegorization, to which he refers, may have been acquired orally or through reading. However, he owes his most profound insights to "his own soul, which oftentimes is God-possessed and divines where it does not know" (Cher. 27).

A vast range of writings by Philo has been preserved by the Christian Church in the original Greek, others in Armenian translation. The bulk of these writings, dealing with the Pentateuch, can be divided into three series of treatises.[11]

The first series consists of an exposition of the Pentateuch as a legal code. At the opening of the first book of the series *De opificio mundi* (*On the Creation*), Philo explains that the Pentateuch, although a law code, opens with the story of creation rather than with legal material, because this story serves to demonstrate that the laws of the Pentateuch are in harmony with the laws of nature, and that through fulfilling these laws one becomes a "loyal citizen of the world." There follow biographies of the three Patriarchs (and Joseph), whom Philo interprets, in accordance with Platonic theory, as the living embodiments of the law or the archetypes on which the law was modeled by Moses. Another biography is *De Vita Mosis,* the best written of Philo's writings, composed as a separate unit and clearly addressed to a gentile audience. Its first book gives a biographical account of Moses, based on Greek rhetorical standards, and the second deals with him as a lawgiver, a priest, and a prophet. This is followed by the small treatise *De Decalogo (On the Decalogue),* containing the narration of the revelation on Sinai and an exposition of the Ten Commandments. The longest is the concluding treatise *De specialibus legibus (On the Special Laws)* with appendices, which categorizes all the biblical commandments under the various commandments of the Decalogue.

The second series, the *Legum allegoriarum (Allegorical Interpretation),* is a philosophical interpretation of the Pentateuch. This series, consisting of 18 exegetic treatises (others being lost), parallels the first 17 chapters of Genesis, completely disregarding their narrative content and transposing them by way of allegorization into a set of abstract philosophical-mystical concepts, connected by a free play of associations with a wealth of other motifs, brought together from all parts of the Pentateuch. The last treatise, *De Somniis (On Dreams),* draws its basic material from the various dream narratives of Genesis. In this whole series the thread of argument is sometimes lost and the association of ideas is comprehensible only to a reader very well versed in the text of the Bible. It has been suggested that this work is a collection of sermons that Philo delivered in the synagogue on various occasions and afterward loosely joined together.

The third series consists of *Quaestiones et solutiones in Genesin (Questions and Answers on Genesis)* and *Quaestiones et solutiones in Exodum (Questions and Answers on Exodus),* preserved (though not completely) only in Armenian translation. This work is in the form of a Hellenistic commentary, where each paragraph is headed by an exegetic question, answered subsequently by a short literal, and a lengthy allegorical, explanation.

In addition to these three series, there is a group of treatises devoted to purely philosophical topics, that contain only occasional allusions to Jewish motifs. Some of these treatises are in dialogue form, and all are connected with the main concerns of Philo's religious outlook, such as the eternity of the world *(De aeternitate mundi)* (On the Eternity of the World) and providence *(De providentia)* (On Providence). The authenticity of some of the treatises in this group has been contested. These works may have been addressed to young Jewish intellectuals on the verge of apostasy—such as Tiberius Julius Alexander, Philo's nephew, who figures in some of them as a partner in the dialogue— people that could no longer be reached by a direct Jewish appeal. Finally, there are two books on contemporary history, *In Flaccum (Flaccus),* on the pogroms in Alexandria (38 C.E.), and *De Legatione ad Gaium (On the Embassy to Gaius),* which deals with Philo's mission to Rome to protest the erection of statues of the emperor in Alexandrian synagogues and later on in the Temple of Jerusalem. In addition there is *De vita contemplativa (On the Contemplative Life),* the only source about the sect of Therapeutae.

Philosophy. The philosophical substructure of Philo's world view may be defined as a Stoicism with a strong Platonic bent and some neo-Pythagorean influences,[12] although some scholars see him mainly as an opponent of the stoics. The Platonic element in his thought accounts for his separation of the world into a lower, material and a higher, spiritual or intelligible realm. Only in the upper, intelligible realm can ultimate truth be attained. In the concrete world of common experience there is only "opinion" or "probability," which falls between truth and lie. Thus, abstract concepts always range higher with Philo than concrete facts, and his statements about things perceived by the senses have of necessity a provisional and somewhat ambiguous character. Exoteric and esoteric sections can be distinguished in Philo's writings. The exoteric sections are concerned with the literal sense of the Bible, whereas the esoteric ones attempt to disclose the deeper philosophical-mystical meaning of Scripture through allegorical interpretation. For example, in the esoteric sections persons of the biblical narrative are interpreted as "representing" or "suggesting" abstract concepts, while the question of their historicity is left obscure. The central issues of Philo's thought are to be found not so much in the well-planned works of the above-mentioned first series, but in the diffusedly written allegorical commentaries. In summarizing Philo's main ideas a distinction must be made between the realm of "opinion" and the realm of "truth."

While the real destination and the real bliss of man consists in lifting up his soul to a contemplative life and freeing himself from bodily needs and pleasures, the right to this higher life is attained only after honestly fulfilling one's earthly duties in society. Therefore, Moses discharged the levites from their communal task only at the age of 50 (Fuga 37). It was in this spirit that Philo accepted his mission to Rome, and perhaps other political activities, although he deplored the circumstances that compelled him to do so (Spec. Leg. 3:1–6). In his historical writings he sees Providence at work in the rescue of the Jewish people, although in other works he is prone to let the concept of Israel evaporate into an allegorical designation for the "God-seeing" (apparently based on an etymology of the Hebrew term for Israel, *ro'eh el*) mystical man. The tendency to spiritualize the physical reality of Israel may account for Philo's very favorable attitude to proselytes, who, insofar as they leave their kinfolk and fleshly bonds, are considered as real imitators of Abraham (Spec. Leg. 1:52). He welcomes the widespread acceptance of Jewish religious institutions by gentiles as a proof of the superiority of the Jewish law. Philo maintained that this law was designed by Moses under divine inspiration, following the pattern of the Decalogue, which was given and promulgated by God Himself.

In an appeal to the philosophically educated Jews who, because they regarded the laws as symbols, were negligent in observing them (Migr. 89–93), Philo argues against the abrogation of the law. The immanent weakness of his argument lies in his admission that the physical fulfillment of the biblical prescriptions is only the outward requirement of the law, whereas its real aim is the attaining of its symbolic meaning. Nevertheless, Philo goes to great lengths in pleading for the superior ethical, educational, and social value of Mosaic legislation on the material level as well. In his exposition of Jewish law Philo shows only scant acquaintance with the Oral Law. For example, he is not aware (Virt. 142ff.) of any halakhic extension of the prohibition against cooking a kid in its mother's milk (Qu. Ex. 23:19). The assumption of some scholars that Philo's known deviations from *halakhah* are the result of divergences of Alexandrian from Palestinian *halakhah*, and that Philo mastered the *halakhah* of his own community, is doubtful.

Many more connections can be found between Philo and Palestinian *aggadah,* especially where he does not allegorize. He borrows from the Hebrew tradition not only a wealth of individual Midrashim, but also central midrashic concepts, such as the two *middot* (attributes) of God. Only in one place (Praem. 162–72) does he expound the messianic hope of Israel—so strong in his time—emphasizing its miraculous, and carefully avoiding its more military, aspects. His literary skill and rhetorical education are specially evident in his historical and political writings, where he succeeds in vivid descriptions and analyses of political situations and psychological motivation.

According to the inner meaning of the Holy Writ, uncovered by allegorical interpretation, Moses is a philosopher. However, Philo does not always consider philosophy the highest achievement of mind; sometimes he writes of a third stage above science and philosophy, called wisdom (Congr. 79). This is paralleled by his anthropology, i.e., his enumeration of three types of man—the man who is "earth-born," the man who is "heaven-born" and the man who is "God-born" (Gig. 60). The Platonic surge of the soul from the world of sense perception to that of intelligence is sometimes supplemented by a second soaring from the world of ideas to the Divine itself (Opif. 71). Obviously, this highest sphere, which is not always distinguished from the noetic one, cannot be a relapse into the concrete, but must be an ideal realm beyond the ideas of the second stage. It is the ultimate aim of Philonic thought and striving. Philo is not interested in the traditional topics of Greek science and philosophy in themselves, but only insofar as they are ways to, or expressions for, the realm of the Divine. So, ultimately there are only two realities in Philo's world of truth: God and the soul. The timeless drama between these two poles is the content of Philo's mystical philosophy.

In discussing God's essence Philo maintains an extreme transcendentalism, surpassing even that of Plato. He describes God as ". . . transcending virtue, transcending knowledge, transcending the good itself and the beautiful itself" (Opif. 8), and as ". . . better than the good, more venerable than the monad, purer than the unit . . . " (Praem. 40). Whereas in lower levels of Philo's thought, God is endowed with goodness and other attributes, and activity figures as His "property" (I. Leg. Alleg. 5), on the most abstract level he insists that God is "without quality" (*ibid.* 36), has no name, and is unknowable. This last tenet is not meant in an agnostic way; on the contrary, man has to strive to know

God and God is the only object worth knowing. But whereas it is easy to know that God is, we cannot know what He is (Spec. 1:32). Nevertheless Philo often encourages a thorough research into understanding God's essence; although this can never be successful, the research itself is utterly blissful.

It has not yet been sufficiently acknowledged that the definite transcendentalist trend in Philo's discussion of God's essence is balanced by a strong immanentistic trend, based on the Stoic model, in his discussion of God's relation to the world and the soul. The Stoic scheme lends itself to a philosophic formulation of the working of divine powers inside things and even more inside the human soul. Since such an involvement of God in the world is in contradiction to His absolute apartness, the two aspects must be reconciled by an ontological differentiation that comes close to splitting the otherwise strongly maintained unity of God. This is the background of Philo's doctrine of the "intermediary powers." The Logos, which for the stoics defined the Godhead, comes to be distinguished from God Himself, without being ontologically disconnected from Him. At times the Logos is identified by Philo with the mind of God, and thus it may be considered as another name for God Himself (Opif. 24). At other times, however, it is symbolized by the high priest (II Som. 185ff.), and is characterized as being "midway between man and God" (II Som. 188). In a similar way, the doctrine of God's two "powers," mercy and justice, is built up into a system of intermediaries, whose activities can be referred to as God's own deeds, but sometimes are clearly meant to exonerate God from direct responsibility for severe acts of punishment (Decal. 177), which presupposes their being distinguishable from Him. Thus Abraham's three guests (Gen. 18:2) are identified (*Quaestiones et solutiones in Genesin*, 4:2) as God and His two powers. Only at a close look does Abraham discover they are one person.

These and cognate hypostases are instrumental in establishing God's relation to the world. Although Philo teaches that the world is created by God, God's direct contact with the defiling quality of matter is avoided by the interposition of the Logos or the "world-creating power" (Op. 21). In accordance with contemporary interpretation of Plato's *Timaeus* Philo maintains that creation is carried out in two successive stages, as is illustrated in the biblical narrative; the first day of creation represents God's conceiving in His Logos the noetic world of ideas that

later serves as a model for the creation of the material world, represented by the other five days. In the creation of man, the only creature
capable of doing evil, God needs the cooperation of subservient powers.

Man is composed of body and soul, body connecting him with matter
and soul with God. Thus, he has to make a fundamental choice as to the
direction of his life. The alternative is identified by Philo with the struggle of the Stoic sage for the control of his passions by reason, and so
the whole of Stoic ethics becomes integrated into Philo's religious
philosophy. However, behind the moralizing tenor of many passages
lurks a religious pathos. The narration of the sin in the Garden of
Eden is allegorically interpreted as the drama of man's fall. The most
violent of passions, lust, is represented by the snake, who appeals
not to reason (Adam) but to the senses (Eve), and succeeds with their
help in subjugating reason too. Therefore (Gen. 2:24), man leaves his
father (God) and his mother (wisdom) and clings to his wife (sensuality)
and they are made into one flesh (II L.A. 59). It should be noted that
this interpretation of the sin takes no account of the express prohibition
by God, which constitutes the real issue in rabbinical exegesis. The recon-
ciliation between the soul and God is described by Philo in two ways:
God's descent into the human soul and the soul's ascent to God. In both,
the interplay of transcendence and immanence in the concept of God is
of decisive importance. God the exalted, superior to every thinkable
human category, comes to merge with the human soul, or the soul
surpasses even the summit of Plato's ideal heaven—this is what happens in the union between God and man. The basic identity of human
and divine spirit, implied in Stoic physics, here gives scientific expression to an enthusiastic mystical experience. What under stoic presuppositions was just a truism, becomes under the Philonic constellation
a paradox of overwhelming power.

In order to prepare himself for God, man has to strip himself of
earthly bonds, to leave "his land, his kinfolk and his father's home"
(Gen. 12:1), i.e., his body, his senses, and his faculty of speech, and to
segregate himself from these as much as possible for a living man (Migr.
1ff.). The sharp contrast between the self-loving and the God-loving
man is symbolized by Cain and Abel, a contrast utterly foreign to the
Stoics who view the "self" of man as his divine part.

Unlike the moral struggle of the Stoic sage, which is intended to
lead to "apathy" and freedom from the passions, the entering of the

Divine into man makes him jubilant and surge into a frenzy (Plant. 38). The "stream from Eden," the wine of the godly cupbearer (II Som. 254), drives the soul into ecstasy, for it fills it with an unearthly quality, called by names like "the holy spirit." Thus, the soul seeks more than intellectual knowledge, when it wants to "know what God is," although rationalistic terminology is often applied. The real aim is better indicated when Philo speaks of "reaching" God. The three Patriarchs are the archetypes of three main routes to "virtue," meaning ultimately union with God, namely, learning, nature, and training, respectively. Abraham proceeds from erudition (Hagar) to virtue (Sarah), whereas Isaac as the perfect nature reaches the mystical goal without interposing an intellectual endeavor, and Jacob is rewarded for his asceticism by the fact that the "Lord" (Justice) becomes to him "God" (Mercy; I Som. 163, alluding to Gen. 28:21), meaning that God discloses to him His higher spheres.

Here there is an additional function of the doctrine of intermediaries. These intermediaries present themselves to the ascending soul as so many stages on its way to God. Although the soul cannot advance to God Himself, it may be able to reach one of His "powers," whose number is variously given. This is developed in an allegory of the six towns of refuge (Num. 35), which are made (Fuga 86ff.) to represent a sequel of stations on the way to God, located partly on this and partly on the other side of the river, i.e., partly accessible and partly inaccessible to the soul. Schemes like this are variously adumbrated by Philo but do not harden into a fixed pattern.

In Jewish tradition man is said to relate to God in two ways—in fear and in love. Philo considers fear not only inferior to love (as do the rabbis, especially the school of R. Akiva) but sometimes as completely wrong (since fear is reckoned by the Stoics as one of the passions that have to be overcome), deriving from an inadequate, vulgar idea of the Godhead (corresponding to the literal sense of Scripture).[13] The proper attitude of the sage is love, understood as Platonic eros, but surpassing the world of ideas and directing itself to God Himself (Opif. 71). This comes close to the erotic aspect of Hellenistic mysticism, and indeed, Philo indulges in sexual imagery, as for example in an allegory that he repeats a few times, always with extreme mysterious secrecy (Cher. 43ff.), on the biblical mothers, of whom it is said that "God opened their womb." He interprets this phrase as referring to the fatherhood of

God and the virgin birth, it being understood that in this context the mothers themselves are to be regarded as purely allegorical figures. However, Philo usually shrinks from the idea of a full consummation of the mystical "holy marriage," so that usually the stress is shifted in Philo from the blissful union with God to the experience of eros itself, which is conceived as a state of highest bliss.

While Philo maintains at times that this apex of bliss is reached by elevating the soul from noetic fulfillment to a last soaring to the Divine, as symbolized in the figure of Abraham, at other times he views religious perfection as independent of philosophical perfection, as in the symbol of Isaac, or even as sharply contrasted with it: "When the light of God shines, the human light sets: when the divine light sets, the human dawns and rises" (Heres 264).

Sometimes (III Leg. Alleg. 136) it is hinted that this love is a gift from God; Philo often reinterprets accomplishments ascribed to the Stoic sage, such as steadfastness, peace, and kingliness, as divine gifts, by which God grants the perfect man a share in His own nature. To these virtues he adds pistis (meaning both "faith" and "faithfulness") that is here for the first time made into a value concept and is likewise transformed into a property of God's own essence; so, this "faith" means a blissful state of mind and not just faithful acceptance of certain creeds. Philo regards prophecy too as a divine gift. Whereas on the level of "opinion" it is praised as valuable prescience of future events (II V. Mos. 18ff.), in esoteric writings this popular aspect, which incorporates the biblical aspect of prophecy as a mission to the people, is abandoned. Here prophecy is an act of ecstasy, where man is overflooded with divine light. No perceptible message is connected with experience, for in its consummation "ears are made into eyes" (I. Som. 129) and the message vanishes into flashes of light. Moses looking on from the top of Nebo into the "promised land" (Migr. 44) is the most sublime symbol for this meaning of prophecy.

Influence. Apart from Josephus, no ancient Jewish source mentions Philo, although there are traces of Philonic influence in Midrash. The first medieval Jewish writer who mentions him is Azariah dei Rossi[14] who Hebraizes his name into Jedidiah.

Philo had a much greater influence on Christianity—not on the New Testament itself but on the Church Fathers, Clement of Alexandria,

Origen, Ambrose, and many others. They drew eagerly on his allegorical interpretations and adopted many of his concepts, especially on his relating of Platonic and Biblical ideas. However, owing to their different approach, many of his abstract concepts, such as wisdom, Logos, and faith, were concretized in Christianity.[15]

[1] For a fuller picture the reader may refer to the indexes of biblical passages appearing in Saadiah Gaon, *The Book of Beliefs and Opinions*, transl. by S. Rosenblatt (1949); Judah Halevi, *The Kuzari* transl. by H. Hirschfeld (1964); Moses Maimonides' *Guide for the Perplexed*, transl. by S. Pines (1963) and M. Friedlander (1904 and reprinted 1952); Joseph Albo, *Sefer Ha-Ikkarim*, transl. by I. Husik (1930).

[2] See the essay by Saul Lieberman in *Biblical and Other Studies*, Ed. Alexander Altmann (1963).

[3] H. A. Wolfson, *Philo* Vol. I, p. 92 (1947).

[4] See G. Scholem's *Major Trends in Jewish Mysticism* p. 40 ff. (1941 and reprinted), his *Jewish Gnosticism, Merkabah Mysticism and Talmudic Tradition* (1960) and his *Kabbalah* (1973).

[5] H. A. Wolfson, *Philo* Vol. I, pgs. 3–27 (1947).

[6] Ibid, Vol. I, p. 94 note 39.

[7] The *Letter of Aristeas* is a Hellenistic Jewish work (2nd century B.C.E.) written in Greek. The account that it gives of the preparation of the Septuagint is more legend than history.

[8] See R. H. Charles *Apocrypha and Pseudepigrapha* (1913) for the *Books of Maccabees* and other works of this period (in English).

[9] H. A. Wolfson, *Philo* Vol. I, pgs. 287–289.

[10] This is a subject of disagreement among scholars. See S. Belkin's *Philo and the Oral Law* (1940) which argues that Philo was familiar with both Hebrew and the Jewish scholarship of his day. For an opposing view see E. R. Goodenough's *An Introduction to Philo Judaeus* (1940 and 1962) and H. A. Wolfson's *Philo*, 2 vols. (1940) and S. Sandmel, *Philo's Place in Judaism* (1956).

[11] The standard abbreviations of Philo's works are:

PHILO	
Abr.	*De Abrahamo*
Aet.	*De aeternitate mundi*
Agr.	*De agricultura*
Alex.	*Alexander (de animalibus)*
Cher.	*De Cherubim*
Conf.	*De confusione linguarum*
Congr.	*De congressu eruditionis gratia*
Decal.	*De decalogo*
Det.	*Quod deterius potiori insidiari soleat*
Ebr.	*De ebrietate*

Flacc.	*In Flaccum*
Fuga	*De fuga et inventione*
Gig.	*De gigantibus*
Heres	*Quis rerum divinarum heres sit*
Hyp.	*Hypothetica*
Immut.	*Quod Deus sit immutabilis*
Jos.	*De Josepho*
Leg. Alleg. (L. A.)	*Legum Allegoriaum*
Leg. ad Gaium	*Legatio ad Gaium*
Migr.	*De migratione Abrahae*
Mut.	*De mutatione nominum*
Opif.	*De opificio mundi*
Plant.	*De plantatione*
Post. C.	*De posteritate Caini*
Praem.	*De praemiis et poenis*
Prob.	*Quod omnis probus liber sit*
Prov.	*De providentia*
Qu. Ex.	*Quaestiones in Exodum*
Qu. Gen.	*Quaestiones in Genesin*
Sacr.	*De sacrificiis Abelis et Caini*
Sobr.	*De sobrietate*
Som.	*De somniis*
Spec. Leg.	*De specialibus legibus*
Virt.	*De virtutibus*
V. contempl.	*De vita contemplativa*
V. Mos.	*De vita Mosis*

The complete edition of Philo's writings in the original Greek with an English translation is to be found in the Loeb Classical Library Series (F. H. Colson and G. H. Whitaker translators) 10 vols, 1929–62. Two supplementary volumes containing English translations of the writings preserved in America were added by Ralph Marcus (translator) in 1953. A small selection of Philo's writings in English translation selected and translated by H. Lewy can also be found in H. Lewy et al., *Three Jewish Philosophers* (1960).

[12] For works on Stoicism, Neoplatonism and Pythagoreanism readers are referred to the bibliography of this book.

[13] For a discussion of the 'Fear of God' and the 'Love of God' in talmudic literature see Solomon Schechter, *Some Aspects of Rabbinic Theology* (1909; reissued 1961).

[14] Azariah dei Rossi, *Me'or Einayim* (1886) pgs. 90–129.

[15] For more on Philo's influence on Christian thought see H. A. Wolfson's *The Philosophy of the Church Fathers* Vol. I (1956 and 1964); J. Danielou, *Philon d'Alexandrie* (1958); H. Chadwick, "Philo and the Beginnings of Christian Thought" in *The Cambridge History of Later Greek and Early Medieval Philosophy* (1967).

Part Two

MEDIEVAL PERIOD

INTRODUCTION

Medieval Jewish philosophy began in the early tenth century as part of a general cultural revival in the Islamic East, and continued in Muslim countries—North Africa, Spain, and Egypt—for some 300 years. The Jews of the period spoke, read, and wrote Arabic and thus were able to participate in the general culture of their day. Although Jews produced a rich literature on biblical and rabbinic subjects and much poetry, they did not produce an extensive scientific and philosophical literature of their own. The extant literature was adequate for their needs, and their major speculative efforts were devoted to investigating how Judaism and philosophy were related. Most of their philosophic works were written in Arabic. Toward the end of the 12th century the setting of Jewish philosophy began to change. The Jewish communities in the Islamic world declined, and communities hospitable to philosophic and scientific learning developed in Christian lands, particularly Christian Spain, southern France, and Italy. As a result, Arabic was gradually forgotten, and since, with some notable exceptions, Jews had little occasion to learn Latin, Hebrew became the language of Jewish works in philosophy and the sciences. Thus, whereas in Muslim countries Jews were part of the mainstream of general culture, in Christian lands they had to foster a general culture of their own.

In this period, while Jews continued to write works investigating the relation of Judaism and philosophy, they now also produced an extensive literature devoted to purely philosophic topics. As a first step they translated into Hebrew the extensive Arabic philosophical literature of the previous period. Then they commented on the newly translated works, summarized them in compendia and encyclopedias, and composed their own treatises and books. Jewish philosophy during this period was largely based on sources from the Islamic philosophic tradition, but some Jewish philosophers were also influenced by the

27

views of Christian scholastics. The second period in medieval Jewish philosophy lasted until the early 16th century.

The philosophic literature available during the Islamic period was based on works studied in the late Hellenistic schools. As the Islamic empire expanded, these schools came under Muslim rule, and the works studied in them were soon translated into Arabic. At times these translations were made from Greek originals, but more often from intermediary Syriac translations. A number of works were translated more than once. The translators, most of whom were Nestorian and Jacobite Christians, were active from about 800 until about 1000.[1] Of Platonic works translated, the most important were the *Timeaus, Republic,* and *Laws,* but Arabic translations of some other dialogues are extant. Perhaps the most important influence was exercised by the works of Aristotle, all of which were known, except for the *Dialogues* and *Politics.* Together with the works of Aristotle there were translated works by his commentators Alexander of Aphrodisias, Themistius, Theophrastus, Simplicius, and John Philoponus. There were also translations of works by Galen, some of which are no longer extant in the original Greek. The Neoplatonic tradition was represented by the *Theology of Aristotle,* a collection of excerpts from Plotinus' *Enneads,* and the *Liber de Causis,* a collection from Proclus' *Elements of Theology,* as well as by other Neoplatonic writings, some of which have been discovered only recently. There were also translations of the Hermetic writings. In addition, philosophers of the period were familiar with Epicurean, Stoic, and skeptic teachings which, however, reached them through the reports of other authors rather than through translations of original works. Jewish philosophers were similarly influenced by the works of Islamic philosophers of the period, including Al-Kindī, Al-Rāzī, Al-Fārābi, Avicenna (Ibn Sīnā), Al-Ghazālī, Avempace (Ibn Bājja), and Averroes (Ibn Rushd). However, Averroes influenced medieval Jewish philosophy during its second period rather than its first. Jews were familiar, also, with the collection known as the "Epistles of the Brethren of Sincerity," and they knew the writings of Sufi mystics.

MU'TAZILITE KALĀM

Paralleling Islamic philosophers, Jewish philosophers of the Islamic period may be divided into four groups: followers of the Mu'tazilite branch of the Arabic theology known as Kalām, Neoplatonists, Aristotelians, and philosophical critics of Aristotelian rationalism. At times, doctrines from several schools were mixed in the work of a single philosopher.

ISLAMIC THINKERS

Mu'tazilite Kalām theology arose in Islamic circles toward the end of the eighth century. Its views developed out of reflections on problems posed by Scripture. The two major problems were the unity of God and God's justice, and because of their concern with these problems, Mu'tazilites were also called "Men of Unity and Justice." The first problem arose from the observation that the Koran affirms that God is one, yet describes Him by many attributes; the second, from the observation that God is omnipotent and omniscient (which seems to imply that God causes everything in the world including man's actions), yet punishes man for his wrongdoing. To solve the first problem, the Mu'tazilites set out to show that God can be described by many attributes without violating His unity; to solve the second, that, although God is omnipotent and omniscient, man's freedom and hence responsibility for his actions are not precluded. These two interests were broadened to include discussions of other aspects of God and human nature.

Mu'tazilites also addressed themselves to more theological problems, such as the nature of different kinds of sinners and the afterlife. Since the Mu'tazilites' speculations derived from a concern with scriptural problems, they did not formulate a systematic philosophy as the Neoplatonists and later the Aristotelians did. Philosophy was for them a way of solving scriptural difficulties, and they made use of any philosophical argument that might be of help. Hence, their philosophic speculations were eclectic, and a philosopher would make use of Platonic, Aristotelian, or Epicurean arguments as the need arose. Characteristic of Muʿtazilite works is their division into sections devoted to the unity of God and His justice. Also characteristic are proofs of the existence of God based on proofs of the creation of the world and the division of scriptural commandments into rational and traditional. In reaction to the Muʿtazilites, a more orthodox kind of Kalām known as Ashʿarite (founded by al-Ashʿarī, d. 935), arose.[2] While Ashʿarite Kalām was known to Jewish philosophers and is cited by them, it appears that there were no Jewish Ashʿarites. The Ashʿarites were known for their insistence on the absolute omnipotence and omniscience of God, which led them to deny the existence of laws of nature and human free will. However, to safeguard God's justice and man's responsibility they formulated the doctrine of "acquisition," according to which man, while not causing his acts, can do them willingly or unwillingly.

SAADIAH GAON

Saadiah was the greatest scholar and author of the geonic period and an important leader of Babylonian Jewry. He was the first medieval Jewish philosopher. Saadiah was born in Pithom (Abu Suweir), in the Fayum district in Egypt. Little is known about his family except that his opponents slandered his father because he was not a scholar and earned his living from manual labor. While there is no doubt that in his youth he already displayed outstanding talents both as an author and in communal activity, there is scant information about his teachers, whether in Jewish studies or in Greco-Arabic philosophy. The Arab writer Mas'udi states that when Saadiah was in Ereẓ Israel, he studied under Abu Kathir Yaḥya b. Zechariah al-Katib of Tiberias. However, earlier than that, when he still lived in Egypt, he had already written two books and corresponded with R. Isaac b. Solomon Israeli of Kairouan. It is therefore certain that when he left Egypt he was already well educated in both Jewish and secular studies.

From 921 Saadiah appears as the leading protagonist in an ongoing bitter struggle between Aaron Ben Meir, head of the Jerusalem academy, and the leaders of the Jewish communities in Babylonia. The immediate cause of the dispute was a technicality over the fixing of the calendar. However the larger issue at stake which promoted the dispute into a major clash was whether the sages of Palestine or Babylonia were to be the supreme leaders of world Jewry.

The controversy grew in bitterness and invective and Ben Meir lost ground. The action of the Babylonian scholars in defending their tradition prevented people from following the head of the Palestinian academy, and caused some who had previously followed Ben Meir to desert him. The duration of the schism after 923 and the manner in which it was resolved cannot be determined. Ben Meir continued as head of the academy but Saadiah and the Babylonian leaders had won.

It would appear that immediately on his arrival in Babylonia in 922, Saadiah was appointed head of the yeshivah of Pumbedita. After the Ben Meir controversy had subsided, Saadiah found time for literary work and several of his works were written in the 920s. When the question of the continuation of the academy of Sura was under discussion, Saadiah's name was proposed. After a complicated series of political machinations and attempts to appoint others, Saadiah was appointed head of the Sura[3] academy by the Exilarch David ben Zakkai, in the spring of 928. Saadiah's tenure at the head of the academy was surrounded by difficulties and political and personal struggles with the Exilarch. For a time Saadiah was even forced to relinquish the Gaonate and for most of the remainder of his life he was the center of a storm of controversy. He died in 942.

Saadiah was a pioneer of rabbinic literature, if not the first in this field he was the first to write "books" in the modern sense of the word. He was also the first to give his halakhic works the form of monographs, assigning a separate one to each topic of Hebrew law: a book on the Laws of Gifts, another on the Laws of Commercial Transactions, and so on. He was likewise the first to set a standard pattern for his books of halakhic decisions by dividing each one into sections and subsections. Every subject begins with a brief definition of the topic under discussion, followed by various details and talmudic proofs of them. Saadiah's halakhic books are thus distinguished by their systematic structure and logical order and by a lengthy detailed introduction which he prefaced to each book of halakhic decisions. Saadiah was the first to write halakhic works in Arabic, which had in his days replaced Aramaic as the principal language spoken by the Jews in Babylonia.

Saadiah's Philosophy. Saadiah's major philosophic work, written in Arabic, *Kitāb al-Amānar wa-al-I'tiqādāt,*[4] is the earliest Jewish philosophic work from medieval times to have survived intact. It was translated into Hebrew by Judah ibn Tibbon in 1186 under the title *Sefer ha-Emunot ve-ha-De'ot* (Constantinople, 1562), and in this version exercised a profound influence on Jewish thought. In 1970 a new Hebrew translation was prepared by Y. Kafaḥ and published together with the Arabic original.[5]

Saadiah belonged to the school of the Muʿtazilites, but it is evident that he was also influenced by Aristotelianism, Platonism, and Stoicism. In line with Muʿtazilite thought, Saadiah in *Sefer ha-Emunot ve-ha-De'ot* did not attempt to establish a complete philosophical system resting upon an independent foundation, but rather set out to find rational proof for the dogmas of the Oral and Written Law. Saadiah explains that he wrote this work in order to provide his fellow Jews with spiritual guidance in the face of the confusion which the multiple sects and religious disputes of the tenth century had created among the people, and to combat heretical views, such as those of Ḥīwī al-Balkhī.[6]

The *Emunot ve-De'ot* (as it is usually referred to) is a polemical work, in which Saadiah, in addition to clarifying and expounding his own views, devoted much space to disproving opposing theories. Saadiah believed that it was a religious obligation to provide a rational basis for the Law, in order to dispel doubts and refute views at variance with those which he accepts. Saadiah's importance lies in his being the first medieval Jewish philosopher to attempt to reconcile the Bible and philosophy, reason and revelation.

In the introduction to the *Emunot ve-De'ot,* in an attempt to refute the skeptics and to show that one can achieve a knowledge of the truth by means of speculation, Saadiah presents a psychological and epistemological account of the reasons for doubt, and explains why men in their search for the truth become involved in error. He identifies three sources of knowledge: (1) sense perception, (2) self-evident principles, such as the approval of telling the truth and the disapproval of lying, and (3) inferential knowledge gained by syllogistic reasoning. He attacks the claim of the skeptics that these sources of knowledge are not to be relied upon, but at the same time discusses the errors that one may make in utilizing them, and the steps that one must take in order to insure their reliability. There is, in addition, a fourth source of knowledge, reliable tradition, i.e., confidence in the truth of the reports of others, which is indispensable for the functioning of human society. In Judaism reliable tradition has special significance in that it refers to the transmission, through Scripture and the oral tradition, of God's revelation to the prophets. Saadiah maintains that while one can arrive at a knowledge of the truth by means of speculation, revelation is necessary in order to impart the truth to those who are incapable of rational investigation, as well as to provide guidance for those who are involved in speculation. Even while engaged in speculation one must not set aside the doctrine contained in Scripture.

Saadiah believes that there is a correspondence between reason and revelation, and that one cannot refute the other. Therefore, one must reject the validity of any prophet whose teachings contradict reason, even if he accompanies his teachings with miracles. Those biblical statements which appear to contradict the results of rational investigation (e.g., anthropomorphic descriptions of God) must be regarded as allegories. Saadiah points out that in interpreting anthropomorphic expressions allegorically he is not subordinating revelation to reason, but is actually following revelation, which teaches that God is incorporeal.

In typical Mu'tazilite fashion, Saadiah opens the body of his work with a discussion of creation. He maintains that the world was created in time, that its creator was other than itself, and that it was created *ex nihilo*. He presents four proofs for creation, the first based on Aristotelian premises, the other three drawn from the *Kalām*. In the first proof, invoking the principles that the world is finite in its dimension, and that a finite body cannot possess an infinite force, Saadiah concludes that the force preserving the world is finite and consequently that the world itself must be finite, i.e., must have a beginning and an end. In the second proof, on the basis of the fact that that which is composed of two or more elements must have been put together at some point in time, Saadiah argues that the world, which is composed of various elements, must have been created at some point in time. In the third proof Saadiah argues that the world is composed of various substances all of which are the bearers of accidents. Since accidents originate in time, the world itself must have originated in time. The fourth argument is taken from the nature of time. Were the world uncreated, time would be infinite. But infinite time cannot be traversed, and hence the present (or any other finite) moment could never have come to be. But the present clearly exists, and hence time cannot be infinite. It follows that the world must have had a beginning.

Having advanced these four proofs for creation, Saadiah proceeds to refute 12 other cosmogonic theories which differ from his own. These range from theories which, while accepting the principle that a creator created the world in time, deny that it was created out of nothing, through that which upholds the eternity of the world, to theories which are sceptical about the possibility of human knowledge and hence about demonstrating either the creation or eternity of the world (*Emunot ve-De'ot*, 1:3).

Saadiah's concept of the nature of God is based upon his view of God as creator. God is the cause of all corporeal existence, He cannot Himself be corporeal, for if He were corporeal, there would have to be something beyond Him which was the cause of His existence. Since God is incorporeal, He cannot be subject to the corporeal attributes of quantity and number, and hence cannot be more than one. Turning to the question of divine attributes, Saadiah demonstrates that an analysis of the concept of God as creator leads to the attribution of three essential qualities to Him: life, power, and wisdom. The attribution of these qualities to God does not imply a plurality in God. In reality all these qualities are united in Him, but we are forced to speak of them as separate because of the limitation of human language (*Emunot ve-De'ot*, ch. 2). The creation of the world was not the result of a need or compulsion on the part of God, but an act of free will. In creating the world God wished to benefit His creatures by giving them the opportunity of serving Him through the observance of His commandments, by means of which they could attain true happiness (*Emunot ve-De'ot* 1:4).

The laws given by God to Israel may be divided into two categories: the rational laws *(mitzvot sikhliyyot)*, which have their basis in reason and which man would have discovered by means of reason even if they had not been revealed, and the traditional laws *(mitzvot shimiyyot)*, ritual and ceremonial laws, such as the dietary laws, which do not have their basis in reason. The acts to which the traditional laws refer are neither good nor evil from the point of view of reason, but are made so by the fact that they are commanded or prohibited by God. All the rational laws can be subsumed under three basic rational principles: First, reason demands that one express gratitude to one's benefactor. Hence, it is reasonable that God should demand that man render thanks to Him through worship. Second, reason demands that a wise person not permit himself to be insulted. Hence, it is reasonable that God should prohibit man from insulting ·Him, i.e., should prohibit man from taking His name in vain, or from describing Him in human terms. Third, reason demands that creatures should not harm one another. Hence, it is reasonable that God prohibit men from stealing, murdering, and committing adultery, and harming one another in various other ways. While the individual traditional laws do not have their basis in reason, these laws as a class can also be subsumed under a principle of reason. It is reasonable for a wise man to give unneccessary employment to a poor man merely in order to be able to pay him and thereby confer a benefit upon him. Thus, it is reasonable that God should present man with various ceremonial laws in order to be able to reward man for observing them. While the basis of the traditional laws is the fact that they are commanded by God, it is possible upon careful examination to discern even in these laws a certain intrinsic value and rationality. For example, the commandment to refrain from work on the Sabbath provides man with an opportunity to devote himself to spiritual matters. Revelation is obviously necessary in order for man to arrive at a knowledge of the traditional laws. It is also necessary in the case of the rational laws for reason grasps only abstract principles and general norms. The details necessary for the concrete application of these principles are communicated by means of revelation (*Emunot ve-De'ot*, ch. 3).

Saadiah views man as a composite of body and soul. The soul is composed of very fine material, and has three essential faculties: appetite, which controls growth and reproduction; spirit, which controls the emotions; and reason, which controls knowledge.[7] The soul cannot act on its own, and is therefore placed in the body, which serves as its instrument. By means of his actions, i.e., by means of the performance of the divine commandments, man can attain true happiness. One may ask why God does not reward man without his having to undergo hardship and suffering in this world. Saadiah explains that the only real reward is that which man wins for himself through actions for which he is responsible. It is precisely the quality of infinite goodness in God which demands that man be given the opportunity to win his own reward (*Emunot ve-De'ot* 6:4). It follows that man must have freedom of choice, for if he did not, he would not be responsible for his actions, and God's rewarding and punishing him would be unjust. A further indication that man possesses freedom of choice is the fact that he feels that he is free to act, and does not feel anything preventing him from acting. Saadiah attempts to reconcile the paradox of free choice with God's foreknowledge by stating simply that God's knowledge is not a cause of man's actions, and hence does not restrict his freedom of choice. God merely knows what the outcome of man's deliberation will be (*Emunot ve-De'ot* 4:34). The problem which troubles Saadiah more is the question of theodicy—why the evil prosper and the good suffer. His solution lies in the balance between suffering in this world and the reward in the next. The righteous who suffer in this world will be rewarded in the *olam ha-ba* (world to come).

In the latter part of *Emunot ve-De'ot* Saadiah discusses in detail the doctrine of *olam ha-ba*, which was the natural extension and corollary of his resolution of the problem of theodicy. He also discusses the related eschatalogical doctrines of the resurrection of the dead, the nature and role of the Messiah and messianic age, and the doctrine of redemption.

Saadiah argues that the soul is a unified substantial entity (ethereal yet luminous), qualitatively different from the body, possessing both power and knowledge, which exists independently of a body. It is an accepted and standard argument of medieval philosophy, derived primarily from Platonic sources (e.g., Phaedo) and neo-Platonic sources (e.g., Philo, Plotinus, Augustine), that such a description of the soul vouchsafed its continuous existence. Unlike neo-Platonic accounts, however, Saadiah links this account of the soul to the Jewish eschatological belief in the resurrection of the body. Taking this belief literally, Saadiah argues that the soul remains in a sort of limbo-like state until it will be re-united with the body in the days of messianic fulfillment. Messianic fulfillment means to Saadiah not an other-wordly metaphysical state but a future historic convolution which will make manifest the messianic promises of the Prophets, especially those concerned with the People of Israel, its land, and its Temple.

Saadiah's Influence. Saadiah is one of the dominant figures in the development of Judaism and its literature. Although he had predecessors in some of the branches of that literature in which he engaged, he was the first to weld these numerous and diverse studies into a complete system. He provided a powerful impetus to all those who followed in his footsteps in the various branches of that literature, and there is hardly one of the outstanding figures in them who does not pay generous and laudatory tribute to his pioneering work. In philology, Menahem b. Jacob ibn Saruq speaks of "the accuracy of his interpretations and the comprehensiveness of his linguistics"; the renowned grammarian Jonah ibn Janah praises his great work in that field; the mathematician and astronomer Isaac b. Baruch ibn Abbatio states that "he was greater in science than I am"; to Abraham ibn Ezra in his biblical commentary he is "the *gaon*" par excellence, and in his devastating criticism of the *paytanim* (to Eccles. 5:1), he singles out Saadiah as an exception. Maimonides disagreed with his philosophical views in many fundamental points, but states "were it not for Saadiah the Torah would have well-nigh disappeared from the midst of Israel" *(Iggeret Teiman).* His halakhic works penetrated to the Franco-German center and to the tosafists. He is the most authoritative geonic source, a fact which incidentally is evidence that his Arabic works were early translated into Hebrew, in versions which are no longer extant. Saadiah influenced Jewish Neoplatonists, such as Bahya ibn Paquda, Moses ibn Ezra, and Abraham ibn Ezra. Jewish Aristotelians such as Abraham ibn Daud also borrowed some of his ideas. The influence of Saadiah declined with the appearance of the *Guide of the Perplexed,* in which Maimonides attacks *Kalām* philosophy, alluding to Saadiah, although never mentioning him by name. However, in the 14th and 15th centuries, Maimonides' philosophical opponents drew upon Saadiah's work, and *Sefer ha-Emunot ve-ha-De'ot* was influential until the Haskalah period.

OTHER RABBANITE FOLLOWERS OF KALĀM

Although Saadiah remained the major Jewish exponent of Mu'tazilite Kalām, other Jewish philosophers made use of kalamic teachings. In Rabbanite circles, kalamic influences were evident until the rise of Aristotelianism in the 13th century, while among Karaites, Kalām

רבינו סעדיה גאון זל   צט

אדרוס טובה. ומטטסוא מטא את כלם סלא כדרך סנטאו ולטכך סאזן כתבתי זה.
וא תתמה סהטעולב ככוי כאנ מא וכער ודס כטטטסה כפה כאכן העלוון הוא המפתח
ומסדיק כל הכפס כך להכדיל אף אפי היכל סהוא מחזרו ומרוס על כל כפת העולס
מחוקק את כל סעולם ומטאו בטכמלו כלים. במטנה כבפר מרככה מפרס כדרך
כבודו סל כורא מקומו. סהוא זרח על כרוב המיוחד מנד מערכי סאין סב פרטו
ענן: סכעכטעלות. יהקקן פי לטל עטה דמות טורתן. חבכן כאחירתו. נרכן
פעמי סקדי זו. פעמי סקדים זו. ולקמן מפרט לה. סמיון פעמים דנוטות פ:מיס
רפוות. לבור בטן. ולימד התמורות כדפרי. וכר בהס ככבים כעולבלקמן מפרט
לה חכלל סלם. ומים כסנכ ז ימי הסבוע. וסערים כנפט. ז סעריס וכקכים יס
כראם כ עיוס. כ אוכים. כ כחירו. ופהא וככלם ככנ ז זכרים וז כקכות. כיּנד
נרכן וכו. מי ב אבכיב כוכות כ כתים. ג כוכותו ל כוון וב כנוןאב כ ח. ג כוכות
וג כנון אבג אבנ כנא אבנ כ אבנ נ אבכ נ בא. פדם דסילדבר עולה למכן כתיס כך
חסבון היומות האחרות כנון כנד ז לפעמים נ סהס יכ. ולרם ראה רמז הפכוכב.
כינד ז אקת הרי סתיה. ג לפעמוס סכים הרינ ז לפעמים הרו כד. ה לפעמים
כד הריקז. דכור סלו אותיות ולפתמיס סק. כתכבות וכקקראותו וזהו ה כוכות
סקז ועולין תסז. ז לפעמים תסכ עולס ס חלטים ואר בעיס סרו כענין זן אדכ עולם
למסבן נדול עד הס חדל למפור כי אין מספר. וזה המסכון סלה כך כלא נקוד
אך כנקוד אין חקר ואין מספר. ואס כמטא חכם ומוכה חטבנון סהיס עוסה מכב
אותיות דכור אחד ניו בנ ל כאתיותיו וככ קונקרליו וכחטבנון הזה דכרי כלכולים ודברים
כדולים מלא דכור כני דכור סלוש יד כדכור פי סכיס כדכור אכזנו זה כזה יסמטס
לא יסמטס. לא יסמטס ויסמטעהיס מוטא כל סלטונות סכארץ אבל אוכו כעולס אא
מי סאין לו סני זהו לטון מה ם. ולעלהטכן. וזו ככבי סכעולם תכלל טלם. וזה סדר
תסלוכה כל ימות הסנס. כאצג חלם כלולות. הלם כלבא כומים. ומין אס כל
מי. וכל אחד מסמס סטה אחדו כ מזלות תחתיס. פירוס עגול אמטי ראסון
סמכוזיר. ולכן כוירתי תלי
כתוך ז ככבים. וז ככבים
כתוך יב מזלות. וכן סכיּנו
א טכנכיכ ב. ג על נכי ז.
ז על נכי יב. והז יב ככבוס
כמטלכס כיּוס כך   מ
מהלכס כלולה לכד ממה
ולככה סהם מטתני מהלך
חיל אם. מדי יום יוס כאסר
בירתי וכמו סאפרס לקמן
כל סד מעט התלי והנגלגל
וסס עלה תלי בנגלגל כמלך
על כטאו וזה כירו: כו   ה   כו

Illustrated page from Saadiah's commentary on *Sefer Yezirah*, Mantua, 1567

provided the dominant philosophy throughout the Middle Ages. David ibn Marwān al-Mukammiṣ, probably an older contemporary of Saadiah, combined kalamic, Platonic, Aristotelian, and Neoplatonic teachings in his 'Ishrūn Maqālāt ("Twenty Treatises"), a work only partially preserved. Al-Mukammiṣ cites the kalamic formula: "God is knowing, but not with knowledge; living, but not with life," interpreting it to mean that God's attributes are identical with each other and with His essence. Following the Neoplatonists, he adds that God's attributes must be understood as negations.

Kalamic and Greek philosphic influences are also found in the Bible commentary (extant in fragments) of Samuel b. Hophni (d. 1013), head of the academy of Sura. He also held that God's attributes are identical with His essence, and, again following the Muʿtazilites, he teaches that only prophets can work miracles.

KARAITES

Karaite philosophers were stricter in their adherence to the principles of Muʿtazilite Kalām than the Rabbanite followers of that school. In the 11th century the outstanding Karaite philosophers were Joseph b. Abraham al-Baṣīr and his disciple Jeshua b. Judah, whose views were similar. Their rationalism goes beyond that of Saadiah, as can be seen from their opinion that rational knowledge of God must precede belief in revelation. In their view, only after it has been established that God exists, that He is wise, and that He is omnipotent is the truth of revelation guaranteed. A similar rationalism is manifest in their conception of ethics: they maintained that various specific moral principles are self-evident upon reflection, e.g., that good should be done and evil avoided, that one should be grateful, and that one should tell the truth. This awareness is independent of revelation, since even those who deny God and revelation adhere to these principles. The moral law is binding not only for man but also for God. These two philosophers argue with great subtlety for the creation of the world, but unlike Saadiah, they accept the kalamic doctrine that everything is ultimately composed of atoms.

In the late Middle Ages Aaron ben Elijah of Nicomedia, author of Eẓ Ḥayyim ("Tree of Life," written in 1346), was the outstanding Karaite thinker. Though his work appeared some 150 years after

Maimonides' *Guide,* he was still adhering to the philosophy of the Kalām. In fact, his work was a kind of Kalām critique of the *Guide.* Aaron held that kalamic doctrines are in accord with biblical teachings, while Aristotelianism, pagan in origin, conflicts with biblical teachings on many points. Against Maimonides, Aaron argued that the Kalām proofs for the creation of the world are valid, that God can be described by positive attributes, that providence extends not only to man but also to animals, that evil is not merely a privation of good, and that the soul, not only the acquired intellect, is immortal (for Maimonides' views see below). Following Maimonides, he distinguished the prophecy of Moses from that of other prophets. He was critical of the kalamic doctrines that God created the world by means of the "created will" and that animals will be rewarded in the hereafter, and also of kalamic conceptions of law.

NEOPLATONISM

Through medieval Arabic translations of Greek texts, which began to appear at the same time that the Jews were entering the main stream of Arabic intellectual and cultural life, Plato and Platonism became generally known to Jewish thinkers.

Among the dialogues reported to have been translated into Arabic were the *Republic*, the *Timaeus*, and the *Crito*. Quotations in Arabic from the *Republic, Timaeus, Laws,* and *Symposium*, among others, have been identified. Another source was the synopses of certain of the Platonic dialogues by Galen. Maimonides quotes from Galen's "commentary" on the *Laws*,[8] and his contemporary and friend Joseph ibn Aknin quotes from Galen's *Summary of the Republic*.[9]

However, it was mainly through the works of his later interpreters and followers that the doctrines of Plato had an effect on Jewish intellectuals in the Islamic cultural sphere, first of all through quotations and interpretation of Platonic doctrine occurring in the body of Aristotle's writings, and secondly through Neoplatonic interpreters of Plato, mainly Plotinus and Proclus. The doctrines of Plotinus became known through the medium of the pseudepigraphical *Theology of Aristotle,* which consists of excerpts from the fourth, fifth, and sixth *Enneads* of Plotinus, as well as other works. The longer version of the *Theology of Aristotle* includes extracts from an as yet unknown Neoplatonic work cited in the works of Isaac Israeli and translated partially into Hebrew by Abraham ibn Ḥasdai in *Ben ha-Melekh ve-ha-Nazir* ("The Prince and the Ascetic"), which itself is a translation of an Arabic work which goes back to the legend of Buddha. Also interpolated in the longer version are texts relating to the doctrine of the Divine Will, which are not Plotinian and had an influence, along with the whole *Theology,* on Ibn Gabirol in his *Fons Vitae.*

The Arabic philosopher Avicenna untilized Neoplatonic sources in the

construction of his philosophic system and had a vast influence on philosophic circles, Jewish as well as non-Jewish. The influence of Neoplatonism
on Jewish mystical (kabbalistic) thought is also very great. A third
major source of Platonic doctrine was through the works of al-Fārābī,
who seems to have been dependent on a tradition of Platonic interpretation which emphasized the political aspect of his thought. The influence
of the *Republic* and the *Laws* as well as the *Statesman* are apparent in
his political works. In his *Philosophy of Plato and Aristotle*, he summarizes briefly all of the dialogues and considers them from a political point
of view. Extensive excerpts from this work were translated into Hebrew
by the polymath 13th-century historian of philosophy, Shem Tov ibn
Falaquera. Maimonides in his *Guide* leans heavily on al-Fārābī in his
attempt to explain the relationship which should obtain between philosophy and religion. Plato indirectly thus influenced the whole course
of later Jewish medieval philosophy, which was mainly a reaction to the
position taken by Maimonides in his *Guide*. Maimonides' esotericism in
the *Guide* may also have been influenced by the tradition of Platonic
esotericism common in Arabic philosophic literature.[10]

The *Politics* of Aristotle was not known in the Arabic west, where
Plato was the major classic of political philosophy. Averroes composed
an *Epitome of the Republic* in which he expresses interesting personal
views, more openly than he would in works addressed to a more religious
audience, on the relation between philosophy and politics. This work,
along with Averroes' *Middle Commentary on the Nicomachean Ethics*,
was translated by Samuel b. Judah of Marseilles into Hebrew in the 14th
century, and marks the first time that a classical work of political
philosophy was translated into Hebrew. The work was soon summarized
by Joseph ibn Kaspi, Samuel's contemporary, and exercised some
influence on the course of later Jewish philosophy. In the 16th century
the Jewish physician Jacob Mantino translated it from Hebrew into Latin
and it appears in the standard Latin editions of Averroes' works.

Neoplatonism was characterized by the doctrine of emanation, which
states that the world and its parts emanated from a first principle, God,
in a manner analogous to the emanation of rays from the sun or streams
of water from a living fountain. To safeguard the absolute unity of God,
Neoplatonists posited a first emanation, identified by some with wisdom
(logos) and by others with will, which was between God and the world.
Drawing on an analogy between man, the microcosm, and the world, the

macrocosm, Neoplatonists posited a number of spiritual substances, such as intellect, soul, and nature, between the first emanation and the world. Some Neoplatonists also held that the spiritual world, no less than the visible, is composed of matter and form. Neoplatonism is marked by the insistence that God is completely above the created order and thus can be described only by negative attributes. Some Neoplatonists held that the world proceeds by necessity from God and is contemporaneous with Him, while others, making concessions to Scripture, affirmed that the world is the product of God's will and is posterior to Him. In their conception of man, Neoplatonists subscribed to the duality of body and soul. The human soul, being spiritual and self-subsistent, is independent of the body and having descended from the supernal world, reverts to its source by means of ethical and intellectual purification (or by theurgy; e.g., Iamblichus). The stages of ascent were commonly designated (after Proclus) the *via purgativa* (purification), *via illuminativa* (illumination), and *via unitiva* (union), the highest stage, a kind of *unio mystica* (mystical union) and apotheosis, being the sole means by which the One is apprehended. In its individuation and investiture in the body, the soul is devalorized; release from the fetters of the body in ecstasy or in death is equivalent to salvation, this philosophical soteriology tending toward combination with a doctrine of metempsychosis.

Neoplatonism is thus seen to be a religious movement and a doctrine of salvation as well as a philosophical system. As such, it was potentially an antagonist and an ally of the monotheistic faiths. Ancient Neoplatonism (excluding the school of Alexandria) was hostile to Christianity: Porphyry and Julian wrote refutations of Christianity; Iamblichus, Proclus, and Damascius were implacable opponents of Christianity. Indeed, Neoplatonism as a philosophical interpretation of pagan mythology (e.g., Iamblichus and Proclus) represents the dying gasp of ancient paganism. The fundamental postulates of Neoplatonism conflict with those of the monotheistic faiths: an impersonal first principle, rejection of creation and revelation, the conception of man as essentially soul, and the attendant soteriology-eschatology (including metempsychosis) involving submergence of the individual soul in the universal soul. Nevertheless, for monotheistic philosophers the contradictions were not insurmountable. In fact, the method of figurative interpretation cultivated by ancient Neoplatonists (after the Pythagoreans and Stoics) in order to identify pagan mythological themes with philosophical ideas was employed by monotheistic philosophers in order to read their neoplatonic doctrines into the text of Scripture. The ladder of Jacob's dream was thus interpreted as a symbol of the soul's ascent e.g., by Ibn Gabirol,[11] creation became a metaphor for eternal procession. Revelation and prophecy were discussed in terms reminiscent of the *unio mystica*. This identification was not without some basis in ancient Neoplatonism either, if one considers the aspect of grace or divine initiative implicit in *Enneads* 5:3, 17 and 5:5, 8, or the use of the Chaldean Oracles and Orphic Hymns by Porphyry and Iamblichus. Assimilation to the divine, the goal of philosophy according to the neoplatonic introductions to Aristotle of the Alexandria school, resonated with similar ideals of the monotheistic traditions. The deep spirituality of Neoplatonism promoted the kind of synthesis with religious feeling that finds moving expression in Ibn Gabirol's poem, *Keter Malkhut*.

ISAAC ISRAELI

Neoplatonism in Jewish philosophy appeared at the same time as the Kalām. The first Neoplatonist was the renowned physician Isaac b. Solomon Israeli (c. 855–c. 955), who flourished in Kairouan. Influenced by the Islamic philosopher al-Kindī and various Neoplatonic writings, he composed *Kitāb al-Ḥudūd* (*Sefer ha-Gevulim;* "Book of Definitions"), *Kitāb al-Jawāhir* ("Book of Substances"), *Sefer ha-Ru'aḥ ve-ha-Nefesh* ("Book on Spirit and Soul"), *Sha'ar ha-Yesodot* ("Chapter on the Elements"), and *Kitāb al-Ustuquṣṣāt* ("Book on the Elements"). In Latin translations some of these works influenced Christian scholastic thought. According to Israeli, God, the Creator, in His goodness and love created the world in time and out of nothing. The means of creation were His power and His will, which for Israeli are attributes of God, not separate hypostases. Two simple substances, first matter and first form, or wisdom, come directly from God. It appears that these two principles combine to form the next hypostasis, intellect, but Israeli also affirms that first matter and form have no separate existence but exist only in the intellect. Intellect is followed by three distinct hypostases of soul—rational, animal, and vegetative. The next hypostasis is nature, which Israeli identifies with the celestial sphere.

This hypostasis is the last of the simple substances and holds a position intermediate between these substances and the perceptible world. The four elements of the lower world are produced from the motion of the celestial sphere. Israeli distinguished three stages in the creation of the world: creation proper, which produces only first matter, first form, and intellect; emanation, which produces the four spiritual substances; and causality of nature, which produces the world below the heavens. Israeli's philosophy of man is based on the neoplatonic notion of the human soul's return to the upper world from which it came. The soul's ascent proceeds in three stages: purification, which consists of turning away from appetites and passions; illumination by the intellect, which produces wisdom defined as knowledge of eternal things; and union with, or adherence to, supernal wisdom (not God), at which stage the soul becomes spiritual. Union with supernal wisdom can be accomplished even in this life. Israeli identifies union with the religious notion of paradise, and he holds that the punishment of sinners is that their souls cannot ascend to the upper region but are caught in the fire extending below the heavens. Israeli distinguishes between philosophy, which is the quest for wisdom, and wisdom, which is the final goal. Discussing the prophet, Israeli sees no sharp distinction between him and the philosopher: both are concerned with the ascent of the soul and with guiding mankind toward truth and justice. Israeli distinguishes three kinds of prophecy, which are in ascending order: voice *(kol)*, spirit *(ru'aḥ)*, and speech *(dibbur)*. Many of Israeli's ideas are cited and developed in the commentary on *Sefer Yeẓirah* by his disciple, Dunash ibn Tamim.

SOLOMON BEN JUDAH IBN GABIROL

The main source of information on Solomon ibn Gabirol's life is his poems, but frequently these provide little more than hints or bare facts.

Ibn Gabirol was apparently born in Malaga—or at any rate he lived there and regarded it as his native city, but as a child he was taken to Saragossa, where he acquired an extensive education. Orphaned at an early age, Gabirol complained of his weak physique, small stature, and ugliness, and it is apparent that he was frequently ill in his childhood, suffering particularly from a serious skin disease. Beginning to write poetry at an early age, at the latest 16, his self-esteem, at times verging on arrogance, brought him into frequent conflict with influential men of his day, whom he attacked virulently. Since he wanted to devote his life to philosophy and poetry, he was dependent on the support of wealthy patrons, a subservience against which he rebelled from time to time. It is thought that he wrote *Tikkun Middot ha-Nefesh* ("The Improvement of the Moral Qualities") in 1045, and soon afterward he seems to have left Saragossa; from then on few details are available on his life and work. According to Ibn Ezra, Gabirol died in Valencia at the age of 30, while Abraham b. David states that he died in 1070, when he was approximately 50. However, the most exact date seems to be that given by Ibn Sa'id: 450 A.H. or 1057–58, when he was between 35 and 38. There are many legends surrounding his life which have come down to us which attest to the awe in which the man and his works were held after his death.[12]

In one of his poems, Gabirol boasts of having written 20 books, but only two are extant that can certainly be attributed to him: *Mekor Ḥayyim* (The Fountain of Life) and *Tikkun Middot ha-Nefesh*. The difficult task of recovering and identifying Gabirol's poems, which were scattered in prayer books, anthologies, and single pages dispersed in many libraries, was first undertaken in the 19th century by J. L. Dukes, S. D. Luzzatto, S. Sachs, and H. Brody, who brought out the first collection of his verse. The discovery in the *Genizah* in the early part of the 20th century of an ancient index of poems by Gabirol, Ibn Ezra, and Judah Halevi proved that there had been a very early collection of Gabirol's poems, and later a complete *divan* was found in manuscript (Schocken 37).

In his poetic works Gabirol displays his great knowledge of biblical Hebrew and his linguistic virtuosity, while avoiding the complexity of many of his predecessors. Employing images and idioms from Arabic poetry, he fuses them into an original style. In spiritual tone his poetry is shaped by Bible and talmudic literature as well as by early mystical Midrashim. In its mystical tendencies, his work is closely akin to Sufi poetry. Both his scientific knowledge, especially of astronomy, and his Neoplatonic leanings are evident in his poems.

In accordance with contemporary tradition, most of Gabirol's secular poetry was composed in honor of patrons whom he describes in extravagant panegyric. In his "wisdom poetry" he depicts himself as devoting his life to knowledge in order to prepare his soul to rejoin the "Source of Life" on its release from its bodily prison. Knowledge has two aspects consisting both of the effort of the intellect to scale the heights of the heavenly spheres and of the soul's introspection. At first pleading with God to let him live, the poet soon begins to deride the world and time, regarding them as valueless and insignificant obstacles on the way to eternity. From the height of his identification with the infinity of the Godhead and of eternity, he regards with disgust the trials of the world below, the illusions of the senses, and the weakness of the flesh.

In accordance with the rules of rhetoric, some of Gabirol's extensive nature poetry seems to have served as an introduction to his laudatory verse, for the patron's generosity was often likened to the ordained plenitude of nature. It is clear from his nature poetry that he was influenced by the predominantly Islamic culture prevalent in Spain at the time, but within this traditional framework, the fine descriptions are accurately observed.

In another large section of Gabirol's work, his ethical poems, he addresses the reader directly, propounding an ethic based upon individual introspection. These poems deal with the transience of life and the worthlessness of bodily existence in all its aspects as opposed to the eternal values of spiritual life and the immortality of the soul. Gabirol's didactic tendency also finds expression in the many riddles he composed, which were possibly appended to letters, and it is also apparent in the dialogue form in which many of the longer poems were written. This style, developed in medieval Arabic poetry, was also used to introduce variety into the long poems which otherwise tended to be monotonous as a result of the identical rhyming of all the stanzas.

Stylistically, liturgical poets were always the elite of medieval Jewish poetry and Gabirol's works in this genre are the apogee of the tradition. Gabirol composed a substantial number of religious poems in the difficult style of the early school of liturgical poets, possibly because they were commissioned by various communities or synagogues. Despite this, the freshness and vivacity of his imagery is striking. Many of these liturgical poems have been preserved, not only in Sephardi and Ashkenazi prayer books but also in those of the Karaites. It is on the basis of these poems that Gabirol is regarded as the major religious poet of Spanish Jewry. Although his God is a personal deity, to whom he may turn in confession or supplication, Gabirol, unlike Judah Halevi, does not describe his great love for God as the relationship between the lover and the beloved. The poet, who in his secular verse is strong-willed and contemptuous of the base world about him, becomes humble in his religious poetry as he begins to understand himself and man in general. When addressing God, he realizes his insignificance and his inability either to combat desire or to understand the essential evil of the senses for which there is no succor except in the compassion of God *("Adonai, Mah Adam," "Shokhenei Battei Ḥomer")*. At times, these expressions of longing and of profound love for God are akin to the emotions expressed in the love poems *("Shaḥar Aleh Elai Dodi")*.

The concepts and visions in Gabirol's mystical poems are very difficult to reconcile with the philosophical concepts expressed in his other works. In these poems, knowledge of the Divinity can be apprehended only by the elect who have plumbed the mysteries of creation through which God manifests Himself. The very names of God are endowed with mystical significance, becoming potent symbols of the power of the Creator and the wonders of His creation. Many midrashic elements, as well as God's reply out of the whirlwind in Job, join to form a dynamic, mystery-shrouded account of creation breaking forth from the turmoil of primordial chaos into reality and form. There are detailed descriptions of the upper spheres, the curtain of the heavens, and the abode of the angels. The close relationship between imagery and content in some of these poems, suggests that they may have been written in moments of ecstasy.

Judah Al-Ḥarizi has the highest praise for Gabirol's poetry: "All the poets of his age were worthless and false in comparison . . . He alone trod the highest reaches of poetry, and rhetoric gave birth to him in the lap of wisdom . . . all the poets before him were as nothing and after him none rose to equal him. All those who followed learned and received the use of poetry from him" *(Taḥkemoni,* "Third Gate").

Philosophy. Gabirol presents his philosophic views in his major work *Mekor Ḥayyim* ("The Source of Life"). Written in Arabic, but no longer extant in that language, the full work has been preserved in a medieval Latin translation under the title *Fons Vitae*. A Hebrew translation of several extracts by Shem Tov ibn Falaquera (13th century), who claimed that it contained all of Gabirol's thought, is also extant under the title *Likkutim mi-Sefer Mekor Ḥayyim*. In studying *Mekor Ḥayyim,* however, the loss of the Arabic original makes it difficult to explain certain terms.

Mekor Hayyim is written in the form of a dialogue between master and pupil, a style also current in Arabic philosophic literature of that period. However, it is not a typical Platonic dialogue, in which the student discovers true opinions for himself through discussion with the master; instead, the student's questions serve to enable the master to expound his views. *Mekor Hayyim,* divided into five treatises, is devoted primarily to a discussion of the principles of matter and form. The first treatise is a preliminary clarification of the notions of universal matter and form, a discussion of matter and form as they exist in objects of sense perception, and a discussion of the corporeal matter underlying qualities. The second treatise contains a description of the spiritual matter that underlies corporeal form. The third is devoted to demonstrating the existence of simple substances. The fourth deals with the form and matter of simple substances, and the fifth, with universal form and matter as they exist in themselves. The doctrine of matter and form is, in Gabirol's view (*Mekor Hayyim,* 1:7), the first of the three branches of science, the other two being, in ascending order, the science of (God's) will and the science of the First Essence, God. Gabirol states (5:40) that he has written a special book devoted to God's will, but no further evidence of such a book is available.

Gabirol's cosmological system generally has a neoplatonic structure but with modifications of his own. The first principle is the First Essence, which can be identified with God. Next in order of being are the divine will, universal matter and form, then the simple substances— intellect, soul, and nature, and finally the corporeal world and its parts. Gabirol holds that all substances in the world, both spiritual and corporeal, are composed of two elements, form and matter. This duality produces the differences between various substances, but, according to some passages, it is specifically the forms that distinguish one substance from the other, while according to others, it is matter. Matter is the substratum underlying the forms; forms inhere in it. All distinctions between matter and form in the various substances stem from the distinction between universal matter and universal form, the most general kinds of matter and form, which, according to Gabirol's account of being, are the first created beings. However, Gabirol presents conflicting accounts of their creation. According to one account (5:42), universal matter comes from the essence of God, and form, from the divine will, but according to another (5:36–38), both of these principles were created by the divine will. In some passages Gabirol holds that universal matter exists by itself (2:8, 5:32), which deviates from the Aristotelian account of matter, but in other passages he states, in accord with Aristotle's view, that matter is akin to privation, and form to being, and that matter exists only in potentiality (5:36).

All forms, in addition to appearing in various levels of being, are also contained in universal form. Matter and form do not exist by themselves; their first compound is intellect, the first of the spiritual substances, from which the soul emanates, it, too, being composed of matter and form. Hence, as opposed to the Aristotelian views, spiritual matter exists, and it is found in all incorporeal substances. All spiritual, or simple, substances emanate forces that bestow existence upon substances below them in the order of being. Thus, soul is emanated from intellect. There are three kinds of soul, rational, animate, and vegetative, which, besides being cosmic principles, also exist in man. In contrast to the opinion of the Aristotelians, nature as a cosmic principle emanates from the vegetative soul. Nature is the last of the simple substances, and from it emanates corporeal substance, which is below nature in the order of being. Corporeal substance is the substratum underlying nine of the ten Aristotelian categories. The tenth category, substance, is universal matter as it appears in the corporeal world, and the nine other categories are universal form as it appears in the corporeal world.

For soul to be joined to body a mediating principle is required. The mediating principle joining the universal soul to the corporeal world is the heavens; the mediating principle joining the rational soul of man to the body is the animal spirit. The relation of man's body to his soul is also said to be like the relation between form and matter (a parallel which is difficult to reconcile with Gabirol's account of these two principles). The soul comprehends the forms but not matter, since the latter principle is unintelligible. In order to comprehend sensible forms the soul must use the senses, because these forms do not exist in the soul as they are in the corporeal world. The forms which always exist in the soul are the intelligible forms. However, since the soul was deprived of its knowledge as a result of its union with the body, these forms exist in the soul only potentially, not actually. Therefore,

God created the world and provided senses for the soul, by means of which it may conceive tangible forms and patterns. It is through this comprehension of the sensible forms and patterns that the soul also comprehends ideas, which in the soul emerge from potentiality to actuality (5: 41).

All forms exist in intellect, also, but in a more subtle and simple manner than in soul. Furthermore, in intellect they do not have separate existence, but are conjoined with it in a spiritual union. "The form of the intellect includes all the forms, and they are contained in it" (4:14). Intellect, which is composed of universal form and matter, is below these two principles, and therefore can conceive them only with great difficulty.

Above the knowledge of form and matter there is a far more sublime knowledge: that of the divine will, which is identical with divine wisdom and divine logos. This will in itself, if considered apart from its activity, may be thought of as identical with the Divine Essence, but when considered with respect to its activity, it is separate from divine essence. Will according to its essence is infinite, but with respect to its action is finite. It is the intermediary between divine essence and matter and form, but it also penetrates all things. In its function as the efficient cause of everything, it unites forms with matter. The will, which causes all movement, be it spiritual or corporeal, is in itself at rest. The will acts differently on different substances, this difference depending upon the particular matter, not upon the will (5:37). The First Essence, in this case God, cannot be known because it is infinite and because it lacks any similarity to the soul. Nevertheless, its existence can be demonstrated.

The goal to which all men should aspire is defined in *Mekor Ḥayyim* (1:1, 2:1) as knowledge of the purpose for which they were created, i.e., knowledge of the divine world (5:43). There are two ways to achieve this goal: through knowledge of the will as it extends into all matter and form, and through knowledge of the will as it exists in itself apart from matter and form. This knowledge brings release from death and attachment to "the source of life."

Philosophical Sources. On a number of points, Gabirol's philosophy is close to the Neoplatonic system current in medieval thought, for example, the concept of emanation that explains the derivation of simple substances and the concept of the parallel correspondence between different grades of being. Nevertheless, it differs on two very important points from the Muslim Neoplatonism: the concept of form and matter (especially the latter) and the concept of will.

Gabirol's concept of matter is not internally coherent. On the one hand, it reflects distinct Aristotelian influence, but on the other, the occasional identification of matter with essence (*substantia*) suggests a Stoic influence, possibly the result of Gabirol's reading of the Greek physician Galen (second century). A concept that particularly characterizes Gabirol's system is spiritual matter. One possible source of this concept is the Neoplatonist Plotinus (205?–270) in his *Enneads* (2:4), but there is no known Arabic translation of the latter's text. Theorem 72 of Proclus' *Elements of Theology*, which was translated into Arabic, sets forth a view of matter akin to Gabirol's. Like Gabirol, Plotinus and the Greek Neoplatonist Proclus (c. 410?–485) regard matter as the basis of all unity in the spiritual world as well as in the physical. However, they do not maintain that universal form and matter are the first simple substances after God and His will. Pseudo-Empedoclean writings set forth the view that matter (Heb. *yesod*) and form are the first created beings and are prior to intellect. Ibn Falaquera states explicitly that Gabirol followed the views expressed by "Empedocles," that is, in the Pseudo-Empedoclean writings. It is even more likely that Gabirol's views on form and matter were influenced by certain texts of Isaac Israeli or by a pseudo-Aristotelian text.[13]

In the identification of divine will and the logos and in the concept of the omnipresence of will, Gabirol's concept of will finds a parallel in Saadiah Gaon's commentary to *Sefer Yeẓirah* (Book of Creation). There is also a partial similarity of Gabirol's teachings to those of the Muslim Ismaili sect. In the text of *Mekor Ḥayyim* Plato is the only philosopher mentioned.

Tikkun Middot ha-Nefesh, Gabirol's work on ethics, was written about 1045. In this work Gabirol discusses the parallel between the universe, the macrocosmos, and man, the microcosmos. There is no mention in the book of the four cardinal virtues of the soul, a Platonic doctrine which was popular in Arabic ethical writings. Gabirol developed an original theory, in which each of 20 personal traits is assigned to one of the five senses: pride, meekness, modesty, and impudence are related to the sense of sight; love, mercy, hate, and cruelty, to the sense of hearing; anger, goodwill, envy, and diligence, to the sense of smell; joy, anxiety, contentedness, and regret, to the sense of taste; and generosity, stinginess, courage, and cowardice, to the sense of touch. Gabirol also describes the relation between the virtues and the four qualities: heat, cold, moistness, and dryness, which are incorporated in pairs in each of the four elements of which the earth is composed: earth, air, water, and fire.

Gabirol gives poetic expression to the philosophical thought of *Mekor Ḥayyim* in the first part of his poem *Keter Malkhut*.[14] Although the conceptual framework of *Keter Malkhut* is not identical in every detail to that of *Mekor Ḥayyim*, the differences are in many cases only of phrasing or emphasis. The conceptual variations reflect the contradictions apparent in *Mekor Ḥayyim* itself. *Keter Malkhut* opens with praise for the Creator and an account of His attributes: His unity, existence, eternity, and life and His greatness, power, and divinity. God is also described as "Light," according to the neoplatonic image of the deity, "Thou art the supreme light and the eyes of the pure soul shall see thee" (tr. Lewis, 31). Nevertheless, Gabirol stresses that God and his attributes are not distinguishable: we refer to attributes only because of the limited means of human expression.

The next section speaks of divine "Wisdom" and the "predestined Will" *(ha-Ḥefeẓ ha-Mezumman)*, which together parallel the single concept of will *(Raẓon)* in *Mekor Ḥayyim*. "Thou art wise, and from Thy wisdom Thou didst send forth a predestined will, and made it as an artisan and a craftsman, to draw the stream of being from the void . . ." *(ibid.,* 33). His description of the creative activity of the predestined will corresponds with the concept of will in *Mekor Ḥayyim*, but despite the close ties between them, wisdom and will are not as closely identified with each other in *Keter Malkhut* as in *Mekor Ḥayyim*. In *Mekor Ḥayyim* Wisdom is seated upon the Throne, which is the first matter; in *Keter Malkhut* the link between these two substances is not clearly stated: "Who can come to Thy dwelling place, when Thou didst raise up above the sphere of intelligence the throne of glory, in which is the abode of mystery and majesty, in which is the secret and the foundation to which the intelligence reaches . . ." *(ibid.,* 47). Apparently, in *Keter Malkhut* the foundation or element *(ha-Yesod)* is the first matter.

The will is the instrument and the means of creation; after the description of the will the poet goes on to describe the structure of the world according to Ptolemaic cosmology. The earth, "half water, half land," is surrounded by a "sphere of air," above which there is a "sphere of fire." The world of the four elements is circumscribed by the spheres of the moon, Mercury, Venus, the sun, Mars, Jupiter, Saturn, the zodiac, and the diurnal sphere, "which surrounds all other spheres." The distance of these spheres from the world, the length of their orbit, the magnitude of the heavenly bodies found within them, and, particularly, their forces and their influence upon nature, worldly events, and the fate of man are all described according to Ptolemaic and Muslim astronomy. However, beyond the nine spheres there is yet another, which is the result of philosophical abstraction: " . . . the sphere of the Intelligence, 'the temple before it,'" from whose luster emanates the "radiance of souls and lofty spirits . . . messengers of Thy Will" (*ibid.*, 45). Above this sphere is "the throne of glory, in the abode of mystery and majesty," and beneath it is "the abode of the pure souls" (*ibid.*, 47). In this exalted sphere, also, the punishment of sinful souls will be meted out. This part of the poem ends with a description of the soul that descends from the upper spheres to reside temporarily in matter, the source of sin, from which the soul can escape only by "the power of knowledge which inheres" in it (*ibid.*, 50). The concluding section of the poem contains a confession of sins *(viddui)*, and for that reason *Keter Malkhut* was included in the Day of Atonement prayer book of some Jewish rites.

Mekor Ḥayyim is unique in the body of Jewish philosophical-religious literature of the Middle Ages, because it expounds a complete philosophical-religious system wholly lacking in specifically Jewish content and terminology. The author does not mention biblical persons or events and does not quote the Bible, Talmud, or Midrash. To some extent this feature of the work determined its unusual destiny. Among Jewish philosophers *Mekor Ḥayyim* is quoted by Moses ibn Ezra in his *Arugat ha-Bosem.* Abraham ibn Ezra was apparently influenced by it although he makes no direct reference to the work, and Joseph ibn Ẓaddik, the author of *Ha-Olam ha-Katan,* also drew on it. There is also a clear similarity between the views of the Spanish philosopher and kabbalist Isaac ibn Latif and those of *Mekor Ḥayyim.* Traces of Gabirol's ideas and terminology appear in the Kabbalah as well.

On the other hand, *Mekor Ḥayyim* was severely attacked by

Abraham ibn Daud, an Aristotelian, in his book *Emunah Ramah*. Despite these influences, however, *Mekor Hayyim* was slowly forgotten among Jews. In its own time it was not translated into Hebrew, and the original Arabic text was lost.

In the 12th century *Mekor Hayyim* was translated into Latin by Johannes Hispalensus (Hispanus) and Dominicus Gundissalinus. Hispalenus, also known as Aven Dauth, may possibly have been the same Ibn Daud who criticized Gabirol. Gabirol's name was corrupted to Avicebron, and he was generally regarded a Muslim, although some Christians thought he was a Christian. Some Christian thinkers were greatly influenced by *Mekor Hayyim*. Aristotelians, such as Thomas Aquinas, sharply criticized Gabirol's views, but the Franciscan philosophers, who favored Augustine, accepted some of them. Especially important are St. Bonaventura and Matthew of Aquasparta who made a great deal of Ibn Gabirols' views on "form" and "matter." The Jewish philosophers Isaac Abrabanel and his son Judah Abrabanel, better known as Leone Ebreo, seem to have been familiar with some of Gabirol's works. Leone Ebreo, who quotes him by the name Albenzubron, regards him as a Jew, and states his own belief in Gabirol's views. It was only in the 19th century, 350 years after the Abrabanels, that Solomon Munk, the French scholar, rediscovered the Falaquera extracts and through them identified Avicebron as Solomon ibn Gabirol, a Jew. Among modern philosophers, Schopenhauer noted a certain similarity between his own system and that of Gabirol.

BAHYA (Bahye) BEN JOSEPH IBN PAQUDA

Bahya ibn Paquda is the best known of all Jewish moral philosophers. Little is known about the particulars of his life beyond the fact that he lived in Muslim Spain, probably at Saragossa. Bahya was also known as a religious poet. Bahya's major work, *Kitāb al-Hidāya ilā Farāʾiḍ al-Qulūb* was written around 1080.[15] It was translated into Hebrew by Judah ibn Tibbon in 1161 under the title *Hovot ha-Levavot* ("Duties of the Hearts"), and in this version it became popular and had a profound influence on all subsequent Jewish pietistic literature. Several abridgments were made of the Hebrew translation, and the work was translated into Arabic, Spanish, Portuguese, Italian, and Yiddish.[16]

In his *Hovot ha-Levavot* Bahya drew a great deal upon non-Jewish sources, borrowing from Muslim mysticism, Arabic Neoplatonism, and perhaps also from the Hermetic writings. From Muslim authors he borrowed the basic structure of the book as well as definitions, aphorisms, and examples to illustrate his doctrines.

Despite the fact that Bahya borrowed so liberally from non-Jewish sources, *Hovot ha-Levavot* remains an essentially Jewish book. In the introduction to this work Bahya divides the obligations incumbent upon the religious man into duties of the members of the body *(hovot ha-evarim)*, those obligations which involve overt actions; and duties of the hearts *(hovot ha-levavot)*, those obligations which involve not man's actions, but his inner life. The first division includes the various ritual and ethical observances commanded by the Torah, e.g., the observance of the Sabbath, prayer, and the giving of charity, while the second consists of beliefs, e.g., the belief in the existence and unity of God, and attitudes or spiritual traits, e.g., trust in God, love and fear of Him, and repentance. The prohibitions against bearing a grudge and taking revenge are also examples of duties of the hearts. Bahya explains that he wrote this work because the duties of man's inner life had been sorely neglected by his predecessors and contemporaries whose writings had concentrated on religious observances, that is, the duties of the members of the body. To remedy this deficiency Bahya wrote his work, which may be considered a kind of counterpart to the halakhic (legal) compendia of his predecessors and contemporaries. Just as their halakhic compendia contained directions for the actions of the religious man, so Bahya's work contained directions for his inner life. *Hovot ha-Levavot* is modeled after the works of Muslim mysticism, which attempt to lead the reader through various ascending stages of man's inner life, toward spiritual perfection and finally union (or at least communion) with God.

In accordance with Platonic teachings (probably influenced partially by the Epistles of the Sincere Brethren), he maintains that man's soul, which is celestial in origin, is placed, by divine decree, within the body, where it runs the risk of forgetting its nature and mission. The human soul receives aid from the intellect and the revealed Law in achieving its goal. To elucidate this point Bahya makes use of the Mu'tazilite distinction between rational and traditional commandments. He holds that the duties of the members of the body may be divided into rational commandments and traditional (religious) commandments, while the duties of the hearts are all rooted in the intellect. With the aid of reason and the revealed Law the soul can triumph over its enemy, the evil inclination *(yezer),* which attacks it incessantly in an effort to beguile it into erroneous beliefs and to enslave it to bodily appetites. Since the basis of religion is the belief in the existence of God, the first chapter of the work is devoted to a philosophical and theological explication of the existence and unity of God and a discussion of His attributes.

In the second chapter Baḥya examines the order in the universe and the extraordinary structure of man, the microcosm. Such an examination leads to a knowledge of God, and to a sense of gratitude towards Him as creator. In the third chapter he discusses divine worship, which is the expression of man's gratitude to God. To fulfill his duties to God without faltering and to achieve his true goal, man must diligently practice a number of virtues. One of these is trust in God, which is based on the belief that God is good, and that he has a knowledge of what is best for man, and the power to protect him. To trust in God does not mean that one should neglect one's work, leaving everything to Him, but rather that one should conscientiously attempt to carry out one's duties, trusting that God will remove any obstacles which lie in the way of their fulfillment. While man has the freedom to will and choose, the realization of his actions is dependent on God's will. Further, a sound spiritual life requires sincerity, a perfect correspondence between man's conscience and behavior. Man's intentions must coincide with his actions in aiming toward the service of God. Humility, repentance, and self-examination are also essential. Another virtue is asceticism or temperance. Baḥya considers total asceticism, involving the breaking of all social ties, an ideal rarely attained in the biblical past and hardly to be recommended in the present. Actually, he recommends the pursuit of the middle way prescribed by the revealed Law, defining the genuine ascetic as one who directs all his actions to the service of God, while at the same time fulfilling his functions within society. The observance of these virtues leads to the highest stage of the spiritual life, the love of God. True love of God is the ardor of the soul for union with the Divine Light, a concept of a distinctly mystic character. Baḥya does not, however, develop this concept in all its implications. The love of God, in his view, is a synthesis of the degrees of perfection described above, but does not go beyond them. The lover of God, such as described by him, keeps at a distance from his loved one. Despite Baḥya's dependence upon Muslim mysticism, which is here more pronounced than elsewhere in the work, his teaching remains in the line of Jewish tradition, and he cannot be called a mystic in the strict sense of the term.[17] Baḥya's *Ḥovot ha-Levavot* established itself as the single most important Jewish ethical treatise of the whole medieval and early modern period. In one way or another, all attempts to define and understand Jewish ethics and the nature of Jewish spirituality after Baḥya's classic had to deal with the problem of spiritual interiority and recognize its centrality for true piety.

MINOR NEOPLATONISTS

Abraham bar Ḥiyya. Abraham b. Ḥiyya (first half of the 12th century), who lived in Spain and was the author of works on mathematics and astronomy, was the first to write philosophical works in Hebrew. His philosophic ideas, influenced by Neoplatonism and Aristotelianism, are found in his *Hegyon ha-Nefesh ha-Aẓuvah* ("Meditation of the Sad Soul") and in his eschatological treatise *Megillat ha-Megalleh* ("Scroll of the Revealer"). Central to the former work is a discussion of repentance; in general, his interests are more ethical and theological than philosophic. Abraham b. Ḥiyya subscribes to the doctrine of emanation, but, differing from earlier Neoplatonists, he interposes a world of light and a world of dominion between God and the three spiritual substances. His conception of matter and form is Aristotelian: he holds that these principles exist only in the corporeal world, not in that of the simple substances. In *Hegyon ha-Nefesh,* Abraham b. Ḥiyya divides the fates of souls after death into four categories: souls that have acquired intellectual and moral perfection will ascend to the upper world; souls that have acquired intellectual, but not moral, perfection will ascend only to the sphere below the sun, where they will be afflicted by the sun's fire; souls that have acquired moral, but not intellectual, perfection transmigrate to other bodies until they have acquired knowledge; and souls that have neither perfection will perish with their bodies. However, in *Megillat ha-Megilleh,* he denies the transmigration of the soul and makes the afterlife more dependent on moral perfection. In *Megillat ha-Megalleh* Abraham b. Ḥiyya formulates a theory of

history reminiscent of Judah Halevi's theory and of Christian speculation. The history of the world can be divided into six periods corresponding to the six days of creation. There is also an analogue to the Christian
notion of original sin: God created Adam with three souls, rational,
appetitive, and vegetative. Before Adam sinned the rational soul
existed independently of the other two souls, but afterwards it became
dependent on them. After the flood, God freed the rational soul from
its dependence on the vegetative soul, but not from its dependence on
the appetitive soul. However, in each generation the rational soul of
one man achieved independence, and this was the state of affairs until
the time of Jacob. In Jacob the rational soul was so pure that all of
his descendants, first his 12 sons and later all of Israel, received a
rational soul independent of the lower two souls. This is Abraham bar
Ḥiyya's explanation of the election of Israel, though he does not
deny that there may also be righteous persons among the gentiles.

Joseph ibn Ẓaddik. Joseph ibn Ẓaddik of Cordova (d. 1149) was
the author of *Sefer ha-Olam ha-Katan* ("Book of the Microcosm"), an
eclectic Neoplatonic work with Aristotelian and kalamic influences,
apparently written as a handbook for beginners. In the four parts of the
work he discusses the principles of the corporeal world and its constitution, the nature of man and the human soul, the existence of God
(derived from the creation of the world) and His attributes, and human
conduct and reward and punishment. His thought shows similarities to
that of Saadiah, Israeli, Baḥya, Pseudo-Baḥya, and Ibn Gabirol,
though he does not mention them, and he attempts to refute opinions
of the Karaite al-Baṣīr. With Ibn Gabirol, he affirms that spiritual
beings are composed of matter and form, but he defines the matter
of spiritual beings as the genus of a species rather than as a distinct
principle. However, he does not mention Ibn Gabirol's universal
matter and universal form. Like Ibn Gabirol, Ibn Ẓaddik mentions the
divine will, but for him, it appears to be identical with the essence of
God rather than a separate hypostasis. He criticizes Al-Baṣīr's notion
that the divine will is a substance that God creates from time to time.
For his proof of the creation of the world he selects the Kalām proof
from accidents, but he describes God in Neoplatonic fashion as an
absolute unity beyond the world and as incomprehensible. Yet, he also
holds that God can be described by attributes that are identical with

His essence. These attributes in one respect describe God's actions, and in another, His essence; as describing His essence, they must be understood as negations. The attributes of action are important for providing models for human conduct. For example, as God is good and merciful, so man should be good and merciful. A similar orientation is found in his account of human happiness. He begins by saying that the knowledge of the supernal world and God is the goal of human life; but then he seems to consider this knowledge only as preliminary to proper conduct. Ibn Ẓaddik's account of the soul's fate after death is derived from Israeli (see above).

Moses and Abraham ibn Ezra. Moses ibn Ezra (c. 1055–after 1135) was important mainly as a poet and critic, but he presented some philosophic opinions in his *al-Maqāla bi al-Ḥadīqa fī Maʿnā al-Majāz wa al-Ḥaqīqa* (partially translated into Hebrew as *Arugat ha-Bosem*). Ibn Ezra was fond of quoting sayings (often incorrectly attributed) of such authorities as Pythagoras, Empedocles, Socrates, and Aristotle, and he preserved some Arabic quotations from Ibn Gabirol's *Mekor Ḥayyim*.[18] His orientation was Neoplatonic, and he employs the notions that man is a microcosm and everything in the upper world has its counterpart in man; the soul's knowledge of itself leads to the knowledge of the Creator; God is a unity above all unities, and, unknowable as He is in Himself, He can only be known by metaphors; the rational soul is a substance which must take care of the body; and others.

Abraham ibn Ezra (c. 1089–1164) was important as a grammarian, as an author of works on arithmetic and astronomy (including astrology), and as a biblical commentator. He was the author of *Sefer ha-Shem* and *Yesod Mora,* on the names of God and on the commandments, but his philosophic views are scattered throughout his biblical commentaries. He often presented his opinions in enigmatic language. Ibn Ezra was profoundly influenced by Neoplatonic doctrines, which in his formulation have at times a pantheistic ring; for example "God is the One; He made all and He is all." Like Ibn Gabirol he held that everything other than God is composed of matter and form, and he alludes as well to the divine will. Speaking of creation, Ibn Ezra affirmed that the world of the intelligences and angels as well as that of the celestial spheres is coeternal with God, and only the lower world was created (through emanation). The human soul comes into being from the spiritual substance known as the universal soul, and, if worthy, it can become immortal by being reunited with that soul and being absorbed by it. Destruction is the punishment of unworthy souls. Like the Islamic Aristotelians, Ibn Ezra held that God's knowledge extends only to species, not to individuals. God's providence, also general, is transmitted through the influences of the heavenly bodies, but individuals who have developed their souls and intellects can foresee evil influences caused by the celestial spheres and avoid them.

JUDAH HALEVI

The question of Judah Halevi's birthplace is still unsolved, but both Toledo and Tudela have been suggested. Under Muslim rule, Judah Halevi, apparently from a wealthy and learned family, received a comprehensive education in both Hebrew and Arabic. His childhood years were spent during a peaceful period for the Jews of the region. At an early age he traveled to Andalusia with the intention of proceeding to the large Jewish center in Granada. Among the various communities he passed through on his way was Córdoba where he participated in a poetry writing contest (styled after those of the Arabs). He won the competition for imitating a complicated poem by Moses ibn Ezra, who invited Judah Halevi to his home. The two developed a close friendship and Judah Halevi spent some time with him in Granada, in an atmosphere of wealth and culture.

With the coming of the Almoravides from Africa and their conquest of Muslim Spain (after 1090), the position of the Jews in Andalusia deteriorated, and Judah Halevi left Granada. For the following 20 years he traveled through numerous communities. While in Toledo, however, he was disillusioned by the murder in 1108 of his patron and benefactor, the nobleman Solomon ibn Ferrizuel, who had achieved a high rank in the service of Alfonso VI. Judah left Toledo apparently before the death of Alfonso VI (1109) and again began to travel. His fame continued to spread, and the circle of his friends and admirers, to whom he wrote many poems, broadened greatly.

His financial situation was generally sound; it seems that he was only rarely dependent on gifts. Aside from his profession as a physician, he also engaged in trade, apparently with Jewish merchants in Egypt. Active in community affairs, too, he helped to collect money for the ransom of captives. He also wrote laments on the death of many of his friends and acquaintances. Another genre in which he excelled was love poetry.

Of all his ties with various people, Judah Halevi's friendship with Abraham ibn Ezra was especially close and long-lasting. Both wandered through the various cities of Muslim Spain, and at least once traveled to North Africa together. In his biblical commentaries, Abraham ibn Ezra quotes Judah Halevi numerous times in matters of grammar, exegesis, and philosophy.

Erez Israel: Judah Halevi's decision to emigrate to Erez Israel, a gradual one, reflected the highest aspiration of his life. It resulted from a complex of circumstances: intense and realistic political thought; disillusionment with the possibility of secure Jewish existence in the Diaspora; intense longing for a positive, redeeming act; and the prevalent messianic climate, which so affected him that he once dreamt that the redemption would come in the year 4890 (1130 C.E.).

The decision was strengthened by his religious philosophy, developed at length in his book the *Kuzari* and in many of his poems. This philosophy maintained the unity which ensues from the relationship between the God of Israel, the people of Israel—to whom He chose to reveal His truth through His prophets—, Erez Israel—the "Gate of Heaven," the only place where prophecy is possible—, and Hebrew—the language of Israel. From this it clearly followed that the ideal existence for the Jews was attainable only in their own land. Throughout the philosophical and poetic work of Judah Halevi, as in his life, one can sense the intellectual effort to make other Jews conscious of this. In his philosophical work as well as in his poetry, Judah Halevi spoke out harshly against those who deceived themselves by speaking of Zion and by praying for its redemption while their hearts were closed to it and their actions far removed from it.

After intense personal struggles over the issue of Zion, which occupied him in the last period of his life and which find expression in his "Poems of Zion," in the *Kuzari* (mainly in the fifth and final part), and in the *Genizah* letters which date from the same period, he set out for Palestine in 1139. The following year he arrived in Alexandria. Several months later he went to Cairo. His friends tried to convince him to remain in Egypt, claiming that Egypt was as important as Erez Israel, since the first prophecy as well as great miracles took place there. Finally, however, Judah Halevi boarded a ship at Alexandria, bound for Erez Israel, but its departure was delayed by inclement weather. From the elegies written in Egypt and from the *Genizah* letters which mention his death, it can be concluded that he died about six months after reaching Egypt and that he was also buried there. What was denied him in life, however, the famous legend, first mentioned in *Shalshelet ha-Kabbalah,* and later by Heinrich Heine in his *Hebraeische Melodien,* has supplied. It relates that he managed to reach the city of Jerusalem, but, as he kissed its stones, a passing Arab horseman (Jerusalem, in fact, was then under the Crusaders) trampled on him just as he was reciting his elegy, *"Ziyyon ha-lo tishali."*

About 800 poems written by Judah Halevi are known, covering all the subjects commonly found in Spanish Hebrew poetry as well as the forms and artistic patterns of secular and religious poetry.

Outstanding among the 350 *piyyutim* (religious poems) which Judah Halevi composed for all of the Jewish festivals is a large group, which may be entitled *"Shirei ha-Galut"* ("Poems of the Diaspora"). The realism of these poems clearly reflects the tragic events suffered by the Jewish people. Their main value, however, is to be found in the lyric fashioning of his own world by the poet, who identified deeply with the fate of his people and whose poetry afforded true expression to many others.

In discussing the problem of the "end of days," Judah Halevi uses the obscure eschatology of the Book of Daniel. He sometimes expresses depression arising from his fear at the delay of the redemption and of the danger of destruction of his people. In these *piyyutim* Judah Halevi expresses his yearning for redemption in an urgent demand for its realization and in rejoicing over its expected realization. Following an ancient midrashic motif, he allegorically expressed the pain of God's chosen and faithful people, whom He had seemingly forsaken to idolators, in terms of the anguish of a prince whose servants have captured him and whose father delays in rescuing him; in contrast God, the lover, promises to keep His covenant and assures His people of His love and the future redemption. In this section the poetry is replete with descriptions of love and spring taken from the Song of Songs. In these poems Judah Halevi takes a polemical stand against false belief; against the enticements of monks and apostates, the beloved, wounded and insulted, vows unconditional faithfulness to her lover proclaiming happiness in her pains which are but wounds of a lover. He emphasizes the superiority of the Jewish religion, which alone is divinely revealed. The poems are imbued with sometimes strongly contrasting emotions: loneliness and suffering; rejoicing in the light of the past and sufferings in the darkness of the present; despair and security; lust for revenge and yearning for redemption. The strong tensions between these opposites find imagistic expression in such figures as a dove escaping the hunter (the Jewish people carried, in the past, on the wings of eagles); the degradation of the slave (the lost kingdom); the loneliness of the exiled son (the essential chosenness of the people).

Along with *piyyutim* of a national nature on such biblical and historic themes as the description of the miracles in Egypt in the poems for Passover, the miracle of Purim, the *Avodah* for the Day of Atonement, are found lyric poems expressing personal religious experiences. Judah Halevi expresses man's reverence for God, his dread of sin, and the desperate struggle against his carnal nature. He repeatedly admonishes the soul with harsh words, instills in it the fear of judgment and death, entices it with the idea of the reward of paradise, and deters it with the threat of the fire of hell. In this conflict God, a harsh judge, is too lofty to be approached and known. On the other hand, he writes of his happiness with God, which pervades his entire being; his powerful love of and devotion to God increase the light in his soul, mitigate its fear, and protect it from the power of evil. At that time, God is revealed to the heart. Traces of contemporary philosophical views can be discerned in these poems as well as influences of similar motifs in earlier Hebrew poetry. Exalted style is only rarely used; generally the poetic tone is gentle, humble, and quiet. Some poems confront the great paradoxes of religious experience; some combine deep meditation with emotional feeling; others occasionally border on the mystical as the poet ventures into areas of the ancient revelation in quest of his "lover," his God, "and no one answers."

The most famous of the poetic works of Judah Halevi are the *"Shirei Ẓiyyon"* ("Poems of Zion," or Zionides), approximately 35 in number. Their originality is evident in the very topic, which was at that period an uncommon one, but even more so in their varied and beautiful artistry. The poems of longing for Ereẓ Israel express the inner tension between love and pain, between the dream and the reality, and the effort required to bridge the West and East. The poetic disputations exhibit a strong intellectual base, overpowered by personal emotion. At times the controversy is an expression of the poet's own inner uncertainties. To Judah Halevi it seemed that for many life in Spain was a kind of slavery, a pursuit of worthless enticements, and a betrayal of God. He found true freedom in servitude to God and in subservience to His will, realized by his emigration to Ereẓ Israel.

Philosophy. Judah Halevi's philosophy is contained in a single volume entitled *Kitāb al-Ḥujja waal-Dalil fī Naṣr al-Dīn al-Dhalīl* ("The Book of Argument and Proof in Defense of the Despised Faith"). It was translated from Arabic into Hebrew in the middle of the 12th century by Judah ibn Tibbon under the title *Sefer ha-Hokhaḥah ve-ha-Re'ayah le-Hagganat ha-Dat ha-Bezuyah,* generally known as *Sefer ha-Kuzari* ("The Book of the Khazars").[19]

Halevi worked on the *Kuzari* for 20 years, completing its final draft shortly before his departure for Ereẓ Israel. Although Halevi, in one of his letters, states that he was prompted to write this work by having to answer certain questions posed by a Karaite, it deals only marginally with Karaism. It is a polemical work, directed primarily against Aristotelian philosophy—which Halevi, while being one of the first to recognize the threat it posed to the Jewish faith, greatly respected—and secondarily against Christianity and Islam. While the *Kuzari* is an apologia rather than a systematic philosophic treatise, it is based upon an original, crystallized, and unified conception of Judaism, developed by Halevi in the course of a thoroughgoing confrontation with philosophy.

The work is called the *Kuzari* after the king of the tribe of the Khazars in 9th century Russia whose conversion to Judaism provides the literary framework of the work. After being told by an angel in a dream that, while his intentions were acceptable to God, his actions were not, the king, in an effort to discover how he should lead his life, invites first an Aristotelian philosopher, and then representatives of Islam, Christianity, and Judaism, to discuss with him their respective beliefs. This literary framework enables Halevi to compare the teachings of Judaism with those of Aristotelianism, Islam, and Christianity, in an effort to prove the superiority of Judaism.

The *Kuzari* is divided into five parts. In the first part the philosopher, the Christian, and the Muslim expound their views. The king is with the philosopher, and when he realizes that Christianity and Islam are both based on Judaism, he calls in a Jewish scholar. The following four parts are devoted mainly to the dialogue between the king and the Jew. In the second part the king questions the Jewish scholar concerning the attributes of God. The king's question in regard to the attributes of God is the correct question in terms of medieval philosophical thought where no question, except perhaps that of creation, so exercised the minds of philosophers. However the reply of the Jewish scholar is in reality not a reply to this question but a way of changing the nature of the discussion to consider another type of issue altogether. The scholar is more concerned with the experience of God gained through prophecy than with the theoretical knowledge of God. Thus, he directs the discussion to the circumstances in which prophecy arose, and to the particular qualities of the people of Israel, of Erez Israel, the Temple, and the Hebrew language. Halevi, in contradistinction to the general universalist emphasis of medieval philosophy, Jewish and non-Jewish alike, develops a doctrine which holds that Israel alone among the nations possesses the gift of prophesy. Among other things, this unique faculty accounts for Israel's "chosen-status" and its special position in the natural and cosmic scheme. In order for Israel to develop its religious nature to the full it requires the proper environment. This environment is, of course, the Holy Land (Erez Israel) which, due to its various natural and supernatural qualities, makes it uniquely appropriate for the people of prophecy. The third part deals with the details of the worship of God in Judaism. The scholar explains that worship in Judaism consists in fulfilling the biblical commandments, which originated in divine revelation, and which cannot be interpreted or applied except by means of the authoritative tradition. This last point leads to a detailed argument against Karaism. In the fourth part the scholar discusses the names of God, distinguishing between *Elohim* and *Adonai,* the former being a general term denoting the god who is known through philosophical reasoning, the latter, a proper name, denoting the God of Israel who is known only through revelation and prophecy. He explains prophecy as the experience of being in the presence of God or the *Shekhinah,* an intermediary being between God and man— an experience brought about by the special "inner sense" of the prophet. He goes on to discuss the uniqueness of the people of Israel, and the "inner sense" which enables them to approach the divine presence. Halevi, in order to show that all science originated with the Jews, and that the Jewish people from its inception did not lack any human perfection, concludes this chapter with a summary of, and commentary on, *Sefer ha-Yeẓirah* ("The Book of Creation"), which he regarded as a major scientific work, and which he attributed, as did others at the time, to Abraham the Patriarch. In the fifth and final part of the book he takes up the polemic with the philosopher whom he did not properly challenge in the first part. The Jewish scholar, in an ironic vein, presents his pupil with a sketch of the Aristotelian philosophy of his day, at the same time exposing its weaknesses. While Halevi seems better acquainted with the doctrines of Aristotelianism than were his predecessors, it would be wrong to assume that he studied Aristotle's works directly. It has been shown, for example, that his exposition of Aristotelian psychology is based on a work by Avicenna.[20] Halevi's criticism of Aristotelianism is highly reminiscent of al-Ghazālī's criticism of philosophy in the *Incoherence of the Philosophers (Tahāfut al-Falāsifa').* Halevi also presents his pupil with an outline of the arguments of the Kalām, of which he does not approve any more than he does of Aristotelianism. Though he considers these arguments useful for polemics, he believes they have no great intrinsic value.

Halevi's teachings are based on the concept of immediate religious experience and its superiority over deductive reasoning. However, he does not negate the value of metaphysical speculation, recognizing that, in the absence of direct experience, it is the only way of learning the truth. Halevi regards Aristotle's system as the finest achievement of the human intellect. Even Aristotle conceded that deductive reasoning cannot refute experience. Since Aristotle based his system on ordinary sensory experience, while the prophets based their teachings on the special experience contained in revelation, Aristotle's conclusions are valid only in regard to mathematics and logic, but have no validity in regard to divine law. Thus, in contrast to the philosopher, who defines the prophet as one who has attained the highest degree of perfection in conjunction with the perfection of the imaginative faculty, Halevi defines the prophet as one who, by means of special "inner sense," is able to apprehend spiritual reality, in the same way as the ordinary man, by means of the external senses, apprehends physical reality. The prophet, because he experiences directly the presence of God, can become much closer to God than the philosopher who has an indirect theoretical knowledge of Him. The mission of the prophet is not to instruct men in eternal truths, but to teach them the deeds whose performance leads to the experience of God's presence. This is indeed the purpose of the Torah, Judaism being the only religion which seeks to instruct men in correct and righteous actions, rather than speculative truths. The prophetic faculty is a faculty beyond ordinary human reason, and constitutes a generic distinction between the prophet and the ordinary man, parallel to the distinction between man and animals. This faculty is hereditary and unique to the people of Israel. It is only through the intermediacy of Israel that the other nations can approach God, just as it is only through the intermediacy of the prophets that the people of Israel can come close to Him. This is the cornerstone of Halevi's doctrine of particularity of the people of Israel.

In his polemic against Christianity and Islam, Halevi contends that a prophetic religion, possessing the evidence of the prophetic experience, has no need to authenticate itself by means of rational proof. What Halevi objects to in Christianity and Islam is not the irrationality of their claims, but the fact that they cannot base their doctrines on an unequivocal historical revelation such as the one granted to Israel at Sinai, when 600,000 people were granted the experience of prophecy, and found with a certitude that the intellect cannot attain, that God spoke to man and commanded him to observe the laws of the Torah. Christianity and Islam must, therefore, have recourse to the historical tradition of Judaism. Halevi recognizes the presence of authentic Jewish elements in Christianity and Islam, and the vital role that these religions play in history. However, insofar as they have diverged from the Torah and sought to supplant it, they are falsehoods which can neither be substantiated by the tradition of Israel, nor claim authentic historical validity for their own traditions. Halevi in his view of history attempts to explain the paradox of a "chosen people" suffering exile and oppression, and to show that in spite of the sufferings of the Jewish people, Judaism is the religion par excellence. The function of history is to bring creation to completion in the acceptance of the true worship of God on the part of all mankind. This is a gradual process.

Ha-Inyan ha-Elohi ("the divine influence," a technical term used by Halevi in a variety of senses, including that of an intermediary between man and God) is initially known to only a few individuals (Abraham, Isaac, and Jacob), then to an entire family (the children of Jacob), and then to an entire nation (the people of Israel), who will eventually make it known to mankind as a whole. This history of the people of Israel at this stage represents the true history of mankind. This is demonstrated by the fact that only in the history of the people of Israel is divine providence directly manifest, both in times of unnatural success and in times of unnatural suffering. The successes and failures of other nations can be explained in natural terms, without the manifestation of divine providence. When the other nations recognize the divine influence they too will become part of the true history. This, evidently, is the meaning of the suffering of Israel in exile. Israel is like a seed which appears to be rotting in the ground, but is in reality preparing for life and growth. Thus, unusual suffering is not evidence of the inferiority of the Jewish faith, but of its superiority. The suffering of Israel is the public sanctification of the name of God, and its purpose will be understood at the time of deliverance. It must be noted that Halevi did not believe in a deterministic historical development. Deliverance will only come about when God's commandments are performed by men who willingly submit to divine authority.

Influence: The *Kuzari* is a popular work which exercised a great influence on Judaism throughout history. It was particularly influential in kabbalistic circles in the 13th century, and among the anti-Aristotelians in the 14th and 15th centuries. In more recent times it had a marked influence on Ḥasidism. Some philosophers of the 19th and 20th centuries, such as Samuel David Luzatto, Franz Rosenzweig, and Abraham Isaac Kook, saw in the *Kuzari* the most faithful description of the particular qualities of the Jewish religion.

Title page of *Mi Kamokha* by Judah Halevi, Venice, 1586.

ARISTOTELIANISM

Aristotle achieved a unique rank in the estimation of Muslim and Jewish medieval philosophers, who often refer to him simply as "the philosopher." Maimonides stated that Aristotle had "reached the highest degree of intellectual perfection open to man, barring only the still higher degree of prophetic inspiration."[21] While Aristotelian influences made some inroads into medieval Jewish philosophy from its beginning (when it followed the teachings of the Kalām and Neoplatonism), Aristotelianism, in varying forms, became the predominant trend from Abraham ibn Daud (12th century) to the middle of the 17th century.

Jewish Aristotelianism may be divided into two periods. From the 9th until the end of the 12th century, Jews, living in the Muslim world and knowing Arabic, had available to them the Aristotelian literature existing in that language; from the 13th century on, Jews, living in the Christian world and using Hebrew for their philosophic writings, depended on Hebrew translations of Aristotelian works. During the first of these periods, the works of Aristotle (with the exception of the *Politics,* the *Eudemian Ethics, Magna Moralia,* and the *Dialogues*) together with many of the Greek commentaries on his works, became known through Arabic translations which were made between about 800 c.e. and 1000 c.e.[22] In addition, Jews became familiar with the teachings of Aristotle, at times interspersed with Neoplatonic doctrines, through the summaries, commentaries, and independent works of such Islamic philosophers as al-Fārābī, Avicenna, and Ibn Bājja (Avempace). In the Islamic world, Aristotelian studies were put on a firm footing as early as the 10th century when al-Fārābī, in his *The Philosophy of Plato and Aristotle,* outlined the differences between the two philosophers. The Aristotelian orientation established by al-Fārābī was shared by two 10th-century Jews of Mosul, Ibn Abi Saʿīd al-Mawṣilī and his pupil Bishr ibn Samʿān[23] though, as has

71

been noted, Jewish philosophy did not become predominantly Aristotelian until Abraham ibn Daud. This philosopher, in his *Emunah Ramah* (The Exalted Faith), attacked the Neoplatonic metaphysics of Solomon ibn Gabirol, and expounded an Aristotelianism derived from the teachings of Avicenna. During the Islamic period, Aristotelianism reached its highpoint with Maimonides, who tended toward the teachings of al-Fārābī.

The opening of the second period was marked by Hebrew translations, from the Arabic, of works by Aristotle, by Hellenistic commentators and by Islamic commentators and compilers. These Hebrew translations brought about knowledge of the following works by Aristotle: The logical writings (*Organon*, lit. "instrument"; Heb. *Keli*); *Physics* (*Ha-Shema ha-Tivi*); *De Caelo* (*Sefer ha-Shamayim ve-ha-Olam*); *De Generatione et Corruptione* (*Sefer ha-Havayah ve-ha-Hefsed*); *Meteorologica* (*Otot ha-Shamayim*); *De Animalibus* (*Sefer Ba'alei Ḥayyim*); *De Anima* (*Sefer ha-Nefesh*); *De Sensu et Sensato* (*Sefer ha-Ḥush ve-ha-Muḥash*); *Metaphysica* (*Sefer Mah she-Aḥar ha-Teva*); and the *Nicomachean Ethics* (*Sefer ha-Middot*).[24]

Of special attraction to Jewish translators, commentators, and philosophic authors were the works of Averroes, most of whose commentaries on Aristotle were translated from Arabic into Hebrew between 1189 and 1337, some of them twice. In fact, the Hebrew translations of Averroes became the major source for the knowledge of Aristotle in Jewish circles.

In addition to Hebrew translations of genuine Aristotelian works, there also existed Hebrew translations of a number of works, which though not written by Aristotle, were attributed to him. There were *Liber de Pomo* (*Sefer ha-Tappu'aḥ*), purporting to prove that Aristotle had changed his views in his old age, which Maimonides rejected as spurious; *Secretum Secretorum* (*Sod ha-Sodot*) or *Pseudo-Politics* (*Sefer ha-Hanhagah*),[25] *Liber de causis*, based on Proclus' *Elements of Theology;* and *Theology of Aristotle,* representing excerpts from Plotinus' *Enneads,* which, except for a few quotations, has been lost in Hebrew translation. The Aristotelian literature in Hebrew, in turn, gave rise to Hebrew commentaries and to summaries. In addition, independent works in Hebrew were based on it.

Aristotelianism was based on the premises that the world must be known through observation and that this knowledge is gained through study of the various speculative and practical sciences. The speculative sciences, which deal with the nature of reality, are divided into physics, mathematics, and metaphysics; the practical sciences, which deal with human conduct, are divided into ethics, economics, and politics. Logic is the prerequisite instrument of all the sciences. The physics of the Aristotelians is based on an analysis of the many changes taking place in the world. These changes are explained through the four causes, the material, efficient, formal, and final causes. The world is divided into the celestial and the sublunar regions. The sublunar world is one of generation and corruption, and everything in it is ultimately reducible to the four elements, earth, water, air, and fire. Sublunar beings are divided into minerals, plants, animals, and rational beings, and all of them are composed of matter and form. By contrast, the celestial region, not subject to generation and corruption, is immaterial and the only motion occurring within it are the locomotions of the celestial spheres. The celestial region is made up of its own element—the so-called fifth element. It consists of the various celestial spheres in which are set the sun, moon, planets, and fixed stars. Each sphere consists of a body governed by an incorporeal soul and intelligence. The earth is fixed at the center of the universe and the celestial spheres revolve around it.

All organic beings, plants, animals, and human beings are governed by an internal principle of motion called a soul. In man, the most complex organic being, the soul possesses nutritive, sensory, appetitive, imaginative, and rational faculties, or powers. The highest faculty is the rational, and to develop it is the purpose of human life. The rational faculty starts as the potential intellect and through exercise becomes the actual intellect and, finally, the acquired intellect. The agent in the production of human knowledge is the active intellect, which in the Islamic and Jewish traditions is identified with the lowest of the celestial intelligences. The active intellect also produces prophecy in men who have the required preparation.

While there are some variations in particulars, Islamic and Jewish philosophers subscribe to this general scheme. Metaphysics is viewed as the study of being qua being, that is, of the highest categories, and also as a study of the incorporeal beings, that is, of God and the incorporeal intelligences, which are identified with the angels of Scripture. Morality is viewed as the acquisition of the moral and intellectual virtues. The moral virtues, which, generally speaking, consist of following the mean, are acquired by habituation and thereby become second nature. They are a prerequisite for the attainment of the intellectual virtues, the final goal. While in their ethics Aristotelians followed the traditions of Aristotle, in their political philosophy they followed Plato. They accepted the notion Plato set forth in the *Republic* that mankind may be divided into three classes, men of gold, men of silver, and men of bronze, and identified the first class with the philosophers, who can understand by means of demonstration, and the other two classes with those who can only follow arguments of persuasion. For Plato, the state is founded by a philosopher-king, who in the Islamic and Jewish traditions is identified with the legislative prophet.

Jewish Aristotelianism is a complex phenomenon, the general trends of which can be seen from some of its characteristic discussions. Jewish Aristotelianism differs from the antecedent types of medieval Jewish philosophy in its heightened awareness of the boundaries of faith and reason. Jewish Kalām and Neoplatonism used a variety of rational arguments to establish the truth of revelation, without seeing, on the whole, any sharp boundaries between philosophy and religion. By contrast, Jewish Aristotelians held that philosophic speculations must proceed without any regard to theological doctrines. They recognized as valid only demonstrative arguments, that is to say, arguments based on the standards for such arguments laid down by Aristotle.[26] Once the content of faith and reason had been delineated independently, it could be asked how the two realms are related. According to one view, represented by Maimonides, the teachings of religion and philosophy could be harmonized only in part. For example, Maimonides maintains that while many doctrines, such as the existence of God and His unity, can be demonstrated scientifically, the doctrine of *creatio ex nihilo* cannot, and one therefore has to be guided by prophetic revelation (*Guide*, 2:15). By contrast, Jewish Averroists like Isaac Albalag, Joseph Caspi, and Moses of Narbonne (Narboni) opposed the tendency to harmonize faith and reason. Thus, for example, they accepted the doctrine of the eternity of the world, holding that it had been demonstrated by Aristotle.

A central and most crucial issue in Jewish Aristotelianism was the question of creation. Aristotle based his notion that the world is eternal on the nature of time and motion[27] and on the impossibility of assuming a genesis of prime matter. In contrast to the Kalām theologians, who maintained the doctrine of temporal creation, the medieval Muslim philosophers interpreted creation as eternal, i.e., as the eternal procession of forms which emanate from the active or creative knowledge of God. The task with which the Jewish Aristotelians were faced was either to disprove or to accept the notion of the world's eternity. Maimonides offers a survey and refutation of Kalām proofs for creation, and advances his own theory of temporal creation (*Guide,* 2:17), for which he indicates the theological motive that miracles are possible only in a universe created by a spontaneous divine will (2:25). He rejects the emanationist theory of the Muslim Aristotelians since it fails to account for the origin of matter (2:22). In the course of the subsequent discussion, the more radical Aristotelians veered toward the Muslim philosophers' position, namely, the doctrine of eternal creation. Isaac Albalag, echoing Avicenna, regarded eternal creation as much more befitting to God than temporal creation. Levi ben Gershom maintained the notion of creation in time, but denied the possibility of a temporal origination of prime matter (*Milḥamot,* 6:1, 7). Crescas, on the other hand, sought to combine the concept of *creatio ex nihilo* with that of eternal creation of the world by God's design and will (*Or Adonai,* 3:1, 4–5). In the period following Crescas, when there was greater emphasis on the possibility of miracles, the doctrine of temporal creation gained greater adherence.

Closely allied to the problem of creation is that of divine providence. The Muslim philosophers, who accepted the doctrine of eternal creation, understood Aristotle to teach that providence is identical with the operations of nature, which safeguards the permanence of the species, but is unconcerned with individuals. To bring the Aristotelian position more into harmony with the teachings of religion, Ibn Daud (*Emunah Ramah,* 6:2) makes the point, later elaborated by Maimonides (*Guide,* 2:17), that divine providence extends to individual men according to their degree of intellectual perfection. The question of divine providence and the related problem of God's knowledge gave rise to a concurrent problem, that of divine foreknowledge and man's free will. Narboni shows that God's foreknowledge does not necessarily preclude man's free action. Crescas, on the other hand, adopts a determinist position, but states that this does not invalidate the divine commandments (*Or Adonai,* 2:5, 3). The topic of providence is linked with that of reward and punishment in the hereafter, which, in turn, raises the question of individual immortality. Since Jewish Aristotelianism inherited not only Aristotle's own rather ambiguous doctrine of the soul, but also the discussions of the Greek commentators and Muslim philosophers that revealed sharp disagreement in the interpretation of Aristotle, there was a division among the Jewish philosophers with relation to the soul's immortality, which stemmed from their differences of opinion with regard to the nature of man's material (potential) intellect at birth. Ibn Daud follows Avicenna in regarding the soul as an individual eternal immaterial substance capable of survival after death (*Emunah Ramah,* 1:7). Maimonides' position is somewhat ambiguous. He affirms, on the one hand, the immortality of the individual soul (*Guide,* 1:41, 70; 3:22, 27, 54), but adopts, on the other, the description of the material intellect at birth as a "mere disposition" (1:70) and also speaks of the numerical unity of all souls (1:74, 7), from which it would appear to follow that immortality is collective.[28] In the post-Maimonides period, the discussion was dominated by Averroes' theory of the ultimate elimination of the individual coloring of intellect and the absorption of the individual intellect into the universal Agent Intellect. Levi ben Gershom, however, rejects the doctrine of the unity of souls and affirms the individual immortality of man's acquired intellect (*Milḥamot,* 1:1–14). The ultimate felicity of man, he says, consists in the enjoyment of the intellectual perfection achieved during life. No further increase of knowledge is possible after death. Crescas expresses the general mood of the anti-Aristotelianism of his period and attacks the intellectualist orientation in his statement that the ultimate felicity lies in the love of God (*Or Adonai,* 2:6, 1–2).

ABRAHAM BEN DAVID HALEVI IBN DAUD

This Spanish historian, philosopher, physician, and astronomer is the first medieval Jewish Aristotelian. Born in Córdoba, he spent his formative years in the home of his maternal uncle, Baruch b. Isaac Albalia, who was his teacher. Though little is known of his life until 1160 it is evident from his writings that he received a well-rounded education, including rabbinics, Bible, Hebrew poetry, and Greek and Jewish philosophy. He was also familiar both with the New Testament and the Koran. In the wake of the Almohad conquest of Spain, he fled to Castile, where he settled in Toledo, the city with which he was most deeply associated, until his death there as a martyr in c. 1180.

Historical works: Ibn Daud's major historical work, *Sefer* (or in some Mss. *Seder) ha-Kabbalah* (The Book of Tradition) was written in 1160–61, the very same year in which his philosophical treatise, *Al'Aqīda al-Rafī'a* (The Exalted Faith) was written. The two were intimately related to one another. Both were polemical treatises, the one defending Judaism through history, the other through philosophy. In actuality, *Sefer ha-Kabbalah* is only the first portion of a work that has three sections, although it is by far the best known of the three and had the greatest influence over the generations. It is essentially a history of Jewish tradition, oriented primarily against Karaite teaching, and seeking to prove that it is only within Rabbanite traditions that Scripture fulfills itself. The work was primarily directed to those who had an understanding of Arabic scholarship. It is not the writing of history that was Ibn Daud's basic intent, but rather the ulitization of history in order to dispute with the pious heretic of the time, the Karaite.

Appended to *Sefer ha-Kabbalah* are two additional historical compositions. The first of these is entitled *Zikhron Divrei Romi,* a history of Rome from the time of its foundation until the rise of the Muslim Empire. Its basic purpose was to attack Christianity by claiming that the New Testament was a late fabrication of Constantine. The second appendix is called *Divrei Malkhei Yisrael be-Vayit Sheni* (a history of the kings of Israel during the Second Temple period). The latter work is also polemical in tone and is directed at the Sadducean heresy of the Second Temple period, the prototype in Ibn Daud's view of the Karaite heresy of his day. The text is the least original of his work, for it is essentially a paraphrasing of portions of *Josippon,*[29] a tenth-century composition of an Italian Jew. Nonetheless it was the first to be translated into a European language and was known to European Christian readers. *Sefer ha-Kabbalah* had influence down to modern times as an authority on the history of Spanish Jewry and its comments on the talmudic period particularly influenced the 19th-century Jewish historians. Although it is no longer regarded as objective history it remains a significant source for the life and thought of 12th-century Spain.[30]

Philosophy: Ibn Daud was the first Jewish philosopher to introduce a strict form of Aristotelianism. This type of philosophy had already become dominant among the Muslims, but Jewish thinkers still followed Neoplatonism. In taking the step toward Aristotelianism Ibn Daud was the precursor of Maimonides, but Maimonides' fame eclipsed that of Ibn Daud to such an extent that his work fell into complete oblivion in the following generations. This explains why it was not translated into Hebrew before the end of the 14th century[31] and was mentioned only occasionally, e.g., by Ḥasdai Crescas (*Or Adonai*, 1 :1, introduction). Maimonides himself does not mention his predecessor, but in some places appears to have made use of his philosophical interpretation of the Bible. Ibn Daud for his part refers only to Saadiah Gaon and Solomon ibn Gabirol (*Emunah Ramah,* ed. Weil, p. 2) of the older Jewish philosophers. From his Aristotelian point of view he considered Saadiah's achievement inadequate, despite his respect for him, and he subjected Gabirol's Neoplatonism to severe criticism. It is doubtful that he knew of Judah Halevi's *Kuzari,* although his thought approaches Halevi's at several points.

Ibn Daud was one of the most rationalistic of Jewish philosophers. In his view true philosophy is in complete accord with the Torah, because the Torah contains everything brought to light by human reason subsequent to its revelation. Only those whose concern with philosophy is superficial and who lack the strength to contemplate religion and knowledge at the same time find philosophy disturbing to their belief, but the true thinker recognizes the correspondence between them (*ibid.,* 2). The doctrines of Judaism contain implicitly all the knowledge that other peoples acquire only after thousands of years of endeavor (*ibid.,* 4). To this rationalistic view of the Torah, which had been advocated by Saadiah before him, Ibn Daud adds the concept of the Islamic Aristotelians that the acquisition of metaphysical knowledge is the real purpose of man; he, therefore, focuses on the philosophical interpretation of religious concepts (*ibid.,* 44–45). On the other hand, in the introduction to *Emunah Ramah* (*ibid.,* 4) he justifies the simple faith untroubled by doubt with the statement that moral conduct is also the purpose of philosophy. His work is thus primarily aimed at substantiating philosophically the basic religious concepts.

The true philosophy, according to Ibn Daud, is the Aristotelian philosophy, particularly as interpreted by Avicenna. Avicenna borrowed its proofs for the existence of God and derived from it a definition of God, in one respect, as the Prime Mover and, in another, as the "necessarily existent" whose existence is included in His essence. All motion requires a moving cause, and since the sequence of causes cannot regress infinitely, it must have its origin in a first unmoved mover (*ibid.*, 17–19). To this proof, which originated with Aristotle, Ibn Daud adds one formulated by Avicenna known as the proof from necessity and contingency. According to this proof the existence of all beings other than God is contingent (possible), not necessary; and contingent beings must have their origin in a being necessary through itself (*ibid.*, 47), who is God. Following Islamic Aristotelians, he deduces from the necessary existence of God His absolute unity (simplicity) and uniqueness—unity, because any plurality in God would require the existence beyond Him of a unifying principle, which would contradict His necessary existence; and uniqueness, because the absolute unity of God precludes the existence of two different necessary beings, and two completely like beings would necessarily have to be identical (p. 49). Thus he reaches the Neoplatonic concept of God as the absolute One. With this concept of God's unity in the sense of simplicity, Ibn Daud had to reject the possibility of any positive attributes of God[32] and maintain that the Divine Being is unknowable in any positive fashion. All attributes ascribed to God, including unity and existence, have only a negative significance or concern only the relationship of God to the multiplicity of things (*ibid.*, 51–57).

Like Avicenna, Ibn Daud held that the Aristotelian definition of the soul as the form of an organic body does not necessarily imply that the existence of the human soul is dependent upon the existence of body, as are all other forms. The soul is an immaterial, purposive element which directs and vitalizes the material body. The human soul is able to continue after death without the body because the activities of its noblest part, the intellect, are independent of the body altogether. In this respect, too, he follows Avicenna, in whose view the human intellect is not a mere predisposition inherent in the body, but a substance independent of the body (*ibid.*, 38–39). He therefore does not limit immortality to the acquired intellect, which develops from the act of cognition, but considers the rational soul as such immortal. However, the human soul achieves true cognition only under the influence of the Active Intellect, which is the lowest of the cosmic intelligences that issue from God, and which rules the sublunar world.

Ibn Daud adopted a naturalistic interpretation of prophecy. He regards it as the highest stage of union between the human intellect and the Active Intellect, one of the intelligences of the supernal world responsible for developing man's intellect from its original state of mere potentiality to a state of actuality (*ibid.,* 70–72). Ibn Daud nevertheless adheres to the belief that prophecy is found solely among the Jewish people and in the Holy Land (*ibid.,* 74). He does not try reconcile the two points of view. Nor does he make an attempt to harmonize the Jewish belief that the world was created by the will of God *ex nihilo* and the Aristotelian view that the world flows necessarily from God and is coeternal with Him. He retains the concept of creation without disproving, as Maimonides later did, the Aristotelian arguments for the eternity of the world. Less dogmatic is his attitude to the emanation theory introduced to the Aristotelian system by the Islamic Aristotelians. According to this theory, a being similar to God in unity emanates directly from God, and from this being the multiplicity of things is gradually emanated. Ibn Daud categorically rejected this conclusion, but seems to have accepted the basic assumption that only one single being can issue directly from God, though he views this emanation not as a necessary process but as a free act of creation (*ibid.,* 62–68). However, this interpretation, too contradicts another one of his assertions, namely, that matter was created by God.

Ibn Daud moved furthest from Jewish philosophical tradition in his treatment of the problem of human free will and divine omniscience. The difficulty confronting medieval philosophy was the apparent incompatibility of free will with the omniscience of God. Ibn Daud saw no way out of it other than by qualifying God's omniscience. His view is that what is left to the free decision of man exists in a state of mere possibility until this decision has been made. Evidently following Alexander of Aphrodisias, Ibn Daud maintained that what is in essence merely possible must also be perceived by God as merely possible, and it does not limit His knowledge if He can perceive the objectively possible and undecided only as such (*ibid.,* 96–98).

The conclusion of Ibn Daud's book contains a brief description of ethics, in which Platonic and Aristotelian elements are combined. In his view philosophic ethics corresponds to the commandments of the Torah, which provide the most perfect expression of philosophic principles. Virtue and happiness, the two ends of Greek moral philosophy, are now predicated as the ends achieved most readily and perfectly through adherence to Torah. Again, Ibn Daud's fundamental rationalism with regard to religion is apparent. Besides religious doctrines, the Torah comprises ethical rules and precepts for family and public life, but also the laws concerning sacrifices and similar regulations, which are not rationally comprehensible. These elements, though not valuable in themselves, have value in that they demand teach and produce obedience to God and the Kingship of Heaven. For Ibn Daud all the various parts of the Torah are graduated in such a way that the principles of religion and metaphysical and moral truths form the summit and the ceremonial laws the base (*ibid.*, 102).

MAIMONIDES

Maimonides, the most illustrious figure in Judaism in the post-talmudic era, and one of the greatest of all time, was born in Cordoba, Spain. His father Maimon was *dayyan* of Cordoba and himself a renowned scholar. As a result of the fall of Cordoba to the Almohads in 1148, when Moses had just reached his 13th birthday, and the consequent religious persecution, Maimon was obliged to leave Cordoba with his family and all trace of them is lost for the next eight or nine years, which they spent wandering from place to place in Spain (and possibly Provence) until in 1160 they settled in Fez.[34] Yet it was during those years of wandering, that he laid the strong foundations of his vast and varied learning and even began his literary work. Not only did he begin the draft of the *Sirāj*, his important commentary on the Mishnah, in 1158, but in that same year, at the request of a friend, he wrote a short treatise on the Jewish calendar (*Ma'amar ha-Ibbur*) and one on logic (*Millot Higgayon*) and had completed writing notes for a commentary on a number of tractates of the Babylonian Talmud, and a work whose aim was to extract the *halakhah* from the Jerusalem Talmud. He also continued his general studies, particularly medicine; in his medical works he frequently refers to the knowledge and experience he gained among the Muslims in North Africa.[35] Here also he wrote his *Iggeret ha-Shemad* ("Letter on Forced Conversion") also called *Iggeret Kiddush ha-Shem* ("Letter of the Sanctification of the Divine Name"). Although in the opening lines of the *Iggeret ha-Shemad* he most strongly deprecates the condemnation of the forced converts by "the self-styled sage who has never experienced what so many Jewish communities experienced in the way of persecution," his conclusion is that a Jew must leave the country where he is forced to transgress the divine law : "He should not remain in the realm of that king; he should sit in his house until he emigrates . . ." And once more, with greater insistence: "He should on no account remain in a place of forced conversion; whoever remains in such a place desecrates the Divine Name and is nearly as bad as a willful sinner; as for those who beguile themselves, saying that they will remain until the Messiah comes to the Maghreb and leads them to Jerusalem, I do not know how he is to cleanse them of the stigma of conversion."[36]

Maimon and his sons acted in accordance with this advice, as certainly did many others. Maimonides' departure from the country of the Almohads is commonly assumed to have taken place in 1165. R. Maimon and his family escaped from Fez, and a month later they landed at Acre, where they remained for some five months visiting Jerusalem and other holy places. The family then left Erez Israel and sailed for Egypt. After a short stay at Alexandria they moved to Cairo and took up residence in Fostat, the Old City of Cairo.

Maimon died at this time either in Erez Israel or in Egypt. It has been suggested that the reason for the choice of Alexandria was the existence at that time "outside the town" of "the academy of Aristotle, the teacher of Alexander" to which "people from the whole world came in order to study the wisdom of Aristotle the philosopher." It is not certain what prompted the move to Cairo. That Maimonides' influence was decisive in virtually destroying the hitherto dominating influence of the Karaites who were more numerous and wealthy than the Rabbanites in Cairo is beyond doubt and in the 17th century Jacob Farajī, a *dayyan* in Egypt, states that it was this challenge which impelled Maimonides to move to Cairo.[37]

For eight years Maimonides lived a life free from care, supported by his brother David who dealt in precious stones. He was able to devote himself entirely to preparing his works for publication and to his onerous but honorary work as both religious and lay leader of the community. His *Sirāj,* the commentary to the Mishnah, was completed in 1168. The following year his brother David drowned in the Indian Ocean while on a business trip. Maimonides then had to seek a means of livelihood. Rejecting the thought of earning a livelihood from Torah[38] he decided to make the medical profession his livelihood.

In 1185 he was appointed one of the physicians to al-Faḍil, who had been appointed vizier by Saladin and was virtual ruler of Egypt after Saladin's departure from that country in 1174. In this capacity Maimonides' fame began to spread. About 1177 he was recognized as the official head of the Fostat community.

These were the most fruitful and busy years of his life. It was during those years, busy as he was with the heavy burden of his practice and occupied with the affairs of the community, writing his extensive correspondence to every part of the Jewish world (apart from the Franco-German area), that he wrote the two monumental works upon which his fame chiefly rests, the *Mishneh Torah* (compiled 1180) and the *Guide of the Perplexed* (1190),[39] as well as his *Iggeret Teiman* (Letter to Yemen) and his *Ma'amar Tehiyyat ha-Metim* (On Resurrection of the Dead).

Iggeret Teiman and Ma'amar Tehiyyat ha-Metim. The two major works will be described below, but something must be said of the two letters. The Arab ruler in Yemen instituted a religious persecution, giving the Jews the choice of conversion to Islam or death. Not only did many succumb, but there arose among those Jews a pseudo-Messiah, or a forerunner of the Messiah who, seeing in these events the darkness before the dawn, preached the imminent advent of the Messianic Age. In despair the Jews of Yemen turned to Maimonides, who probably in 1172 answered their request with the *Iggeret Teiman*.[40] It was addressed to Rabbi Jacob b. Nethanel al-Fayyumi, with a request that copies be sent to every community in Yemen. Deliberately couched in simple terms, "that men, women, and children could read it easily," he pointed out that the subtle attack of Christianity and Islam which preached a new revelation was more dangerous than the sword and than the attractions of Hellenism. As for the pseudo-Messiah, he was unbalanced and he was to be rejected. These trials were sent to prove the Jews.

The effect of the letter was tremendous. In gratitude for the message of hope, combined with the fact that Maimonides also used his influence at court to obtain a lessening of the heavy burden of taxation on the Jews of Yemen, the Jews of Yemen introduced into the *Kaddish* a prayer for "the life of our teacher Moses b. Maimon".[41]

This remarkable tribute, usually reserved for the exilarch, has an indirect connection with the third of his public (as distinct from his private) letters, the *Ma'amar Tehiyyat ha-Metim* ("On Resurrection":

1191).[42] Maimonides wrote the letter with the greatest reluctance. It was the direct result of his *Mishneh Torah* and constituted his reply to the accusation leveled against him that in this work he denied, or did not mention, the doctrine of personal resurrection which was a fundamental principle of faith among the Jews of his time. An objective study of his work does lend a certain basis to the allegation. It is true, as he indignantly protests, that he included this doctrine as the last of his famous Thirteen Principles of Judaism, but in his *Mishneh Torah* the undoubted emphasis is on the immortality of the soul and not on individual bodily resurrection. That the allegation was not based upon mere malice or envy of his work is sufficiently proved by the fact that anxious queries were addressed to him from the countries in which he was most fervently admired, Yemen and Provence, and Maimonides answered them. Abraham b. David of Posquières, Maimonides' great critic, wrote: "The words of this man seem to me to be very near to him who says there is no resurrection of the body, but only of the soul. By my life, this is not the view of the sages" (Comm. to Yad, Teshuvah 8:2).

Maimonides died in 1204. There were almost universal expressions of grief. Public mourning was ordained in all parts of the Jewish world. In Fostat mourning was ordained for three days and in Jerusalem a public fast and the Scriptural readings instituted concluded with the verse "the glory is departed from Israel, for the Ark of the Lord is taken" (I Sam. 4:22). His remains were taken to Tiberias for burial, and his grave is still an object of pilgrimage.

Maimonides as halakhist. Maimonides is one of the greatest halakhists in the tradition. Maimonides sets out to explain to the general reader the meaning of the Mishnah, without having recourse to the involved and lengthy discussions in the *Gemara,* the language of which was more difficult than the Mishnah itself. Out of the mishnaic and other tannaitic texts and corresponding passages in the *Gemara,* often widely scattered throughout the Talmud, Maimonides evolves the underlying principles of the subjects discussed, which a particular Mishnah, chapter, or entire tractate presupposed. Following his explanatory glosses to the mishnaic passage, Maimonides gave the halakhic decision in each Mishnah based on his reading of the discussion in the *Gemara.*

Of special significance are the lengthy introductions he included in his commentary. The general introduction which heads his commentary to the order of *Zera'im* is in reality an introduction to and history of the Oral Law from Moses until his own days. The introduction to *Avot*, known as the *Shemonah Perakim* ("Eight Chapters") is a philosophical and ethical treatise in which its author harmonized Aristotle's ethics with rabbinical teachings. In the introduction to Mishnah *Sanhedrin* (10:1), which begins with the words "All Israel has a portion in the world to come," Maimonides dealt at length with the fundamental doctrines of Judaism which he formulated in the Thirteen Articles of Faith. The publication of the critical editions of the responsa[43] of Maimonides[44] affords a better opportunity to appraise his role in the communal life of the Jews of Egypt and neighboring countries. The responsa, which were in the language of the questioner, whether Hebrew or Arabic, number 464; some of them soon found their way into halakhic literature. From these responsa one learns of the growing tension between the *gaon* of Baghdad and Maimonides in connection with traveling on the high seas on the Sabbath, prohibited by Samuel b. Ali but permitted by Maimonides.[45]

The bitter experience of his youth failed to nurture in Maimonides rabid anti-Muslim feelings, and he consistently declined to classify Muslims as idolators. Even the ritual practices connected with the Ka'ba stone in Mecca did not in his opinion deny Islam the purely monotheistic nature. In reply to an inquiry by Saadiah b. Berakhot about the authenticity of the gnostic work, *Shi'ur Komah*, Maimonides writes: "Heaven forfend that such work originated from the sages; it is undoubtedly the work of one of the Greek preachers . . . and it would be a divine act to suppress this book altogether and to eradicate its subject matter."[47]

Of special interest is a responsum to Obadiah the Proselyte,[48] who inquired if he was permitted to say in the blessings and prayers, "Our God and God of our Fathers," "Thou who has chosen us," "Thou who has worked miracles to our fathers," and similar expressions. Maimonides' responsum, apart from its halakhic merit, is a unique human document displaying grave concern for the feelings of this lonely proselyte who was so unsure of himself. Obadiah was advised that he was to recite all those prayers in the same way as one born a Jew, that he must not consider himself inferior to the rest of the Jews.[49] These responsa, although confined to halakhic decisions, nevertheless display Maimonides' views on matters of doctrine and fundamentals of Judaism and are important for gaining a complete view of Maimonides' view of Judaism and Jewish law. Maimonides found all previous attempts at enumerating the traditional 613 commandments unsatisfactory. He therefore composed the *Sefer ha-Mitzvot* ("Book of Commandments")[50] in which he gave his own enumeration of the 248 positive and the 365 negative commandments. As an introduction to this work, he laid down 14 principles which guided him in the identification and enumeration of the commandments.

The *Sefer ha-Mitzvot* was not an end in itself but an introduction to the *Mishneh Torah*[51] ("Repetition of The Law"), on which Maimonides labored for ten successive years.

Maimonides set for himself the task of classifying by subject matter the entire talmudic and post-talmudic halakhic literature in a systematic manner never before attempted in the history of Judaism. The *Mishneh Torah* was divided into 14 books, each representing a distinct category of the Jewish legal system. (In Hebrew 14 is *yad* and hence the alternative name of the work *Yad ha-Ḥazakah,* i.e., "the strong hand.")

Even though the *Guide of the Perplexed* was written after the completion of the *Mishneh Torah,* Maimonides succeeded in incorporating many of its philosophic and scientific aspects into this purely halakhic work. Philosophy and science were handmaidens to theology. Hence Book I contains a complete system of metaphysics, Book 3 the astronomical calculations for reckoning the calendar, and Book 14 a discussion of the doctrine of the Messiah and a refutation of Christianity, Islam, and their founders. These digressions, which technically speaking are not halakhic in essence but rather ethical and philosophic, occur frequently in the halakhic writings of Maimonides.

Unlike the commentary to the Mishnah and *Sefer ha-Mitzvot* which were written in Arabic, the *Mishneh Torah* was written in a beautiful and lucid Hebrew.

Philosophy. Maimonides is, by general agreement, the most significant Jewish philosopher of the Middle Ages, and his *Guide of the Perplexed* is the most important philosophic work produced by a Jew. The Arabic original, *Dalālat al-Ḥā'rīn,* was completed about 1200 and shortly thereafter was twice translated into Hebrew as *Moreh Nevukhim.* The first translation, a literal one, was made by Samuel ibn Tibbon with Maimonides' advice and was completed in 1204. The second, a freer

Traditional portrait of Maimonides from Ugolimus'
Thesaurus Antiquatum Sacrarum, Venice, 1744.

The tomb of Maimonides in Tiberias.

translation, was made by the poet Judah al-Ḥarizi a little later. In its Hebrew translations the *Guide* determined the course of Jewish philosophy from the early 13th century on, and almost every philosophic work for the remainder of the Middle Ages cited, commented on, or criticized Maimonides' views.

While the *Guide* contained the major statement of Maimonides' position, his philosophic and theological views appeared in a variety of other writings, among which the most important are the three lengthy essays in his commentary to the Mishnah (see above), the first book of the *Mishneh Torah, Sefer ha-Madda* which is devoted to God and His attributes, angelic beings, the structure of the universe, prophecy, ethics, repentance, free will and providence, and the afterlife, and the last section of the same work, *Hilkhot Melakhim,* which includes a discussion on the Messiah and the messianic age.

In his philosophic views Maimonides was an Aristotelian, and it was he who put medieval Jewish philosophy on a firm Aristotelian basis. But in line with contemporary Aristotelianism his political philosophy was Platonic. In his works he quotes his authorities sparingly,[52] but in a letter to his translator Samuel ibn Tibbon[53] he indicated his philosophic preferences explicitly. In this letter he advises Ibn Tibbon to study the works of Aristotle with the help of the Hellenistic commentators Alexander of Aphrodisias and Themistius and of Maimonides' contemporary Averroes. It appears, however, that Averroes commentaries reached Maimonides too late to have any influence on his *Guide.* He recommends highly the works of the Muslim al-Fārābī, particularly those on logic, and he speaks of the writings of the Muslim Avempace (Ibn Bāja) with approval. The works of Avicenna (Ibn Sīnā) in Maimonides' view are also worthy of study, but they are inferior to those of al-Fārābī. Of Jewish philosophers he mentions only Isaac Israeli, of whose views he disapproves, and Joseph ibn Ẓaddik, whom he praises for his learning, though he states that he knew only the man, not his work. He also mentions some other philosophers of whose views he disapproves. Al-Fārābī, Avempace, and Averroes interpreted Aristotle rationalistically, and it appears that Maimonides preferred their interpretations to the more theologically oriented one of Avicenna, though he relied on Avicenna for some of his views.[54]

Maimonides considered himself in the tradition of the Aristotelians, adapting and developing their teachings in accord with his own views;

but he differed from them in the works he produced. While the Muslims had composed commentaries on Aristotle's works, summaries of his views, and independent philosophic treatises, Maimonides produced no purely philosophic work of his own, the early *Treatise on Logic* excepted. He held that the extant philosophic literature was adequate for all needs (Guide 2, introd., proposition 25, and ch. 2), and he devoted himself to specific issues, particularly those bearing on the interrelation of philosophy and religion.

Fundamental to Maimonides' approach is a division of mankind into two groups: an intellectual elite, who, using reason, can understand by means of demonstrative arguments, and the masses (including those scholars who study only religious law), who, using imagination, understand by means of persuasive arguments. In the light of this distinction Maimonides' works may be divided into two kinds: *Guide of the Perplexed,* addressed primarily to an intellectual elite, and his other writings, addressed to the masses.

This distinction had one further consequence for Maimonides. Maimonides identified *ma'aseh bereshit* (the account of the creation) and *ma'aseh merkavah* (the account of the divine chariot of Ezekiel) with physics and metaphysics respectively. According to the Mishnah, however (Ḥag. 2:1) one may not teach the former to two persons, nor the latter even to one, unless he is wise and able to understand by himself. Maimonides codifies this as *halakhah* (i.e., legally correct and binding) (Yad, Yesodei ha-Torah, 2:12; 4:10–13) and in his commentary to the Mishnah gives as the reason for the prohibition the current philosophical opinion that the teaching of abstract matters to someone who cannot grasp them may lead to unbelief.

This prohibition against the public teaching of *ma'aseh merkavah* and *ma'aseh bereshit* posed a problem. How could he write the *Guide,* a book devoted to these esoteric topics, when putting something in writing is equivalent to teaching it in public? Maimonides solved this problem by making use of certain literary devices. First, Maimonides addressed the book to his disciple, Joseph ben Judah ibn Sham'un, who after studying with him left for Baghdad. Hence, the *Guide* in its formal aspect is a personal communication to one student. Moreover Maimonides, in a dedicatory letter at the beginning of the *Guide,* relates Joseph's intellectual history, showing that he had acquired some philosophic wisdom and that he was able to reason for himself. Hence, Joseph had fulfilled the conditions necessary for studying the esoteric disciplines.

But Maimonides was well aware that persons other than Joseph would read his work. Hence, he had to make use of other devices. Invoking modes of esoteric writing also current among Islamic philosophers, Maimonides wrote his work in an enigmatic style. Discussing the same topic in different passages, he would make contradictory statements about it. He describes this method in the introduction to the *Guide*, where he speaks of seven types of contradictions which appear in literary works, stating explicitly that he will make use of two of them. It is left to the perceptive reader to discover Maimonides' true views on a given issue.

The enigmatic nature of the *Guide* imposed great difficulties on medieval and modern commentators, and two schools of interpretation arose. Some, while aware of Maimonides' method, consider him a philosopher who attempted to harmonize the teachings of religion with those of philosophy. Others, however, considered Maimonides a philosopher, whose views were in agreement with those of the rationalistic Aristotelians, and who expressed religious opinions largely as a concession to the understanding of the masses. For example, Maimonides, according to the first interpretation, believed that the world was created, while according to the second, his true view was that the world is eternal.

With all these distinctions in mind one may proceed to an exposition of Maimonides' philosophy based largely on the *Guide of the Perplexed*.

Maimonides wrote his work for someone who was firm in his religious beliefs and practices, but, having studied philosophy, was perplexed by the literal meaning of biblical anthropomorphic and anthropopathic terms. To this person Maimonides showed that these difficult terms have a spiritual meaning besides their literal one, and that it is the spiritual meaning that applies to God. Maimonides also undertook in the *Guide* the explanation of obscure biblical parables. Thus, the *Guide* is devoted to the philosophic interpretation of Scripture, or, to use Maimonides' terms, to the "science of the Law in its true sense" or to the "secrets of the Law" (Guide, introd.).

Maimonides' first philosophical topic is God. In line with his exegetical program he begins by explaining troublesome biblical terms, devoting the major portion of the first 49 chapters of the first part of the *Guide* to this task. Representative of his exegesis are his comments on the term "image of God" (*zelem Elohim*), found in the opening section of Genesis. Some have argued, Maimonides states, that since man was created in the image of God, it follows that God, like man, must have a body. He answers the objection by showing that the term *zelem* refers always to a spiritual quality, an essence. Hence, the "image of God" in man is man's essence, that is his reason but not physical likeness (Guide 1: 1).

Maimonides then takes up the question of God's attributes (Guide 1:50–60). The Bible describes God by many attributes, but it also states that God is one. If He is one in the sense of being simple, how can a multiplicity of attributes be ascribed to Him? Medieval philosophers held that attributes applied to substances are of two kinds: essential and accidental. Essential attributes are those that are closely connected with the essence, such as existence or life; accidental attributes are those that are independent of the essence and that may be changed without affecting the essence, such as anger or mercifulness. Medieval logicians generally agreed that accidental attributes introduce a multiplicity into that which they describe, while they disagreed concerning essential attributes. Some held that essential attributes are implicity contained in the essence and, hence, do not introduce multiplicity; others held that they provide new information and, hence, produce multiplicity. Avicenna was an exponent of the latter view, holding that essential attributes, particularly existence, are superadded to the essence. Maimonides accepted Avicenna's position on this point. Maimonides came to the conclusion that accidental attributes applied to God must be interpreted as attributes of action, that is, if it is said that God is merciful, it means that God acts mercifully; and essential attributes must be interpreted as negations, that is, if God is said to be existing, it means that he is not nonexistent.[55]

Prior to Maimonides, Islamic and Jewish Kalām philosophers had offered arguments for the existence, unity, and incorporeality of God and for the creation of the world. Maimonides summarized the teachings of the Kalām philosophers in order to refute them (Guide 1:71–76). In the case of the existence, unity, and incorporeality of God, Maimonides held that these are legitimate philosophic issues, but that the Kalām philosophers, relying on categories of the imagination rather than reason, had not solved them correctly. In the case of creation he held that to demonstrate the creation or eternity of the world lies outside the competence of the human mind.

Maimonides prefaces his own proofs[56] for the existence, unity, and incorporeality of God with 25 metaphysical and physical propositions, which he considers to have been demonstrated in the philosophic literature of his days. To these he adds a 26th proposition, namely, that the world is eternal. However, it appears that this proposition does not reflect Maimonides' own belief concerning the origin of the world (see below), but serves, rather, a methodological function. It can be seen readily, Maimonides implies, that if it is assumed that the world is eternal, the existence of God can still be demonstrated (Guide 2, introd.).

To demonstrate the existence of God, Maimonides makes use of four proofs current in his day: from motion, from the composition of elements (also a kind of argument from motion), from necessity and contingency, and from potentiality and actuality (causality). The common structure of all of them is that they begin with some observed characteristic of the world, invoke the principle that an infinite regress is impossible, and conclude that a first principle must exist. For example, Maimonides begins his first proof, that from motion, by noting that in the sublunar world things constantly move and change. These sublunar motions, in turn, are caused by celestial motions which come to an end with the motion of the uppermost celestial sphere. The motion of that sphere is caused by a mover that is not moved by another mover. This mover, called the Prime Mover, is the last member in the chain of causes producing motion. Maimonides uses the following example as an illustration. Suppose a draft of air comes through a hole, and a stick is used to push a stone in the hole to close it. Now the stone is pushed into the hole by the stick, the stick is moved by the hand, and the hand is moved by the sinews, muscles, etc., of the human body. But one must also consider the draft of air, which was the reason for the motion of the stone in the first place. The motion of the air is caused by the motion of the lowest celestial sphere, and the motion of that sphere, by the successive motions of other spheres. The chain of things moved and moving comes to an end with the last of the celestial spheres. This sphere is set in motion by a principle which, while it produces motion, is itself not moved. This is the Prime Mover, which for Maimonides is identical with God.

Maimonides then turned to the nature of the Prime Mover. Four possibilites exist: Either the Prime Mover exists apart from the sphere, and then either corporeally or incorporeally; or it exists within the sphere, and then either as distributed throughout it or as indivisible. It can be shown that the Prime Mover does not exist within the sphere, which rules out the last two possibilites, nor apart from it as a body, which rules out the third. Hence, it exists apart from the sphere and must be incorporeal. Maimonides shows, further, that there cannot be two incorporeal movers. Thus, it has been established that the Prime Mover exists, is incorporeal, and is one.

Maimonides' proof from necessity and contingency rests on the observation that things in the world are contingent, and that they are ultimately produced by a being that is necessary through itself. This proof was first formulated by Avicenna and was rejected by Averroes (Guide 2:1).[57]

Maimonides next turned to the incorporeal intelligences, which he identified with the angels to the celestial spheres (Guide 2:2–12), and then to creation (Guide 2:13–26). On the last subject he begins by enumerating three theories of the origin of the world: that of the Torah, that the world was created by God out of nothing; that of Plato and others, according to which God created the world out of preexistent matter; and that of Aristotle, according to which the world is eternal. A major portion of the discussion is devoted to showing that Aristotle's and his followers' proofs of the eternity of the world are not really proofs. From an analysis of Aristotelian texts Maimonides attempted to show that Aristotle himself did not consider his arguments as conclusive demonstrations but only as showing that eternity is more plausible than creation. Maimonides' own position is that one can offer plausible arguments for the creation of the world as well as for its eternity. From this it follows that a conclusive demonstration of the creation or the eternity of the world lies beyond human reason; the human mind can only offer likely arguments for either alternative. However, an examination of these arguments reveals that those for creation are more likely than those for eternity, and on this basis Maimonides accepts the doctrine of creation *ex nihilo* as his own. An additional reason is that Scripture also teaches creation. Maimonides' intellectual daring is apparent in his statement (ch. 25) that had the eternity of the world been demonstrated philosophically, he would not have hesitated to interpret the Bible accordingly, just as he did not hesitate to interpret anthropomorphic terms in the Bible allegorically. He also states that the principle of creation is the most important one after that of God's unity, since it explains the possibility of miracles and similar occurrences. However some interpreters understand Maimonides' esoteric teaching as propounding the eternity of the world.

If the world was created, will it come to an end at some future time? He answers in the negative and adds that the future indestructibility of the world is also taught in the Bible (Guide 2:27–29). Maimonides concludes this phase of the discussion with an explanation of the creation chapters at the beginning of Genesis and a discussion of the Sabbath, which in part is also a reminder of the creation.

In the introduction to the *Guide* Maimonides incidentally discussed the nature of the prophetic experience, likening it to intellectual illumination. In the present section (Guide 2:32–48) he is interested in the psychology of prophecy and its political function. He begins by listing three possible theories of how prophecy is acquired: that of the unsophisticated believer, who holds that God arbitrarily selects someone for prophecy; that of the philosophers, according to which prophecy occurs when man's natural faculties, particularly his intellect, reach a high level of development; and that of Scripture, which specifies the same development of natural faculties but adds dependence on God, Who can prevent someone from prophesying, if He so desires.

Maimonides defined prophecy as an emanation from God, which, through the intermediacy of the Active Intellect, flows first upon man's intellectual faculty and then upon his imagination. While a well-developed imagination is of little significance for the illuminative experience of the prophet, it is central to his political function. In line with the views of the Islamic Aristotelians, particularly al-Fārābī, Maimonides conceives of the prophet as a statesman who brings law to his people and admonishes them to observe it. This conception of the prophet-statesman is based on Plato's notion, found in the *Republic*, of the philosopher-king who establishes and administers the ideal state. For Maimonides the primary function of prophets other than Moses is to admonish people to adhere to the Law of Moses; this requires that the prophets use the kind of imaginative language and parables that appeal to the imagination of the masses. Maimonides characterizes three personality types: the philosopher, who uses only his intellect, the ordinary statesman, who uses only his imagination, and the prophet, who uses both.

Though he discusses the phenomenon of prophecy extensively, Maimonides mentions Moses, the chief of the prophets, only in passing in the *Guide*. However, in his halakhic writings he singles out Moses for special discussion. Moses, he states, differed so much from other prophets that he and they had virtually only the name "prophet" in common. Moses' prophecy is distinguished from that of the other prophets in four ways: other prophets received their prophecy in a dream or vision, Moses received his while awake; other prophets received their prophecy in allegorical form, Moses received his directly; other prophets were filled with fear when they received prophecy, Moses was not; other prophets received prophecy intermittently, Moses received it when he wished.[58] Moses also differed from other prophets and legislators in that he conveyed a perfect law, that is, one that addressed itself not only to man's moral perfection but also to his intellectual perfection by requiring the affirmation of certain beliefs.

Maimonides accepts the Neoplatonic doctrine that evil is not an independent principle but rather the privation, or absence, of good. Like the Neoplatonists and other monists he had to accept this position, for to posit an independent principle of evil was to deny the uniqueness and omnipotence of God. There are three kinds of evil: natural evils, such as floods and earthquakes, which man cannot control, social evils, such as wars, and personal evils, the various human vices, both of which man can control. Natural evils are infrequent, and, hence, the majority of evil in the world, which is caused by man, can be remedied by proper training. Maimonides also argues against those who hold that the world is essentially evil, stating that if one looks at the world at large rather than at one's own pains and misfortunes, one finds that the world as a whole is good, not evil (Guide 3:8–12).

Maimonides discusses divine omniscience and then turns to the related question of divine providence. He distinguishes between general providence, which refers to general laws regulating nature, and individual providence, which refers to God's providential concern for individual men. He lists four theories of providence that he rejects: the theory of Epicurus, which states that everything that happens in the world is the result of chance; that of Aristotle (really that of the commentator Alexander of Aphrodisias), which states that there is only general, not individual, providence; that of the Islamic Asharites, which states that the divine will rules everything—this is equivalent to individual providence extended to include all beings, animate and inanimate; and that of the Mu'tazilites, which states that there is individual providence extending even to animals but not to inanimate objects. Last, Maimonides discusses the attitude toward providence of the adherents of the

Torah. They all accept man's free will and God's justice. To these principles some more recent scholars (Maimonides had in mind the *geonim,* most likely Saadiah) have added the principle of *yissurin shel ahavah* ("afflictions of love"), which explains that God may cause suffering to a righteous person in order to reward him in the hereafter. Maimonides rejected it, however, stating that only an unjust God would act in this manner, and asserted that every pain and affliction is a punishment for a prior sin. Finally, Maimonides gave his own position: there is individual providence, and it is determined by the degree of development of the individual's intellect. The more developed a man's intellect, the more subject he is to divine providence (*Guide* 3:16–21). Maimonides used this theory of providence in his interpretation of the Book of Job, in which the characters of that book represent the various attitudes toward providence discussed above (*Guide* 3:22–23).

Maimonides' final undertaking in the *Guide* is the explanation of the Law of Moses and its precepts. But this account is based on his philosophy of man, which he summarizes only in his *"Shemonah Perakim."* From this summary it is clear that Maimonides' philosophy of man was one current among Muslim Aristotelians. Man is composed of a body and a soul, the soul, particularly the intellect, being the form of the body. The soul, which is unitary, contains five basic faculties: nutritive, sensory, imaginative, appetitive, and rational. Of these faculties, the appetitive and rational are important for the good life and for happiness on earth and in the hereafter. Man attains happiness through the exercise of moral virtues to control his appetites and by developing his intellectual powers. In Maimonides' discussion of morality he follows Aristotle in holding that virtuous action consists of following the mean, but he holds that all should go to the extreme to avoid pride and anger (Yad, Deot, 2:3). While in his halakhic writings Maimonides embraced a morality of the mean, in the *Guide* he advocates a more ascetic life, and he particularly recommends curbing the sexual drive. As in Aristotelian thought, the moral virtues serve only a preliminary function, the final goal being the acquisition of intellectual virtues.[59]

In the *Guide* 3:26–49 Maimonides discusses the reasons for and of the commandments. Maimonides considers a distinction made by Mu'tazilite philosophers, Saadiah among them. These philosophers had divided divine law into two categories: rational commandments, such as the prohibitions against murder and theft, which the human mind can discover without revelation; and revealed commandments, such as prayer and the observance of holidays, which are neutral from the point of view of reason and can be known only through revelation. Maimonides understands this position as implying that the revelational commandments come from God's will rather than His reason. Against this view, Maimonides argues that all divine commandments are the product of God's wisdom, though he adds that some are easily intelligible *(mishpatim),* and others intelligible only with difficulty *(hukkim).* However, Maimonides adds that particular commandments have no rational principle behind them and are commandments only because God willed them.

Maimonides postulates two purposes of the Law: the well-being of the soul (intellect) and the well-being of the body, by which he means man's moral well-being. The former is acquired through true beliefs; the latter, through political and personal morality. The beliefs which a man must accept are graded according to his intellectual ability. There are also true beliefs, such as the existence of God, His unity, and His incorporeality, which everyone must accept regardless of intellectual ability; and there are beliefs, such as that God gets angry at those who disobey Him, which have primarily a political function and are considered necessary beliefs. Ordinary men will accept the Law only if there are promised rewards or threatened with punishment, and it is the function of the necessary beliefs to provide such motivation. They are unnecessary for the philosopher, who obeys the Law because it is the right thing to do regardless of consequences.

Although reasons for general moral laws can readily be found, it is more difficult to explain the numerous ritual laws found in the Bible. Maimonides explains many of them as reactions to pagan practices, and he makes uses of his extensive familiarity with such books as the *Nabatean Agriculture,* which describe such practices. Thus, for example, he explains the biblical prohibition against wearing garments made of wool and linen combined as a reaction to a pagan practice requiring priests to wear such garments. Maimonides also considers certain commandments as concessions to historical situations, such as those dealing with sacrifice. Worship without animal sacrifices is preferred, but it would have been unrealistic to require the Israelites leaving Egypt to give up sacrifices altogether. Hence the Bible commanded sacrifices, restricting, however, the times and places for them and permitting only priests to offer them. We should not infer from this, however, that Maimonides believed in a progressive development of Jewish law; in fact, he codifies all of rabbinic law in his *Mishneh Torah*. The *Guide* concludes with a supplementary section on the perfect worship of God and man's perfection.

Eschatology is barely mentioned in the *Guide,* although Maimonides developed it fully in other works. Following traditional Jewish teachings, he deals with the Messiah and messianic times, the resurrection of the dead, and *olam ha-ba* ("the world to come"). He proceeds characteristically by stripping these occurrences of supernatural qualities as much as possible. The Messiah is an earthly king, descended from the house of David. He will bring the Jews back to their country, but his major accomplishment will be to bring peace and tranquility to the world, thereby facilitating full observance of God's commandments. The Messiah will die of old age and be succeeded by his son, the latter, by his son, and so on. No cataclysmic events will take place during messianic times, but the world will continue in its established natural order. Maimonides calculated the year of the coming of the Messiah *("Iggeret Teiman")* although he generally opposed speculations of this kind.[60]

During messianic times the dead will be resurrected with body and soul reunited though later they will die again.[61] Undoubtedly, the central notion of Maimonides' eschatology is his account of *olam ha-ba* ("the world to come"). In his view the intellect, but not the body, has an afterlife, and in that afterlife the intellect is engaged in the contemplation of God. Generally, he speaks of incorporeal intelligences (plural), implying that immortality is individual, but there are passages which suggest that immortality is collective, that is, in the world to come there exists only one intellect for all mankind.[62]

Maimonides' intellectualism is reflected in the formulation of 13 principles that in his view every member of the Jewish community is bound to accept. These 'principles of faith' can be found in all standard daily prayer books *(Siddur)* and are recited by the orthodox in their morning prayers. These principles are known to most people through the *Yigdal Elohim Ḥai* hymn which is widely used in synagogues and which set Maimonides' *Principles* to rhyme to facilitate their memorization. Did Maimonides intend these principles as a means of developing the intellects of the masses, thus enabling them to share in *olam ha-ba,* or as a political expedient, that is, to make the masses aware of intellectual issues so that philosophers can live safely in their midst? Proponents of both views are found among Maimonides' interpreters[63] and it is impossible on the evidence we have available to conclusively decide the issue.

Influence. Maimonides' *Guide,* as has been noted, profoundly influenced the subsequent course of medieval Jewish philosophy. Among the extensive literature that arose were numerous full and partial commentaries on the *Guide,* most of them still unpublished.

MINOR ARISTOTELIANS

During the early 13th century some philosophers were still active in the Islamic world. Joseph b. Judah ibn Aknin (flourished in Morocco), Maimonides' younger contemporary, composed a number of talmudic and philosophic works, among them a commentary on the Song of Songs, a commentary on *Avot,* and a work on moral philosophy, *Ṭibb al-Nufūs al-Salīma wa-Muʿālajat al-Nufūs al-Alīma* ("The Hygiene of the Healthy Souls and the Therapy of Ailing Souls"), which contains an interesting account of the content and order of religious and secular studies among Jews. Joseph b. Judah ibn Sham'un (d. 1226), the disciple for whom Maimonides wrote his *Guide,* composed a small metaphysical work on the necessary existent, how all things proceed from it, and on creation. The early portion of the work follows Avicennian Aristotelianism, and the latter portion, the teachings of Kalām. It is likely that the kalamic section predated Ibn Sham'un's acquaintance with Maimonides. Abraham b. Moses b. Maimon (1186–1237), Maimonides' only son, followed the teachings of his father and defended them against opponents. However, in his *Kitāb Kifāyat al-ʿAbidīn* ("Comprehensive Guide for the Servants of God"), he advocates a Sufi-like Jewish pietism.

In southern France, Samuel ibn Tibbon, the translator of the *Guide* and other works, composed *Perush me-ha-Millot ha-Zarot,* a philosophical glossary for the *Guide,* philosophical commentaries on Ecclesiastes and Song of Songs, and *Ma'amar Yikkavu ha-Mayim* (on Gen. 1:9), devoted to physical and metaphysical topics. He favored the allegorical interpretation of the Bible, and is said to have held that the Bible was primarily for the masses.

Jacob Anatoli (13th century), active as a translator at the court of the emperor Frederick II, wrote *Malmad ha-Talmidim,* a philosophical commentary on the Pentateuch. In this work he quotes the Christian scholar Michael Scot (he even cites Emperor Frederick II) and he shows acquaintance with Christian literature and institutions. He followed the allegorical interpretation of Scripture and preached philosophical sermons publicly. This earned him the anger of the anti-Maimonists.

Shem Tov b. Joseph Falaquera (c. 1225–c. 1295), translator and author of many works devoted largely to ethics and psychology, also wrote *Moreh ha-Moreh,* a commentary on Maimonides' *Guide.* In this commentary he corrects Ibn Tibbon's translation of the *Guide* on the basis of the Arabic original, and he cites parallel passages from the works of Islamic philosophers, particularly from Averroes. In his *Iggeret ha-Vikku'aḥ,* a dialogue between a philosopher and an opponent of philosophy, he justifies the study of philosophy. In his *Sefer ha-Nefesh* he follows Avicenna, but in his encyclopedic work *De'ot ha-Pilosofim* he follows Averroes. He translated and condensed Ibn Gabirol's *Mekor Ḥayyim* from Arabic into Hebrew.

Joseph ibn Kaspi (c. 1279–c. 1340), prolific author of biblical commentaries, lexicographic works, and books on philosophy, wrote a commentary on the *Guide,* consisting of an exoteric and esoteric part entitled, respectively, *Ammudei Kesef* and *Maskiyyot Kesef.* This commentary was influenced by that of Shem Tov b. Joseph Falaquera and in turn influenced later commentaries on the *Guide.* He accepts doctrines associated with the teachings of Averroes, such as the identity of religion and philosophy, the eternity of the world, and the natural interpretation of miracles, but he tries to modify these doctrines in a way that distinguishes him from such extreme rationalists as Moses of Narbonne and Levi b. Gershom.

Hillel ben Samuel. Hillel b. Samuel (c. 1220–1295), one of the first Jewish philosophers in Italy, translated from Latin to Hebrew the Neoplatonic work *Liber de causis* and composed *Tagmulei ha-Nefesh* ("The Rewards of the Soul"). Since he knew Latin, he was able to draw on the opinions of Christian scholastics, particularly those of Thomas Aquinas. In Aristotelian fashion, Hillel defined the soul as the entelechy of a natural organic body, but, following Avicenna and the Neoplatonists, he held that the soul is a substance that emanates from God through the intermediacy of the supernal soul. He also cites Averroes' opinion that there is only one universal soul for all men, from which individual souls emanate like rays from the sun. However, on the question of the material or potential intellect he criticizes Averroes, using arguments offered by Aquinas. Averroes had argued that there exists only one such intellect for all men, but Hillel argued that each person has his own material intellect. On the question of the active intellect, Hillel accepts the opinion of the Islamic and Jewish Aristotelians, for whom the active intellect was the lowest of the celestial intelligences; in this he differed from Aquinas, who held that each person has his own active intellect. According to Hillel, only the rational part of the soul is immortal, and its ultimate happiness consists in union with the active intellect. In its immortal state the soul retains its individuality. Hillel also composed a commentary on Maimonides' 26 propositions.

Isaac Albalag. Isaac Albalag (second half of 13th century, probably lived in Spain) translated Al-Ghazālī's *Maqāṣid al-Falāsifa* (a compendium of the teachings of Avicenna) into Hebrew and presented his own views in a commentary on the work entitled *Tikkun ha-De'ot.* A follower of Averroes, who accepted such doctrines as the eternity of the world, he has also been described as a proponent of the theory of the "double truth," advocated by Latin Averroists. Like the Latin Averroists he distinguished between two coexistent independent truths, philosophic truth and prophetic truth, and he held that the two can contradict one another. However, he does not cite in his work any instance of such contradiction. His outlook is not completely clear, but it seems that his own view on a given topic is always that of philosophy. He maintained that speculative truths are the province of philosophy, not of Scripture. The Torah has as its sole purpose the moral and political guidance of the masses and contains no speculative truths, even by implication. Nevertheless, Albalag offers philosophic interpretations of the Bible; for example, he explained the story of creation in accordance with the doctrine of the eternity of the world. In a somewhat different vein, he states that if philosophic and prophetic truths contradict each other, both should stand, and one should say that the prophetic truth is unintelligible.

Abner of Burgos and Isaac Pollegar. The first half of the 14th century saw a debate concerning the freedom of the will initiated by Abner of Burgos. Abner, who converted to Christianity, presented his views in *Minḥat Kena'ot;* although the work was written after his conversion, it seems clear that he held the same views when he was still a Jew. Following Avicenna, whose opinions he knew through their summary in al-Ghazālī's *Maqāṣid al-Falāsifa,* he held that human acts no less than natural occurrences are causally determined. Although the will has the ability to choose between alternatives, any given choice is determined, in fact, by causes influencing the will. Causal determination of the will is also required by God's omniscience and omnipotence: were human actions undetermined until the moment of decision, God could not foreknow them, and, also, His power would be limited. Abner tried to justify the existence of divine commandments and reward and punishment: divine commandments can be among the causes affecting the will, and reward and punishment are necessary consequences of human actions. Abner viewed biblical and rabbinic statements affirming freedom of the will as concessions to the understanding of the masses.

Isaac Pollegar, who knew Abner personally, attacked his determinism in his *Ezer ha-Dat.* According to Pollegar's solution, which contains difficulties of its own, there is a correlation between the divine and human wills such that at the moment man wills to do a certain act, God also wills that it be accomplished. In willing that the act be accomplished God also knows it. Yet, although this knowledge begins in time, there is no change in God. Whatever the difficulties of this position, it is clear that Pollegar tried to defend the freedom of the will by limiting God's foreknowledge. Levi b. Gershom (see below) solved the problem in a more radical fashion. Holding that God's knowledge extends only to species and not to individuals, he excluded man's action from God's knowledge, thereby safeguarding human freedom.

Moses of Narbonne. Moses b. Joshua of Narbonne (d. after 1362) was another participant in the debate. He wrote commentaries on works by Averroes and other Muslim philosophers (including al-Ghazālī's *Maqāṣid*) and also an important commentary on Maimonides' *Guide.* Although he held Maimonides in high esteem, he criticized a number of his doctrines, which under the influence of Al-Fārābi and Avicenna had a Neoplatonic complexion; he opposes these doctrines with the more strictly Aristotelian teachings of Averroes. His critique of Abner is found in *Ha-Ma'amar bi-Veḥirah,* and he also discusses human freedom in other works. However, his position is not completely clear. In some passages he holds in agreement with Maimonides that God's knowledge extends to particular human acts without determining these acts; in others he holds that God knows only species, not individuals. The latter opinion was probably Moses' real view.

LEVI BEN GERSHOM

Levi ben Gershom (Gersonides) lived primarily in Orange in the first half of the 14th century and briefly at Avignon. Little is known about his life beyond the fact that he maintained relations with some of the most important Christians of his day. His scientific works deal with arithmetic, geometry, trigonometry, and astronomy. His contributions to medieval astronomy and astronomical equipment became particularly well-known. He was also a talmudist and liturgist of some importance.

Levi wrote commentaries on Job (1325), Song of Songs (1325 or 1326), Ecclesiastes (1328), Ruth (1329), Esther (1329), the Pentateuch (1329–38), the Former Prophets (1338), Proverbs, Daniel, Nehemiah, and Chronicles (1338).

His biblical commentaries are the work of an exegete and a philosopher. Certain of his literal explanations are still of interest today. Diverse questions of a philosophical or theological nature are discussed by him, such as the problem of providence, miracles, and the Messiah. From each book of the Bible, Levi extracts the ethical, philosophical, and religious teachings that may be gleaned from the text and calls them *to'alot* or *to'aliyyot.* A collection of these *to'aliyyot* was printed separately (in 1570). In his voluminous commentary on the Pentateuch, Levi attempts to reconstitute the *halakhah* rationally, basing himself on nine logical principles which he substitutes for the traditional 13 hermeneutical rules, and condemning allegorical interpretations.

In one of his first philosophical works, *Sefer ha-Hekkesh ha-Yashar*

(1319), translated into Latin under the title *Liber syllogismi recti*, Levi corrects certain inaccurate arguments of Aristotle in his *Posterior Analytics*. Levi became acquainted with Aristotle's views by reading the paraphrases and commentaries of Averroes, and he himself wrote super-commentaries on a number of them.

In his commentaries on Averroes, which are important for understanding his philosophy, Levi paraphrases the text but frequently inserts notes of varying lengths, preceded by the words: *amar Levi* ("Levi says"). In these notes he develops, criticizes, or corrects aspects of the ideas of Aristotle or Averroes. He manifests an independent spirit in relation to the two philosophers[64] and proves himself an important, creative and astute logician and philosopher.

Philosophy. Levi's major work, to which he constantly refers in his commentaries on Averroes and the Bible, is the *Sefer Milḥamot Adonai* ("The Book of the Wars of the Lord"),[65] begun in about 1317 and completed in 1329. In this work, he treats problems which, in his opinion, have not received a satisfactory solution by preceding philosophers, including Maimonides.

The *Milḥamot* is written in a precise and technical Hebrew but, like Levi's other works, it is characterized by repetitiveness. In almost all the questions analyzed, Levi quotes the opinions of his predecessors— Aristotle, Alexander of Aphrodisias, Themistius, Al-Farābī, Avicen- na—with whom he became acquainted largely by reading Averroes, as well as the opinions of Averroes himself and of Maimonides. He enumerates the arguments that, respectively, support and disprove their theses and, finally, he expounds his own theory. Though lacking a systematic structure, the *Milḥamot* contains an almost complete system of philosophy and theology. However, this work cannot be understood unless one is familiar with Levi's commentaries on Averroes and the Bible, which explain and complement the *Milḥamot* on many points. In order to fully understand the ideas of Levi, one should have recourse to all his philosophical and exegetic works.

Demonstrating the existence of God, Levi rejects the proof, favored by many of his Aristotelian predecessors, according to which the existence of God, as prime mover, can be derived from the various motions existing in the world. In its place he presents a proof based on the orderly processes existing in the world, that is, an argument from design. According to this proof, the observed regularity of processes of generation within the sublunar world leads to the conclusion that these processes are produced by an intelligence. This intelligence is the so-called agent intellect which governs the sublunar world. This intelligence endows matter with its various forms and is aware of the order it produces. The activities of the agent intellect are mediated by the natural heat which is found in the seeds and sperms of plants and animals and this natural heat in turn is produced by the motions of the various celestial spheres. Since these motions contribute to the perfection of the terrestrial world, they must also be produced by intelligences which know them, that is, they are produced by the intelligences of the celestial spheres. From what has been said, it can be seen that the celestial and terrestrial worlds form an ordered, unitary whole and this requires that there exists a supreme being which produces and knows this order. This being is God.

Unlike Maimonides, Levi maintains that it is possible to ascribe positive attributes to God without reducing or changing His absolute unity and simplicity. Admitting that real multiplicity exists only in beings composed of forms and matter, he argues that all the predicates of a proposition dealing with a non-material entity are derived analytically from the subject. According to Levi these predicates are simply an explanation of the subject and introduce no plurality whatever. Opposing Maimonides' doctrine of negative attributes,[66] Levi teaches that man may have a certain positive knowledge of God, based on the observation of His actions. The essential action of God is thinking, and, consequently, the effusion of all forms. All the attributes that man recognizes in his own form are just so many attributes of God. Since the attributes common to both man and God have the relation of cause and effect, it is impossible to consider them absolute homonyms, that is, terms which have nothing in common except their names.

By means of a knowledge that is neither temporal nor changing, God eternally perceives the general law of the universe, that is, those laws governing the movements of the heavenly bodies and, through them, the sublunar beings. God is aware of the fate that awaits all individuals, inasmuch as they are distributed in groups subject to the same celestial determinism which, in principle, governs all the conditions of man. However, this determinism, essentially beneficial, may occasionally cause misfortune. God has therefore accorded man freedom which allows him to liberate himself from the shackles of determinism. An individual who makes use of his freedom is no longer subject to the universal law known by God; he has accomplished an act which is absolutely undetermined and which remains totally unknown to God. God's knowledge, however, does not undergo any modification; it always remains true, since the author of the free act is no longer included in the necessary and universal proposition thought by God. For Levi, God's knowledge embraces all the events of this world, with the exception of free acts that cannot be predicted by any type of knowledge. Levi is convinced that he has finally succeeded in reconciling two contradictory fundamental principles of the Bible: divine omniscience and the freedom of man's will.

The providence of God extends a means of protection that increases in proportion to man's moral and intellectual perfection. Through the determined activities of the stars, God assures a maximum of good to men in general and spares them a maximum of ills. Premonitions, dreams, prophecies and the exercise of free choice save certain individuals from harmful effects of determinism. However, the existence of evil cannot be denied since, at times, the righteous do suffer. But Levi upholds the belief that the true good which is specifically human is the immortality of the soul, and it is this immortality, rigorously proportioned according to one's moral rectitude and intellectual perfection, that constitutes the actual recompense of God.

In opposition to Maimonides who held that the creation of the world can not be demonstrated philosophically,[67] Levi offers philosophic arguments designed to show that the world came into being. One such is that everything produced by a final cause, ordained to a certain end, and serving as a substratum for accidents, cannot exist eternally. Since the world fulfills all these conditions it follows that it cannot be eternal, that is, that it has a beginning in time. He derives the same conclusion from the state of the sciences. Were the world eternal, he argues, the sciences would be more advanced than they are. He holds further that a large number of Aristotle's arguments designed to prove the eternity of the world beg the question. They are based on the assumption that the physical laws discovered within the world are also applicable to its beginning. However, this assumption is fallacious. For while it is true that there are some similarities between processes within the world and creation (Levi here is more moderate than Maimonides who holds a similar view), creation is also unique. Whereas motions in the world take place in time, creation occurred in an instant. However, since nothing can be created out of nothing, the world has a substratum, an eternal body which is nonetheless a relative non-being, in the sense that it possesses no form whatever. This substratum has no "existence" in the proper sense of the word, since all existence derives from form. Thus the theological difficulty that might give rise to the possibility of more than one eternal being is avoided.

God has arranged the universe so that man, the most perfect being of the sublunar world, is accorded the greatest good and is spared the greatest amount of ills possible, as we have already seen. Revelations of different types protect him (premonitions, dreams, etc.). His imagination, under the action of one or several celestial bodies, envisions the menace that certain stellar configurations may place upon him. God has equally furnished man with a practical intellect, from which he learns the indispensable art of self-preservation, and a speculative intellect which permits him to perceive truth and to achieve immortality. The material or potential intellect is not a substance but rather a simple disposition, whose substratum is the imagination. Building on the sensations, the human intellect abstracts concepts; but sensation is only an incidental agent in the production of knowledge, for knowledge in its true sense is the comprehension of intelligibles as they exist in the agent intellect. The human intellect, having understood the intelligible, which is eternal, becomes itself immortal. Differing from Averroes, who maintained that, at this state, the human intellect loses its individuality, Levi held that immortality is individual.

Providence extends particularly to the children of Israel, chosen by God through His covenant with the Patriarchs. Prophecy is a kind of revelation that is superior to all other types of revelation, and differs from them not in degree but in nature. The prophet must necessarily be a preeminent philosopher who grasps the general laws governing changes in the sublunar world as they exist in the agent intellect. By means of his imagination, he applies this knowledge to given individual or communal situations, announcing the good or evil events that may befall a person, a group, or an entire people, as a result of the operation of the laws of nature. He is also capable of predicting a miracle, which is a violation of nature, not, as Maimonides thought, an event included in the laws of nature at the time of the creation of the world. Levi maintains that a miracle is produced at a particular time and place, and that it occurs when the agent intellect suspends normal, natural law, since it no longer applies to certain circumstances Though miracles are not part of the laws of nature, or subject to them, they have their own laws. However, since a miracle is produced by the agent intellect, which can only act upon the sublunar world, no miracles can occur in the translunar world. Thus, for example, the sun did not really stand at the order of Joshua; the victory at Gibeon was attained during the short lapse of time when the sun seemingly stood at its zenith.

Through the intermediacy of Moses, the greatest of all prophets, God gave Israel the Torah, which, through its *mitzvot* and speculative truths, aims to help the children of Israel attain the moral and intellectual perfection which makes immortality possible for them. The commandments have various purposes, which Levi expounds in detail, but the purpose of most of them is to remove materialistic tendencies and teach the existence of forms. Finally, the Torah has revealed certain metaphysical truths that the philosophers have never been able to deduce, namely, the creation of the world and the immortality of the soul.

Levi's eschatology is based on a tradition that there are two Messiahs. After the Messiah son of Joseph dies, having been assassinated, the Messiah son of David will appear. He will be greater than Moses, not because he will promulgate a new Torah, but because he will accomplish a miracle greater than those of Moses: the resurrection of the dead, an event which will convert all peoples of the earth to the true religion. He predicts the coming of the Messiah for the year 1358. During messianic times, the world will follow its usual pattern, men will die as before, but the earth will be filled with knowledge of God and human liberty will be utilized for good ends.

Views on Levi ben Gershom. On account of his boldness and extreme rationalism the suspicion of heresy was fastened to him and Levi became the subject of virulent attacks. Certain of his doctrines became the object of harsh criticism on the part of Ḥasdai Crescas. Shem Tov ibn Shem Tov labeled Levi's major work the "Wars against the Lord." Isaac b. Sheshet Perfet, though recognizing Levi as a great talmudist, maintains that it is prohibited to accept certain of his theories. Isaac Abrabanel, in several of his works, also criticizes him. However, even the most vehement critics of Levi, who very often did not understand his real thought, did not hesitate to borrow some of his ideas and his influence continued to exert itself even as late as the 19th century, when he is mentioned in Malbim's commentary on Job. From the modern vantage point he can be seen to have been the most ardent rationalist in the medieval Jewish tradition who was more willing to accept the implications of this basic Aristotelian system than any of his medieval contemporaries.

Title page of *Sefer Milḥamot ha-Shem* by Levi b. Gershom, Riva di Trento, 1560.

CRITICS OF ARISTOTELIANISM

The extent to which Aristotelian philosophy had saturated and re-defined the discussion of theological and philosophical matters can best be gauged by the reaction to it. Rather than adopting a non-philosophical standpoint, mystical or anti-rational, the serious critics of Aristotelian rationalism accepted the requirement that their critique be framed in philosophical terms and that their objections be grounded in a rigorous logical exposition of the inadequacies of the Aristotelian account of nature and metaphysics. Using the standard canons of argument and analysis, Jewish opponents of Aristotle sought to show, through an internal engagement with the philosopher's thought, that his views were opposed by biblical teaching as well as by sound science. By doing this, critics hoped to legitimatize the veracity and ultimacy of scripture.

ḤASDAI CRESCAS

Ḥasdai Crescas originated from the Spanish town of Barcelona, where his activities as a merchant and communal leader can be traced back to 1367. In that year he was imprisoned, together with R. Nissim Gerondi, his teacher, and R. Isaac ben Sheshet, on a trumped-up charge of desecrating the Host, but was later released. Crescas wrote poetry, and in 1370 participated in a competition between the Hebrew poets of Barcelona and those of Gerona. He was among the delegates of the Catalonian Jewish community who negotiated with the king of Aragon for a renewal and extension of Jewish privileges in 1383. With the accession of John I (1387), Crescas became closely associated with the court of Aragon, and was accorded the title of member of the royal household. In 1387 Crescas was empowered by royal decree to exercise the juridical powers available in Jewish law in order to enforce a ban of excommunication. Shortly afterward he settled in Saragossa, where he served as rabbi in place of Isaac ben Sheshet, who had taken up residence in Valencia. In 1390 John I permitted Crescas to prosecute informers against Jews and to impose punishment on them in accordance with the community's privileges. Soon after, the queen appointed Crescas as judge of all cases concerning informers in the Jewish communities throughout Aragon, but there is no documentary evidence of such an appointment. A son of Crescas suffered a martyr's death in Barcelona in the anti-Jewish riots of 1391.[67]

A document of 1396 shows that Crescas was actively engaged during this period in the general rehabilitation of Spanish Jewry. He also made efforts to reform the system of communal representation in Saragossa, and in 1396 framed regulations (no longer extant) for the community, aimed at strengthening the powers of its administrators. Certain modifications were introduced to them in 1399 by Queen Violante, who extended the responsibility of the administrators and allowed the lower classes a greater share in the representation. However, she continued to entrust Crescas with great authority in constitutional matters. He also helped to effect similar charges in neighboring communities where necessary. His influence was not confined to Aragon. Before 1391 he and Isaac ben Sheshet were approached for advice with regard to the succession of the chief rabbinate of France. He is not known to have engaged in any public duties during the last decade of his life, which he apparently devoted exclusively to his literary activities. After the martyrdom of his son he received permission in 1393 from the king of Aragon to marry a second wife, since his first wife was unable to have any more children. He died at Saragossa.

Crescas had limited time for writing, and what he did write was motivated by his commitment to salvage Judaism in Spain. As part of a campaign to combat the prodigious Christianizing literature aimed at Jews and Conversos he wrote his "Refutation of the Principles of the Christians" (1197–98) in Catalan. This work has survived only in Joseph ben Shem Tov's Hebrew translation entitled *Bittul Ikkarei ha-Noẓerim* (1451).[68] He also composed at least one other Catalan work combatting Christianity which is now lost, and he influenced Profiat Duran to write his *Kelimmat ha-Goyim* ("Disgrace of the Gentiles"), another work criticizing Christianity. The "Refutation" is a non-rhetorical logical critique of ten principles of Christianity: original sin, redemption, the Trinity,

the incarnation, the virgin birth, transubstantiation, baptism, the messiah-
ship of Jesus, the New Testament, and demonology. Even his philosophic
treatise *Or Adonai* ("Light of the Lord"), an anti-Aristotelian classic,
written in Hebrew and completed in 1410[69] was conceived as a polemic.
In this work Crescas attacked Aristotelianism because Aristotelian arguments had been used by Jewish intellectuals to justify their desertion of
Judaism.

Crescas had planned to write a comprehensive work *Ner Elohim* ("Lamp
of God") which was to have been a reaction to the teachings of Maimonides. He envisaged that the work would be composed of a philosophic-
dogmatic part, *Or Adonai* and a halakhic one, *Ner Mitzvah* ("The Lamp
of Mitzvah"); however, the latter section was never written. *Or Adonai* was
directed against the *Guide of the Perplexed,* the main work of Jewish
Aristotelianism. Crescas praised the immensity of Maimonides' learning,
and acknowledged the desirability of his intent, but in justification of his
critique he cited the rabbinic dictum, " . . . wherever the divine name is
being profaned no respect is to be shown to one's master" (Er. 63a). *Ner
Mitzvah* was to have superseded Maimonides' *Mishneh Torah* as a concise
systematization of *halakhah.* The work was to have included Crescas' own
novellae, and was to have incorporated logical and methodological
features lacking in Maimonides' work, namely: alternate halakhic opinions, references to sources, and principles which would permit the application of commandments, general in their nature, to particular cases.
Since this halakhic compendium was never written, Crescas is remembered
as a philosopher, not a halakhist.

Philosophy. The disengagement of philosophy and belief from *halakhah,*
symbolized by the projected two parts of his work, was crucial to Crescas.
For example, Maimonides, combining the two, had interpreted the
opening words of the Decalogue, "I am the Lord" (Ex. 20:2; Deut. 5:6),
as constituting a positive commandment to believe in (or know) the
existence of God. Crescas, by contrast, argued in the preface to his
Or Adonai that it is absurd to speak of a divine commandment to believe
in the existence of God, since such a belief cannot be a commandment
itself, but must be a presupposition for any commandment. Before one
can speak of a divine commandment one must already be convinced
of the existence of a divine commander, God. Furthermore, in Crescas'
psychology belief is involuntary; and one can only be reasonably com-

manded to do what one has the power to choose to do. Once again, therefore, belief in the existence of God is a presupposition of all the commandments, but it itself is not a commandment; it is pre-halakhic.

Or Adonai is divided into four books which analyze (1) the presuppositions or roots *(shorashim)* of Torah, (2) the fundaments *(pinnot)* of Torah, (3) other obligatory beliefs of Torah, and (4) some non-obligatory speculations. Following Maimonides, Crescas counts as roots God's existence, unity, and incorporeality. His analysis is tripartite: (1) a thorough presentation of the alleged Aristotelian roots of Torah, i.e., demonstrations of the 25 supposedly indubitable physical and metaphysical propositions that Maimonides had declared necessary premises of proofs of God's existence, unity, and incorporeality; and explanations of these proofs (cf. *Guide,* 2, Introduction); (2) a disproof of Aristotelianism, i.e., logical refutations of most of the propositions and all of the proofs; and (3) a new investigation of the roots.

Crescas' critique of Aristotelianism was historically momentous; in arguing for the liberation of Torah, he was arguing also for the liberation of science. Crescas refutes the Aristotelian arguments against the existence of a vacuum and suggests that a medium is not a necessary condition of either motion or weight. It is not true that each element possesses an inner tendency toward its alleged natural place: rather, "all movable bodies have a certain amount of weight differing only quantitatively" and "those bodies which move upward do so only by reason of the pressure exerted upon them by bodies heavier in weight." Refutation of the impossibility of a vacuum enables Crescas to argue against the impossibility of infinite incorporeal and corporeal magnitudes and in the process to overthrow Aristotle's definition of place. In Aristotle's theory, according to which the universe in finite, "place" was defined as the adjacent surface of the containing body (*Physics* 4:4); this definition, observes Crescas, involves absurdities, e.g., the outermost celestial sphere has no essential place and the place of the part is sometimes not a part of the place of the whole. In Crescas' conception, space is infinitely extended; it is a vacuum, except where occupied by matter. Thus, space is the place of all matter, and the "place" of a thing is defined as "the interval between the limits of that which surrounds." To the Aristotelian argument that, according to such a definition, places themselves would have an infinite number of movable places, he replies that space is one and its dimensions immovable. Crescas notes that with the refutation of the impossibility of an infinite magnitude, the impossibility of a plurality of worlds is also refuted: there is now place for them. The objection that elements of the world would spill into another is quickly invalidated, even on Aristotelian terms, for each world could have its own proper places for its elements.

Crescas does not explicitly posit the existence of an infinite number of worlds, but it is inferable; he does argue for an infinite number of coexisting magnitudes, and in two theological discussions he refers to *aggadah* about God's travels in (Crescas interprets "providence for") 18,000 worlds (Av. Zar. 3b). He rejects the Aristotelian view that the existence of an infinite number of causes and effects is impossible. In categorically affirming actual infinity, he contends that its denial by Aristotle was based on the fallacious assumption that the infinite is analogous to the finite. However, he argues, while finite magnitudes have boundaries and shape, the infinite by definition has no boundaries and is shapeless; while a finite number can actually be numbered, an infinite number possesses only the capacity of being numbered; while finite whole numbers can be subdivided exhaustively into even and odd, infinite numbers are not to be described by either evenness or oddness. On the other hand, regarding measurability, it is true that the predicates "greater than," "smaller than," and "equal to" are inapplicable to infinite numbers, but they are applicable to the numbers themselves. He rejects the Aristotelian view that the celestial spheres are rational, that is that they possess intelligence, and that their motion is voluntary; he argues that motion of terrestrial as well as celestial elements is natural rather than rational. Having dismissed Aristotle's theory of absolute lightness and weight, and having interpreted motion as a function of weight, he conjectures that the circular motion of the celestial spheres is due to their weightlessness. He rejects Aristotle's identification of form with actuality and matter with potentiality, and proposes that the substratum its "corporeal form." He rejects Aristotle's definition of time as an accident of motion; in his view, time exists only in the soul and is "the measure of the duration of motion or of rest between two instants."

The critique of the Aristotelian propositions was also the critique of the premises of Maimonides' proofs of the existence, unity, and incorporeality of God; and the proofs fall with the propositions. Crescas does, however, recognize one short proof of the existence of God: Regardless of whether causes and effects in the world are finite or infinite, there must be one cause of all of them as a whole. For were there nothing but effects, these effects in themselves would have only possible existence. Hence, in order to bring them into actual being, they need a cause, and this cause is God. He does not accept philosophic proofs for either of the other two roots: God's unity is known only from Torah, "Hear O Israel: the Lord our God, the Lord is one" (Deut. 6:4); His incorporeality is a corollary of His unity. Crescas concludes his dissertation on the roots (shorashim) by remarking that while philosophy cannot establish them, it does agree with them; the argument from design[70] suggested the existence of a Governor to Abraham, but only God's light dispelled Abraham's doubt (cf. Gen. R. 39:1).

Torah, in Crescas' conception, is "the product of a voluntary action from the Commander, Who is the initiator of the action to the commanded, who is the receiver of the action." Fundaments (pinnot) are concepts that follow necessarily (i.e., analytically) from his conception of Torah. They include: 1. God's knowledge of existents, for God could not have commanded the Torah without knowing what he commanded. Crescas argues that God as Creator knows a priori all existents across all time. 2. Providence, for God's voluntary giving of the Torah was itself providential. According to Crescas, God provides for individuals not, as Maimonides taught, in accordance with their intellectual excellence, but on the merit of their love. 3. God's power, for were He powerless, He could not have given the Torah. Crescas argues that He Who created all by virtue of His will is infinitely powerful, neither restricted by nor dependent on nature. 4. Communication between Commander and commanded, i.e., prophecy, for the Torah is the product of such communication. Prophecy, maintains Crescas, is the culmination not of philosophy, as Maimonides taught, but of love for God. 5. Man's power of choice, for the concept of commandment presupposes the commanded's ability to choose to obey. Yet Crescas accepts the philosophic position of determinism, maintaining that two hypothetical individuals with identical backgrounds would in the same situation choose identically. He accepts, also, the theological position of determinism, that God foreknows all, and he affirms the antinomy of the second-century Rabbi Akiva: "All is foreseen, but choice is given" (Avot 3:19). Man, he concludes, has a will, composed of appetite and imagination, though this will is determined by external causes, among them the commandments. Because of this will man is able to choose, and, furthermore, he is responsible for his choice, which, in turn, becomes a cause, determining his reward or punishment. However, a man is not responsible for his beliefs, for belief, in Crescas' analysis, is independent of the will; thus, at Sinai the Israelites, coerced as if God had threatened to crush them with the mountain (cf. Av. Zar. 2b), were not rewarded for believing, but for the voluntary joy attendant on their belief. 6. The purposefulness of Torah, just as objects produced by men have a purpose, so, the Torah, produced by the Prime Intellect (God) must have purpose. It is the purpose of the Torah to effect in the one to whom it is addressed love for man, correct opinions, and physical felicity, which are all subsumed under one final goal—spiritual felicity, the infinite love for God. But even for God, the Commander, the Torah has a purpose, namely to bestow His infinite love upon His creatures.

Against both Platonism and Aristotelianism, Crescas argues that God's love for man is stronger than man's love for God, for God's infinite essence is the source of both loves. Man's love for God results in *devekut* ("conjunction" or "communion") with God; for among spiritual beings, as well as among physical objects, love and concord are the causes of perfection and unity. Love, the purpose of Torah, is the purpose also of man, and, further, of all that is. Maimonides had discredited the question of ultimate purpose, asserting that one could ask the purpose of every proposed purpose. Crescas replies that there is no infinite regress, because, ultimately, goodness is its own purpose, and it follows necessarily from God's essential and infinite goodness that He should boundlessly create good and joyfully will that His creatures attain the ultimate good, *devekut*.

Of the non-fundamental obligatory beliefs, Crescas distinguishes those independent of specific commandments, which include creation, survival of the soul, reward and punishment, resurrection, immutability of the Torah, the distinction between Moses and the other prophets, the efficacy of the Urim and the Thummim,[71] and the Messiah, from those dependent on specific commandments, which include the efficacy of prayer and of the priestly benediction, God's readiness to accept the penitent, and the spiritual value of the High Holidays and the festivals. These beliefs differ only epistemologically from the fundaments: they are *a posteriori,* while the fundaments are *a priori*. One could logically conceive of the Torah without the non-fundamental beliefs but not without the fundamental ones. Yet, since the non-fundamental beliefs are affirmed by the Torah, their denial makes one a heretic. Crescas rejects Maimonides' contraposition of eternity and creation. For Crescas, whether or not the world is eternal is inconsequential; what is crucial is that the world is created *ex nihilo* by the absolute will of God, and that only the existence of God is necessary. Creation need not be in time: God is "creating each day, continuously, the work of the beginning" (liturgy). In his discussion of eternity, as in that of determinism, Crescas accepted a theory considered fatal to religion, and, instead of arguing against it, opted to establish its dogmatic inconsequence, and to show how it could be incorporated into an orthodox theology. In his discussion of the soul, Crescas rejects the Aristotelian theory that only the acquired intellect survives death. He argues that the soul is a simple and incorruptible substance, whose essence is not the intellect but something sublime and inscrutable. Crescas' teaching concerning the Messiah states that he will be greater than Moses and even the angels. Crescas recognizes only the Diaspora of 586 B.C.E.; the period of the Second Temple, being under foreign hegemony, he did not regard as a redemption.

"The Place" *(ha-Makom),* a talmudic appellation for God, strikes Crescas as a remarkable metaphor; as the dimensions of space permeate the entire universe, so does the glory of God. Crescas, differing from Maimonides, speaks of positive attributes of God (e.g., eternity, knowledge, and power), maintaining that terms predicated of God are not employed absolutely equivocally, but amphibolously. Their generic meaning is the same when they are applied to God as when they are applied to created beings; yet, the attributes of created beings are finite, and thus incomparable with the infinite attributes of God. Attributes are infinite also in number; yet all are mental modifications of the attribute of goodness. Crescas considers both the Averroistic and the Avicennian identifications of God's existence with His essence as tautological. For Crescas existence, whether that of God or created beings, is simply extramental non-absence; it is essential to (i.e., a necessary condition of) essence, which, by definition, has extramental reality. Similarly, the attribute of unity, which is simply nonplurality, is essential not only to God, but to every existent substance. All divine attributes are essential in the way that existence, unity, animality, and rationality are essential to man. For Crescas, God is not the *intellectus-intelligens-intelligibile,* and, as is suggested in the astounding conclusion of *Or Adonai,* He even might not be unconditionally inscrutable. He is Goodness, and His happiness is in His infinite creation of good and in His infinite love for His creatures.

Or Adonai was written within the tradition of the Jewish Aristotelianism it sought to refute; it is a continuation of the discussions in Maimonides' *Guide* and Levi b. Gershom's *Milḥamot Adonai*. Crescas' arguments show affinity to the revolutionary physics then being developed at Paris by students of Jean Buridan, especially Nicole Oresme.[72] At times he seems influenced by Thomism, Scotism, and Ockhamist nominalism. However, since he did not write *Or Adonai* for a Latin audience and did not cite Latin schoolmen, the nature of his relationships to these movements is speculative. Aspects of Crescas' discussion of the will seem based on the work of Abner of Burgos, a Jewish convert to Christianity.[73]

Although *Or Adonai* was written for philosophers, not mystics, it is clear that Crescas was influenced by the Kabbalah, especially by the 13th-century Aragonese masters. He cites *Sefer Yeẓirah* and *Sefer ha-Bahir* and often interprets Scripture and Midrash kabbalistically. He emphasizes infinity (although he avoids the kabbalistic term *Ein Sof*), love, and *devekut;* and he dismisses as preposterous the Maimonidean notion that the esoteric studies of *ma'aseh bereshit* and *ma'aseh merkavah* are physics and metaphysics. Aristotelians, such as Shem Tov ben Jospeh ibn Shem Tov, who rejected Crescas' arguments as "figments of the imagination" of a "perverse fool," were convinced that he could not understand Aristotle. Even Isaac Abrabanel, who respected Crescas for his piety, considered his philosophic views often unintelligible or simpleminded. On the other hand, Joseph Jabez praised "Rabbi Ḥasdai, who surpassed in intellect all the philosophers of his time, even the philosophers of Christendom and Islam, and how much more so the philosophers of Israel." Gianfrancesco Pico della Mirandola, quoting Crescas extensively, injected his critique of Aristotelian physics into the Latin literature, which later nurtured Galileo. The *Dialogues of Love* of Leone Ebreo (Judah Abrabanel) might be seen as a poetic adaption of Crescas' metaphysics. Giordano Bruno (1548–1600), the Christian Italian philosopher, seems to have borrowed arguments from him. Spinoza's[74] theories of extension, freedom and necessity, and love are marked by his close study of *Or Adonai*.

JOSEPH ALBO

The dates of Albo's birth and death can only be conjectured. He took a prominent part in the Disputation at Tortosa and San Mateo (1413–14) as a representative of the Jewish community of Daroca (Province of Saragossa). He was still active in 1433, as is evident from Zacuto's report[75] that he delivered a sermon at the circumcision of Abraham Benveniste II at Soria in that year.

Albo's *Sefer ha-Ikkarim* (Book of Principles) is one of the representative Jewish books of his period. It reflects his troubled reaction to the wavering of faith among his fellow Jews which stemmed from the discussions of religious dogma. He keenly felt the need to restore the morale of his people by offering them a reasoned presentation of Judaism and by showing that the basic teachings of the Jewish religion bore the essential character of a "divine law." He brought to his task a wide knowledge of both rabbinic literature and Jewish philosophy. He was also at home in Islamic philosophy (probably through Hebrew versions) and in Latin Christian scholasticism, notably Thomas Aquinas' *Summa Theologica.* In addition, he was versed in mathematics and medicine. He was not, however, an original thinker but prone to eclecticism and homiletical prolixity. The charge of plagiarism which was leveled against him by Jacob b. Ḥabib[76] has been renewed in modern times. It has been suggested that Albo took his main ideas without acknowledgment from his teacher, Ḥasdai Crescas and from Simeon b. Ẓemaḥ Duran.[77] Crescas' *Or Adonai,* which was completed in 1410, was known to Albo when he wrote the first part of his work which contains his fundamental outline of Jewish dogmatics; and it is probable that he knew Simeon b. Ẓemaḥ Duran's formulation of the principles of the Jewish faith in the latter's commentary on Job[78] written in 1405.

The *Sefer ha-Ikkarim* is divided into four parts or *ma'amarim* ("treatises"), the first of which was originally projected as an independent work. The other three parts were added later at the request of friends, and they elaborate upon the three fundamental principles laid down in the first.

Part I of the work opens with a critique of earlier attempts, notably by Maimonides and Crescas, at formulating the *ikkarim* ("principles")

of the Jewish religion. Albo fails to detect any criterion used by
Maimonides in selecting his 13 principles, and questions whether
Crescas' list of six adequately meets the need he professes for laying
down general principles of divine law (pt. 1, introd. and ch. 3). He, in
turn, is eager "to explain those principles which pertain to a divine law
generally, principles without which a divine law cannot be conceived"
(1:3). In the light of this criterion Albo formulates three fundamental
principles of divine law, namely, the existence of God, divine revelation,
and reward and punishment. The same three *ikkarim* had been proposed
earlier by Simeon b. Ẓemaḥ Duran. As Guttmann's[79] detailed analysis
has shown, both Duran and Albo adopted these three principles from
Averroes' *Faṣl al-Maqāl* where they are singled out as examples
of *'uṣūl* ("principles") of revealed law, and where it is stated that
one who denies any of these principles must be considered an un-
believer.

Albo further reflects Averroes' influence in distinguishing between
one who denies these principles of faith and one who, as a result of
erroneous opinions based on false interpretations of Scripture, denies
certain other articles of faith. Thus, in his view, Rabbi Hillel who stated
that the Jews can expect no Messiah in the future (Sanh. 99a), was
guilty of sin for not believing in the coming of the Messiah, but was
not thereby a *kofer be-ikkar* ("heretic"). Albo makes it clear that in
the opinion of the more recent authorities, Crescas in particular, the
belief in the Messiah is not in itself an *ikkar* ("principle") but one of six
emunot ("dogmas") described as *anafim* ("branches") issuing from the
ikkarim (I: 1:23). It is obvious that the relegation of messianic belief to
a rank below that of a "principle" was designed to refute Christian
teaching which made this belief a central one. Albo had already hinted
at this view at the Tortosa Disputation, while other Jewish spokesmen
had adhered to Maimonides' evaluation of the messianic hope as a
cardinal principle of Judaism. Albo, in fact, went so far as to exclaim
that "even if it should be proved that the Messiah had already come, I
would not consider myself less faithful a Jew."

The six "dogmas" which, according to Albo, are obligatory, though
without the status of "principles," are (1) the creation of the world in
time and out of nothing; (2) the superiority of Moses' prophecy to that
of all other prophets, past and future; (3) the validity of the Law of
Moses for all times; (4) the possibility of attaining human perfection by
fulfilling even a single one of the Divine Commandments[80]; (5) the

resurrection of the dead; (6) the coming of the Messiah (*Ikkarim*, I:23).

Of higher rank than these six beliefs "branching" out of the three principles are eight *shorashim* ("derivative principles") which follow necessarily from those same three principles and the denial of which makes one an infidel. Together with the first principles these *shorashim* form the indispensable elements of the Divine Law, all of which makes Judaism identical with the Divine Law *par excellence*. Four of the eight *shorashim* pertain to the existence of God, namely, His unity, incorporeality, independence of time, and His perfection; three pertain to revelation, namely, God's knowledge as embracing the lower (terrestrial) world, prophecy, and the authenticity of the "messengers" or lawgivers proclaiming the Divine Law (Adam, Noah, Moses); and one pertains to the notion of reward and punishment, namely, individual (in addition to universal) providence (1:13–15).

The concept of "Divine Law," which is crucial for Albo, is introduced by him in the context of the discussion of the three kinds of law, namely, *dat tivit* ("natural law"), *dat nimusit* ("conventional law"), and *dat elohit* ("Divine Law"). This scheme was definitely taken over from Thomas Aquinas.[81] Jewish and Muslim philosophy had before then known only the distinction between conventional and Divine Law (cf. Maimonides, *Guide* 2:40). The superiority of the Divine Law over the other two derives, according to Albo, from its purpose "to guide men to the attainment of true felicity, namely, the felicity of the soul and immortality" (1:7). While natural law aims at ordering human society, and while conventional law seeks to improve the social order, the Divine law embraces both *middot* ("conduct") and *de'ot* ("beliefs"). It is, therefore, "perfect, restoring the soul" (Ps. 19:8). Albo expands his exegesis of Psalm 19 to demonstrate the superiority of the Divine Law over the conventional and natural laws. He does so in a manner closely related to Thomas Aquinas' exegesis of the same Psalm. Aquinas' (and Maimonides') influence is also apparent in his treatment of the Divine Attributes.

Albo's work achieved great popularity in Jewish circles. Christian theologians, including Hugo Grotius and Richard Simon, held a high opinion of the work. Some regarded it as a potent apologia for Judaism and rather dangerous to Christianity.[82] Two chapters of the work, containing Albo's critique of Christian teachings (3:25–26), were published in Paris (1566) in a Latin translation by G. Genebrard, together with this translator's attempted refutation of Albo's views.[83]

SHEM TOV FAMILY

The tension of the age is well illustrated by the Shem Tov family. Shem Tov b. Joseph ibn Shem Tov (c. 1380–1441), a kabbalist and opponent of Greek philosophy, attacked in his *Sefer ha-Emunot,* not only such extreme rationalists as Albalag and Levi ben Gershom, but even more fiercely Maimonides himself. His son Joseph b. Shem Tov ibn Shem Tov (d. c. 1480), who greatly admired Aristotle and Maimonides, tried to rehabilitate philosophy by improving its rapport with religious Orthodoxy. He attempted to show that Aristotle really believed in individual providence, and that when Aristotle stated that man's happiness comes through contemplation, he had in mind only happiness in this world, leaving room for happiness in the next dependent on the observance of the Torah. Shem Tov b. Joseph ibn Shem Tov, who bore the same name as his grandfather, continued his father's philosophical interest in a commentary on Maimonides' *Guide* (composed 1488), in which he defends Maimonides against the attacks of Crescas.

ISAAC ABRABANEL

The last Jewish philosopher in Spain was the statesman Isaac Abrabanel (1437–1508), who went into exile with his fellow Jews in 1492. He admired Maimonides greatly (he wrote a commentary on the *Guide*), but, nevertheless he opposed the rationalistic interpretation of Judaism. Thus he held, for example, that prophecy was caused by God Himself, not by the active intellect. His attitude also emerges in his work *Rosh Amanah,* in which he defends Maimonides' 13 principles with great subtlety against all those who had taken issue with them; but in the end he states that only the commandments of the Torah count. Abrabanel's account of history and political life was novel. In his commentary on the beginning of Genesis he held that God willed that man be satisfied with what nature provides and concentrate on cultivation of his spirit. However, men were dissatisfied and produced civilizations to gain further possessions. These civilizations distracted them from their true goal. Abrabanel had a similar attitude toward the state. Man's condition, as ordained by God, was to live in loose associations, but as man's desires increased he organized states. States are evil in themselves, since they detract man from his true goal.

After the expulsion of the Jews from Spain, Jewish philosophy continued in Italy, where it had begun in the 13th century. Abrabanel, in fact, wrote his most important works in Italy. His son Judah Abrabanel, known as Leone Ebreo (c. 1460–after 1523), wrote a general philosophic work entitled *Dialoghi di Amore*.

ELIJAH DELMEDIGO

Elijah Delmedigo (c. 1460–1497), born in Crete, lived for a time in Italy, where he exchanged views with Christian Platonists. He had lectured at the University of Padua, and at the request of the humanist Pico della Mirandola he translated works by Averroes from Hebrew into Latin. He also wrote independent works on philosophic topics, including *Beḥinat ha-Dat* ("The Examination of Religion"), a work based on a treatise by Averroes, in which he investigated the relation of philosophy and religion. Like Averroes, he held that the masses must accept Scripture literally, while philosophers may interpret it. However, he denied philosophers the right to interpret the basic principles of Judaism. Like the Latin Averroists, he envisaged religion and philosophy as independent disciplines that may be mutually contradictory. If this should happen, the philosopher must accept the teachings of religion. He modified this position by maintaining that it is permissible to interpret philosophically doctrines which do not affect a basic principle and by affirming that, in fact, basic principles do not conflict with reason.

Two Jewish philosophers, Gabirol and Maimonides, influenced Christian thought extensively through Latin translations of their major works. Gabirol's *Mekor Ḥayyim* was translated into Latin as *Fons Vitae* in the middle of the 12th century; Maimonides' *Guide* was translated as *Dux (Director) Neutrorum (Dubitantium, Perplexorum)* about a century later. Gabirol's *Fons Vitae*, together with the writings of Augustine and of Islamic philosophers, molded the Neoplatonic component of Christian scholastic thought. William of Auvergne, while disagreeing with some of his views, described Gabirol as "one of the noblest of all philosophers," and he identified Gabirol's (divine) will with the Christian logos. Gabirol is also considered a proponent of the doctrines of the multiplicity of forms, according to which several substantial forms exist within a given substance. However, by far the best known of Gabirol's teachings was his notion that spiritual substances (the angels and the human soul), no less than corporeal substances, are composed of matter and form. This doctrine became the subject of a lively debate among scholastics. Among those who accepted Gabirol's view were Alexander of Hales, Bonaventure, and Duns Scotus; among those who rejected it were Albertus Magnus and Thomas Aquinas. In general the Franciscans accepted this doctrine, the Dominicans rejected it. Among Christian scholastics who were influenced by Maimonides were Alexander of Hales, William of Auvergne, Albertus Magnus, Thomas Aquinas, Meister Eckhart, and Duns Scotus. Aquinas, for example, was influenced by Maimonides in his account of the relation of faith and reason, in his proofs for the existence of God, and in his opinion that the creation of the world in time cannot be demonstrated by philosophic arguments. However, he polemicized against Maimonides' opinion that all essential attributes applied to God must be understood as negations, against his description of the celestial movers, and against his identifying angels with the incorporeal intelligences.

Islamic philosophy and its Greek antecedents provided the foundations for medieval Jewish philosophy during its two phases. There were also Christian scholastic influences on Jewish philosophers who knew Latin: for example, Hillel ben Samuel was influenced by Aquinas and Albalag, by the Latin Averroists. But even those Jewish philosophers who did not know Latin had, in time, access to scholastic thought through Hebrew translations. As was to be expected, the works translated dealt with philosophical rather than theological topics. Among the scholastics from whose works translations were made were Albertus Magnus, Thomas Aquinas, Aegidius Romanus, Peter of Spain, and William of Ockham. S. Pines has advanced the view that while Jewish philosophers do not cite works by late medieval scholastics they were familiar with the problems they discussed.[84]

NOTES TO PART TWO

[1] For an account of these sources see R. Walzer, *Greek into Arabic* (1962). See also H.A. Armstrong, Ed. *The Cambridge History of Later Greek and Early Medieval Philosophy* (1967).

[2] The interpretation of Al-Ash'ari and his later disciple Al-Bāqillānī of Baghdad (d. 1013) became the dominant tradition within Islam.

[3] For full details of this squabble over the academy of Sura and Saadiah's work as the head of the academy see *Encyclopedia Judaica*, vol. 14, col. 545 ff. See also A. Neubauer, *Chronicles*, 2 (1895) p.80 ff; A. Harkavy, *Zikkaron le-Rishonim* vol. I pt. 5 (1832) p. 232 ff. Also, H. Malter, *Life and Works of Saadiah Gaon* (1921, 1970).

[4] *Kitāb al-Amānar wa-al-I'tiqādāt*, ed. by S. Landauer (1880). It was translated into English by S. Rosenblatt in the Yale Judaica Series as *The Book of Beliefs and Opinions* (1948). There is also an abridged English translation by A. Altmann in *Three Jewish Philosophers* (1960).

[5] There exist several manuscripts of an earlier anonymous Hebrew paraphrase of the work, *Pitron Sefer ha-Emunah*, which was probably written by a Palestinian *paytan* of the 11th century (Oxford, Ms. Opp. 1185; Munich, no. 42; Munich, no. 65; Paris, no 669; Parma, de Rossi, no. 769; Vat. no. 266, 269). Saadiah also wrote an Arabic commentary on the *Sefer Yeẓirah* ("The Book of Creation"), entitled *Tafsīr Kitāb al-Mabādi'* (ed. and tr. into French under the title *Commentaire sur le Sefer Yesira par le Gaon Saadya*, by M. Lambert, 1891), which was translated into Hebrew by Moses b. Joseph of Lucena, probably sometime during the 12th century (Ms. Munich, no. 92). References to other Hebrew translations of this work are found in the commentary on *Sefer Yeẓirah* by Judah ben Barzillai al-Bargeloni (ed. by S. J. Halberstam, 1885), and in Berechiah ha-Nakdan's *Meẓaref* (ed. by Gollancz, 1902). Saadiah's philosophical views are also contained in some of his introductions to the Pentateuch (see J. Kafaḥ, *Perushei Rabbenu Sa'adyah Ga'on al ha-Torah*, 1963).

[6] Hīwī al-Balkhī was a 9th century free-thinker and radical Bible critic. He was a main target of many of Saadiah's polemical comments.

[7] This, of course, is the famous tripartite Platonic account of man which Saadiah took over from Islamic Platonism. See Plato's dialogues, *The Republic, Phaedo,* and *Symposium* among others.

[8] *Galeni Compendium Timaei Platonis* ed. by P. Kraus and R. Walzer (1951), p. 101.

[9] See *Galeni Compendium Timaei Platonis* p. 100 and also Abraham Halkin's essay "Classical and Arabic material in Aknin's Hygiene of the Soul" in *PAAJR* 14 (1944) p. 135.

[10] For example, the influence of the Neoplatonic emphasis on 'Emanation' is clearly perceived in Maimonides' *Guide of the Perplexed* where the words for "emanation" occur approximately 90 times in the first two parts of the *Guide*. See D.H. Baneth's article in *Tarbiz* (Hebrew) 23 (1952) p. 178. See also Shlomo Pines' introduction to his translation of the *Guide*, pgs. civ-cv.

[11] See A. Altmann's *Studies in Religious Philosophy and Mysticism* (1969) pgs. 54–55 and A. Nygren's *Agape and Eros* (1953) pgs. 230–237 and 441.

[12] One such legend, found in the commentary to *Sefer Yeẓirah* published in Mantua in 1562, relates how Gabirol made a female *golem* out of wood; another, in *Shalshelet ha-Kabbalah* by Gedaliah ibn Yaḥya (published in Venice in 1587), tells of his death at the hand of an Arab.

[13] See J. Schlanger, *La Philosophie de Solomon Ibn Gabirol* (1968) pgs. 57–70.

[14] *Keter Malkhut*, translated as *The Kingly Crown* by B. Lewis (1961).

[15] *Kitab al-Hidāya ilā Farā'id al Qulub*, Ed. A.S. Yahuda (1912).

[16] In more recent times the work has been translated into English (1962) by M. Hyamson, into German (1856) by M. Stern, and into French (1950) by A. Chouraqui, and again into English from the Arabic original in 1973 by M. Mansoor.

[17] The Neoplatonic and more mystical treatise known as *Kitāb Ma'ani al Nafs*, edited by I. Goldziher (1907) and translated into Hebrew by I. Broyde as *Sefer Torah ha-Nefesh* (1896) which was originally thought to be the work of Baḥya has now been proved to have been the work of another author known as Pseudo-Baḥya.

[18] See Shlomo Pines' articles in *Tarbiz* (Hebrew) 27 (1957–8) pgs. 218–235.

[19] First printed in Fano in 1506, it has been reissued many times. A critical edition of the Arabic and Hebrew text was published by H. Hirschfeld in 1887. An edition of the Hebrew text, prepared by A. Zifroni, appeared in 1960. The *Kuzari* was translated into English by H. Hirschfeld in 1905; reprinted with an introduction by H. Slonimsky (1964); an abridged version with introduction by I. Heinemann was published in 1947. Latin, Spanish, German, French and Italian translations have also appeared. An important Hebrew edition by Judah Even-Shemuel appeared in 1972.

[20] See S. Landauer in *ZDMG* 29 (1875) pgs. 335–418.

[21] Letter to Samuel Ibn Tibbon reproduced in *JQR* 25 (1934/35) p. 380; cf. Averroes' *Commentarium Magnum in Aristotelis de anima* (1953) 3:2, p. 433.

[22] For the history of these translations see R. Walzer, *Greek into Arabic* (1962).

[23] See the article by Shlomo Pines in *PAAJR* 24 (1955) pgs. 103–136.

[24] Most of these works exist only in manuscript form. For details see M. Steinschneider's *Catalogus librorum hebraeorum in Bibliotheca Bodleiana*

(1852–1860) and *Die hebraischen Ubersetzungen des Mittelalters und die Juden als Dolmetscher* (1893). See also the catalogues of Hebrew manuscripts held by the world's major libraries, e.g. the British Museum; the Bodleian (Oxford); the Cambridge University Library; the Hebrew University Library; the State Library in Leningrad; the Harvard University Library; The Catalogue of the Library of Congress (U.S.A.)

[25] The Hebrew version of this text with an English translation was published by Moses Gaster, *Studies and Texts in Folklore, Magic, Medieval Romance.* 3 vols, (1925–28)

[26] Aristotle, *Analytica Posteriora* 73A, 21 ff. and passim.

[27] Aristotle, *Physics* 8:1–3; *Metaphysics* 12:6, 1–2; *De Caelo* 1:10–12.

[28] See Shlomo Pines' introduction to the *Guide for the Perplexed* (963) pgs. cii–civ.

[29] *Josippon* is an anonymous 10th century Italian Hebrew work which claims to give a history of the period of the Second Temple.

[30] *Sefer Ha-Qabbalah* was first published in Mantua in 1514. The definitive critical edition of the text with ân English translation and commentary was published by Gershon Cohen, *Sefer Ha-Qabbalah* (1967).

[31] Ibn Daud's *AlʾAqīda al-Rafi-a* was translated into Hebrew twice in the late 14th century. The first translation was made in 1391 by Samuel ibn Motet at the suggestion of Isaac ben Sheshet and was entitled *Ha-Emunah ha-Nisa'ah* ("The Sublime Faith"). This translation (Mantua ms. 81) was never published. At about the same time another Hebrew version was prepared by Solomon ben Lavi entitled *Ha-Emunah ha-Ramah* ("The Exalted Faith"). This version was published with a German translation by Simon Weil in 1852. The original Arabic version known to have been in existence at the end of the 15th century is lost.

[32] For a discussion of the difficulties and issues relating to the logical and theological status of the term *God* in Jewish thought the reader is referred to the entry under "God, attributes of" in the *Encyclopaedia Judaica*. See also the discussion of this topic in the article on Maimonides in the present volume. For full historical and philosophical reviews of the issue see the works of Husik, Guttman and especially Wolfson given in the bibliography.

[33] One of his works was *Iggeret Neḥamah,* a work which offered comfort to forced converts.

[34] The Moroccan Almohad ruler 'Abd al-Mu'min seems to have become more liberal regarding non-Moslems about this time.

[35] See his *Sefer Ha-Kaẓẓeret* (Treatise on Asthma) published by S. Muntner (1963). This work was written originally in Arabic, *Maqala Fi-al Rabw,* in 1190.

[36] "Iggeret ha-Shemad" in *Ḥemdah Genuzah,* ed. Z. Edelmann, 11B–12A.

[37] See Azulai, letter M150.

[38] See Maimonides' commentary on *Avot* 5:4 and especially his letter to Joseph ibn Sham'un in 1191 in which he notes that: "it is better for you to earn a drachma as a weaver, or tailor, or carpenter than to be dependent on the licence of the exilarch (i.e., to accept a job as a rabbi)". This letter can be found in F. Kobler (ed.) *Letters of Jews through the Ages,* I (1952) p. 207.

[39] This is the view of Z. Diesendruck in *HUCA* 12–13 (1937–38) pgs. 461–497.

[40] *Iggeret Teiman* (Epistle to Yemen), ed. by A. Halkin and an English translation by B. Cohen (1952).

[41] See the "Letter of Naḥmanides to the rabbis of France" in *Kitvei Ramban* edited by C.B. Chavel (1963) p. 341.

[42] *Ma'amar Teḥiyyat ha-Metim* (Treatise on Resurrection), Arabic and Hebrew texts edited by I. Finkel (1938).

[43] Responsa are the answers to questions on points of Jewish law which have been addressed to leading Rabbinic authorities. During the Geonic period (7th to 11th centuries C.E.) this literature became a separate and major source of Jewish law due to the prestige and authority of the Geonim. This process and its legal function continued throughout the medieval and early modern period up to today.

[44] Ed. by A. Freimann, (1934); and again by J. Blau, (1957–61).

[45] Ed. Blau, number 308–9.

[46] Ed. Freimann number 369 = Blau number 448. On this see also Salo Baron in *PAAJR* 6 (1935), p. 83f.

[47] Ed. Freimann number 373 = Blau number 117. On this work see also G. Scholem, *Major Trends in Jewish Mysticism.* (1941) p. 63ff. See also his work on *Jewish Gnosticism, Merkabah Mysticism and Talmudic Tradition* (1960, 1965).

[48] Ed. Freimann number 42 = Blau number 293.

[49] Most of this responsum has been translated into English by F. Kobler, *Letters of Jews through the Ages* (1952); see also S.B. Freehof's *Treasury of Responsa* (1962) pgs. 28–34.

[50] The *Sefer Ha-Mitzvot,* originally written in Arabic, was translated into Hebrew several times. The version by Abraham ibn Ḥasdai is no longer extant and it is the translation by Moses ibn Tibbon, in its critical edition by H. Heller (1946), that is accepted as the standard text of this work.

[51] Responsa, ed. Freimann, number 369 = ed. Blau, number 447.

[52] See *Shemonah Perakim,* introduction.

[53] A. Marx in *JQR,* 25 (1934–35) pgs. 374–381.

[54] For a full discussion of sources see S. Pines, *Guide of the Perplexed* (1963), translator's introduction, lvii–cxxxiv.

55 For a detailed discussion of the problems relating to the attributes of God see the article on "God" in *Encyclopaedia Judaica*. See also the works listed in the bibliography of the present volume, especially those by H.A. Wolfson and also D. Kaufmann, *Geschichte der Attributenlehre* (1877).

56 For a detailed discussion of the proofs for the existence of God in Jewish thought see H.A. Wolfson's article "Proofs for the Existence of God in Jewish Philosophy" in *HUCA* 1 (1924) pgs. 575–596.

57 For a more popular discussion of Maimonides' conception of God and His attributes see *Yad*, Yesodei ha-Torah, 1–2. See also H.A. Wolfson, "Maimonides on Negative Attributes" in *Louis Ginzberg Jubilee Volume* (1945) pgs. 411–446.

58 On the nature of Moses' prophetic qualities see *Hakdamah le-Ferek Helek*, principle 7; *Yad*, Yesodei ha-Torah, 7:6; *Guide for the Perplexed* 2:35.

59 For another discussion of Maimonides' moral philosophy, see *Yad*, Deot.

60 For his opposition to messianic speculation see his *Hakdamah le-Ferek Helek*, principle 12; *Yad*, Melakhim 12:2—uncensored edition.

61 For his affirmation of this doctrine in reply to criticism that he had rejected it, see section in the text entitled: *"Iggeret Teiman* and *Ma'amar Tehiyyat ha-Metim."*

62 For passages which suggest the collective interpretation of immortality see: *Hakdamah le-Ferek Helek; Yad*, Teshuvah 8–10; *Guide* 1:41; *Treatise on Resurrection*.

63 See A. Hyman in A. Altmann (Ed.), *Jewish Medieval and Renaissance Studies* (1967) pgs. 119–144.

64 The reader can gain some idea of Levi's super-commentaries (i.e., commentaries on commentaries) on Averroes by seeing the passages from these commentaries which are cited by H.A. Wolfson in his *Crescas' Critique of Aristotle* (1929).

65 Numerous manuscripts of the *Milhamot* are extant, but the book was printed only twice, and then imperfectly (Riva di Trento, 1560 and Leipzig, 1863). The first four books of the *Milhamot* were translated into German with notes by B. Kellerman (*Die Kaempfe Gottes*, 2 vols., 1914–16), but this translation is unreliable. A French translation of books three and four, based on a critical edition together with an introduction and notes, was made by C. Taouti (1968).

66 For details see chapter on "Maimonides" in this volume and works already cited in the notes.

67 Crescas prepared a chronicle of the massacres in the form of a letter to the Avignon community, dated October 19, 1391. This was published as an appendix to Ibn Verga, *Shevet Yehuda*, ed. by M. Wiener (1855).

[68] *Bittul Ikkarei ha-Noẓerim* was written in 1451 in Spanish. We possess only the Hebrew translation which has been published twice, first in 1860 and again in 1904.

[69] First published in Ferrara in 1555, then in Vienna 1859–60, and Johannesburg in 1861.

[70] For more on the "proofs for the existence of God" see the articles by H.A. Wolfson, "Proofs for the Existence of God in Jewish Philosophy" in *HUCA* Vol I (1924) pgs. 575–596 and "Crescas on the Problem of Divine Attributes" in *JQR* n.s. 7 (1916) pgs. 1–44 and 175–221.

[71] The Urim and Thummim were the apparatus worn by the High Priest during the existence of the Temple and through them he divined the will of God in certain matters.

[72] Jean Buridan (c. 1295–c.1358) a French scholar, was one of the great logicians of the medieval period. For details about his work see *Truth and Consequence in Medieval Logic* by E.A. Moody (1953). His student, Nicole Oresme (d. 1382), was one of the most important medieval scientists and a forerunner, if only obscurely and hesitatingly, of modern scientific emphasis on observation and hypotheses and a rejection of dogmatism and *a priori* accounts which are deductive in character. For details of his work see A.C. Crombie, *Augustine to Galileo: The History of Science A.D. 400–1650* (1952) and P. Duhem's standard work *Le système du monde: histoire des doctrines cosmologiques de Platons à Copernic* (1913–59), 10 vols.

[73] Abner of Burgos, a Jewish convert to Christianity, in the first half of the 14th century argued for determinism in a fashion suggested by Al-Ghazālī's *Maqāsid al-Falasifa*. Abner's views are found in his work *Minḥat Kena'ot* written after his conversion (see above).

[74] For more on Spinoza's debt to Crescas see H.A. Wolfson's *Spinoza* (1934) and his *Crescas' Critique of Aristotle* (1929). See also D. Neumark, "Crescas and Spinoza" in *CCARY*, 18 (1908), pgs. 272–318.

[75] *Yuḥasin* ed. H. Filipowski (1857) p. 226.

[76] Jacob ibn Ḥabib, *Ein Ya'akov* on *Megillah* 2–3.

[77] See J. Guttmann's *Philosophies of Judaism*, Engl. transl. (1964), in which he suggests that Albo was not an original thinker but took his main ideas from Duran and Crescas.

[78] Simeon ben Ẓemaḥ Duran, *Ohev Mishpat* printed in the rabbinic Bible edition *Kehillat Moshe*, 4 (Amsterdam 1727).

[79] See Julius Guttmann's essay "Towards the Investigation of the Sources of the Book of Ikkarim" in *Memorial Volume in honor of Asher Gulak and Samuel Klein;* see also Guttmann's *Philosophie und Theologie von Averroes;* also Julius Guttmann's *Die Stellung des Simon ben Zemach Duran in der Geschichte der judischen Religionsphilosophie* where the relation of Albo

and Duran is discussed in some detail. See also Guttmann *Philosophies of Judaism,* chapter 5.

[80] cf. Maimonides, *Commentary on the Mishnah,* Mak. 3:16.

[81] Aquinas discusses 'natural law' in his *Summa Theologica,* Pt. I of Pt. II (1a IIa e), Qu. 91 Art. 2 and subsequently.

[82] See de Rossi, *Dizionario Storico* (1802) 43–44; also *Bibliotheca Judaica Antichristiana* (1800), 14.

[83] In addition to *Sefer ha-Ikkarim,* Abraham Zaquto records that Albo also wrote a polemical work in Spanish against Christianity but this work has been lost.

[84] See Shlomo Pines, *Scholasticism after Thomas Aquinas and the Teachings of Hasdai Crescas and his Predecessors* (1967). Pines argues that physical and metaphysical notions of Duns Scotus, Buridan, Oresme, Albert of Saxony, and William of Ockham influenced Jedaiah ha-Penini Bedersi, Levi b. Gershom, Joseph ibn Caspi and Ḥasdai Crescas.

Part Three

MODERN PERIOD

THE BRIDGE TO MODERNISM

Modern Jewish philosophy shared with Hellenistic and medieval Jewish philosophy a concern for relating general philosophy to Judaism and it discussed some of the same problems that had been discussed in earlier Jewish philosophy; but, at the same time, it differed from Hellenistic and medieval Jewish philosophy in several respects. For one thing it differed in its conception of Jewish tradition. For Hellenistic and medieval Jewish philosophers, Judaism, with its Oral and Written Law, was the revealed word of God which was binding in its totality for all times. While there were modern Jewish thinkers who accepted the traditional position, most of them considered Judaism a creation of human thought, intention, or feeling, which had developed in history and, which, while containing a perennial core, also contained parts which could be discarded in modern times. Then again, it differed in its conception of science and philosophy. Hellenistic and medieval Jewish philosophers accepted the notion of a geocentric universe with a sharp distinction between its terrestrial and celestial parts—a universe that manifests design and purpose. Modern Jewish philosophers accepted the notion of a heliocentric universe with no distinction between its terrestrial and celestial parts, a universe governed by the necessary laws of nature. Moreover, pre-modern Jewish thinkers saw no sharp distinction between science and philosophy, had strong metaphysical interests, and emphasized that the development of the human mind was the purpose of human life and morality was only a prerequisite for the fulfillment of this goal. Modern Jewish philosophers saw science as distinct from philosophy, and while those following the idealist tradition retained metaphysical interests and emphasized the primacy of intellectual cognition, there were many who denied the possibility

135

(or at least the importance) of metaphysics, emphasizing instead the study of ethics and the centrality of proper conduct for attaining the goal of human life. It can readily be seen that it was easier to reconcile pre-modern philosophy with Jewish teachings than modern philosophy.

The Enlightenment and the Emancipation also had a significant impact on modern Jewish thought. For example, the Enlightenment notion of a religion of reason which, consisting of rational beliefs and practices, was addressed to all men, was adopted by a number of Jewish philosophers of the modern period. Some, Mendelssohn for example, accepted this notion and investigated to what extent historical Judaism was identical with the religion of reason and to what extent different. Others, such as Hermann Cohen, went so far as to maintain that Judaism was the ideal embodiment of the religion of reason. The process of secularization initiated by the Enlightenment also had its impact on Jewish thought. While modern Jewish philosophy was still largely a religious philosophy, there arose Jewish thinkers who attempted to formulate secular philosophies of Judaism and for whom Judaism was a culture or a social philosophy rather than a religious tradition.

The impact of the Emancipation was felt in Western rather than in Eastern Europe, for in the East the Jewish community retained its social (even its political) identity into the 20th century. The progressive political and social emancipation of the Jews posed special problems for Jewish thinkers, one of these being the nature of the Jewish group. While pre-modern Jewish thinkers had no difficulty in accepting the notion that the Jews were a people, many modern Jewish thinkers considered Judaism a religion and the Jews a religious society (*Religionsgemeinschaft*), thereby emphasizing that only their religion distinguished Jews from other citizens. The Emancipation also influenced the concept of the Messiah. Whereas in classical Jewish thought the Messiah was a king from the House of David who would bring the Jews back to their own land, most modern Jewish thinkers gave up the belief in a personal Messiah, speaking instead of messianic times when all mankind would be united in justice and righteousness.

Another factor that influenced modern Jewish philosophy was the emergence of distinct religious groups within Judaism. While in former times, too, there were different groups within Judaism, e.g., Sadducees and Pharisees and Rabbanites and Karaites, Jewish philosophy for the most part moved within the mainstream of classical rabbinic tradition.

However, in the 19th century there developed three distinct groups within Judaism, each of which had its philosophers. Neo-Orthodoxy upheld the classical formulation of Judaism but attempted to make modern culture relevant to Jewish concerns. The positive-historical school (which was to become in the United States in the 20th century the Conservative movement) was committed to classical Jewish tradition but at the same time studied Judaism from a historical-critical perspective, maintaining that Judaism was subject to evolutionary development. Liberal (Reform) Judaism was committed to a program of change, holding that the core of Judaism was ethics (ethical monotheism) and that ritual was subject to abrogation and change.

One further factor was the rise of modern anti-Semitism. In the case of some Jewish thinkers (Hermann Cohen is a notable example) it was anti-Semitism that aroused their interest in Jewish thought. Anti-Semitism also produced in certain thinkers a despair of the promise of emancipation, which, together with the emergence of modern nationalism and classical Jewish messianic expectations, produced Zionism which advocated the reestablishment of a Jewish state, preferably in Erez Israel. In its philosophic component modern Jewish thought followed the main currents of modern and contemporary Western philosophy, rationalism, Kantianism, idealism, existentialism, and pragmatism. There were also influences derived from British empiricism and positivism. Whereas medieval Jewish philosophy consisted of movements which had a certain continuity and structure, modern Jewish thought represents mainly the efforts of individual thinkers. In Western Europe the language of Jewish philosophy was the language of the country in which the philosopher lived, while in Eastern Europe its language was largely Hebrew.

SPINOZA

Baruch (Benedict) de Spinoza became one of the greatest philosophers in the whole of the western philosophic tradition. Spinoza's father fled from Portugal to the Dutch Sephardi community of Amsterdam where he was a successful merchant until his death in 1654. Spinoza became an outstanding student in the school of the Spanish-Portuguese community, probably studying with Saul Levi Morteira and Manasseh

Ben Israel. It has been traditionally claimed that he was led to his irreligious views by studying Latin with a freethinking ex-Jesuit, Van den Enden. Recent studies indicate it is more likely that his heretical views developed out of heterodox controversies within the Amsterdam Jewish community. A generation earlier, Uriel da Costa had twice been expelled from the community for denying the immortality of the soul, and for contending that all extant religions were manmade. In early 1656 Spinoza, a Spanish doctor, Juan de Prado, and a schoolteacher, Daniel de Ribera began to attract attention for their heretical opinions, questioning, among other matters, whether Moses wrote the Pentateuch, whether Adam was the first man, and whether the Mosaic law took precedence over natural law. They may have been influenced by Isaac La Peyrère's *Praeadamitae* which had just been published in Amsterdam. Prado was forced to apologize for his views, and a few days later, on July 27, 1656, Spinoza was excommunicated from the Jewish community.

Spinoza was anathematized and cursed, and all in the Jewish community were forbidden to be in contact with him. He apparently studied at the University of Leiden after his excommunication, and was in Amsterdam with Prado in 1658–59, where a report to the Spanish Inquisition describes them as denying the Mosaic law and the immortality of the soul, and holding that God only exists philosophically. The hostility of the Jewish community, extending, according to 17th-century reports, to an attempt to kill him, led Spinoza to write an apology for his views in Spanish. The work, now lost, was apparently the basis for his later *Tractatus Theologico-Politicus,* his work on Bible criticism. Around 1660 Spinoza left Amsterdam, changed his name to Benedictus (the Latin equivalent of Baruch), became involved with some liberal Protestants, and settled in Rijnsburg where he earned his living grinding lenses. He moved to Voorburg, a suburb of The Hague in 1664, and to The Hague itself in 1670, where he stayed until his death. His correspondence indicates that he was developing his metaphysical system for discussion by a philosophical club in 1663. In the same year he wrote in Latin, *Principles of the Philosophy of René Descartes,* the only work he signed. The work presents Descartes' philosophy in geometrical form, and indicates Spinoza's basic points of disagreement with Cartesianism.

Because of his fame, Spinoza was offered, in 1673, the chair of philosophy at Heidelberg by the Elector Palatine and was promised freedom to philosophize provided that he would not disturb the established religion.

Spinoza declined the post, saying that he preferred his quiet life of philosophical research to teaching, and that he could not control the occurrence of religious dissension. He continued his simple quiet life, writing
and discussing philosophy with Leibniz, among others, but making no
efforts to convert people to his radical views. He managed to live out
his life without belonging to any sect or church. He died of consumption
which may have been aggravated by his lens grinding activity.

In 1670 Spinoza's *Tractatus Theologico-Politicus* appeared unsigned,
presenting his critique of revealed religion, his justification for intellectual and religious freedom, and his political theories. This rationalistic
attack on religion caused a sensation, and was banned everywhere, and
sold with false title pages. Spinoza became notorious, and was constantly accused of being an atheist. To prevent attacks, Spinoza stopped the
publication of a Dutch edition of the *Tractatus*. In 1671 he sent a lengthy
letter to the Jewish leader, Orobio de Castro, defending himself against
the charges of atheism and irreligion.

By 1674 Spinoza had completed his major work, the *Ethics*, and
showed manuscript copies to his friends. He tried in 1675 to have the
work published only to find that theologians blocked this effort on the
grounds that Spinoza was denying the existence of God. Spinoza abandoned plans to have his book printed.

After his death his *Opera Posthuma* appeared, containing his *Ethics*,
the unfinished *On the Improvement of the Understanding*, and the
Political Treatise (completed shortly before his death), a Hebrew grammar,
and a selection of his letters. His Hebrew grammar, *Compendium Gram-
maticae Linguae Hebraeae*, was undertaken at the request of Spinoza's
friends some years before his death but remained unfinished. It pur-
ported to be a self-tutor to Hebrew but in it Spinoza discussed many of
the more complex philological problems of Hebrew grammar. Ten
years later, in 1687, his one scientific work, the *Treatise on the Rainbow*,
appeared.

Spinoza's biblical criticism follows older starts, assembles them for
the first time into a rationalized system, and prepares the way for all later
critical works on the Bible up to the present. His biblical criticism is
closely connected with his philosophical system and political position.
Based on the knowledge of the Bible that he acquired in his childhood,
and developing during long years of reflection, his critical views of the
Bible were expressed in the *Tractatus Theologico-Politicus*, and also in

a few letters and conversations. In opposition to what he considered the misuses of the Bible that he observed in Judaism and Christianity, Spinoza developed what he believed to be the true method of biblical interpretation. Every person has the right to engage in biblical interpretation; it does not require supernatural illumination or special authority. Spinoza's supreme principle, indefatigably repeated by him, is that the Bible must be interpreted on its own terms. The method of the interpretation of the Bible is the same as the method of the interpretation of nature. "For, as the method of interpreting nature consists essentially in putting together a history [i.e., a methodical account] of nature, from which, as from sure data, we deduce the definitions of natural phenomena, so it is necessary for the interpretation of Scripture to work out a true history of Scripture, and from it, as from sure data and principles, to deduce through legitimate inference, the intention of the authors of Scripture." The history of Scripture should consist of three aspects: (1) an analysis of the Hebrew language; (2) the compilation and classification of the expressions (sententiae) of each of the books of the Bible; (3) research as to the origins of the biblical writings, as far as they still can be ascertained, i.e., concerning "the life, the conduct, and the pursuits of the author of each book, who he was, what was the occasion and the epoch of his writing, whom did he write for, and in what language. Further it should inquire into the fate of each book: how it was first received, into whose hands it fell, how many different versions there were of it, by whose advice was it received into the Canon, and lastly, how all the books now universally accepted as sacred, were united into a single whole" (ibid.).

In accordance with this program, Spinoza analyzed the biblical writings in an attempt to determine their authors (ibid., ch. 8–10). He repeated the arguments on the strength of which Ibn Ezra had supposed that the Pentateuch did not derive in its entirety from Moses, and complemented them. Although some of the Pentateuch did originate with Moses (The Book of the Wars of God, the Book of the Covenant, the Book of the Law of God), it was only many centuries after Moses that the Pentateuch as a whole appeared. The Pentateuch, together with the books of Joshua, Judges, Samuel, and Kings, form a single larger historical work, whose author, he conjectures, was Ezra.

Furthermore Spinoza discovers in the Prophets numerous contradictions in their conceptions of natural and spiritual phenomena. He therefore concludes that God adapted his revelation in these matters to the individual prophet, and that philosophical knowledge is not to be found in these works. The content of the revelation to the prophets is rather the right way of life (*ibid.*, ch. 1, 2). The example of Balaam indicates that there were prophets not only among the Hebrews. The election of the Hebrews should not be understood as an indication that they were different from other people in intellect and virtue; their election refers only to their kingdom and it ended with the latter's collapse (*ibid.*, ch. 3). The ceremonies prescribed in the Bible, like the entire Mosaic law, were applicable only during this period and with the termination of the period no longer contributed to ultimate happiness and blessedness (*ibid.*, ch. 4, 5). According to Spinoza, stories in the Bible are not to be believed literally; they are intended to instruct the people, who could not comprehend abstract concepts, definitions, and deductions (*ibid.*, ch. 5). Since nothing can happen that contradicts natural law, the biblical stories of miracles must be explained in a natural way. Spinoza admits that this one question is a conclusion drawn from his own philosophy and not from the Bible (*ibid.*, ch. 6). Spinoza knows that precisely in the application of his method difficulties are encountered in the interpretation of the Bible, many parts of which cannot be solved since we have only an incomplete knowledge of Old Hebrew and of the circumstances of the composition of the biblical books, some of which (namely in the New Testament) do not exist in the language in which they were written (*ibid.*, ch. 7). However, as Spinoza states emphatically, these difficulties do not touch the central content of faith: that there is one God, who demands justice and neighborly love and forgives those who repent. This faith is independent of philosophical thought and leaves complete freedom for it (*ibid.*, ch. 14). In the *Tractatus Theologico-Politicus* Spinoza also presents a political program along with a description of the Hebrew theocracy, which he applies to the contemporary situation in Holland, hinting between the lines at other applications (*ibid.*, ch. 17–19).

His Philosophy. Spinoza has usually been regarded as the modern philosopher whose life is most consonant with his theory. His simple, eminently moral life, devoted to rational enquiry, seems to have developed out of his rejection of ceremonial Judaism and his efforts to find a basis for rejecting scriptural authority. Starting from the heterodox

currents within the Amsterdam Jewish community, Spinoza developed a
critique of Judaism and supernatural religion in the *Tractatus Theologico-Politicus*. Insisting that religious tenets should be judged only on
the basis of reason, Spinoza, using some of the ideas of Abraham ibn
Ezra and La Peyrère, rejected the Mosaic authorship of the Pentateuch,
and the possibility of genuine prophecy. Spinoza then offered a rationalistic metaphysics within which supernatural events could not occur,
and within which the Bible was to be examined as a human document
expressing certain human developments of the past. Insisting that
miracles were impossible, Spinoza argued that nature is governed by
eternal and necessary decrees of God. Nothing can be contrary to natural
laws. If one examined rationally what was meant by "God" and "nature"
it would be clear that nothing supernatural was possible, since God
determined nature lawfully; and if one applied the same methods to
studying Scripture as are employed in studying nature—"the examination of the history of nature, and therefrom deducing definitions of
natural phenomena on certain fixed axioms,"—one would find nothing
mysterious or divine in Scripture. Its moral teachings are compatible
with those of reason (see below).

In *On the Improvement of the Understanding,* Spinoza developed his
rationalistic method. Setting out to search for a good which would
enable him to enjoy continuous, supreme, and unending happiness, he
rejected fame, riches, and ordinary pleasures. As a way to finding this
good, he rejected hearsay or information gained by authority, sense
information, and deductive conclusions based on incomplete or inadequate understanding. True knowledge by which one could achieve
genuine happiness is reached through perceiving things solely through
their essences or proximate causes. In this way one knows why something is what it is, why it has the nature it does, or what made it what
it is. When one possesses this kind of knowledge, scepticism or doubt is
no longer possible. Skepticism is only the result of lack of understanding.
The Cartesian doubt based on the possibility that God may be a deceiver
is dissipated as soon as one has a clear and distinct or adequate idea of
God. When we arrive at definitions of things that really explain their
natures, and which have complete certainty (which Spinoza found in
mathematical knowledge), we can no longer express any doubts or
questions. Such a definition, when of a created thing, explains what
causes it and allows for the deduction of all of its properties. For an

uncreated thing, the definition explains the thing, since it has no causes other than itself (otherwise it would be created) and leaves no room for doubting whether the thing exists or not.

Using this method, Spinoza presented his philosophy in geometrical form in the *Ethics*. Starting with definitions of terms like "God," "substance," "attribute," and "mode," which presumably meet his standards, and with a series of axioms spelling out the nature of causality and existence and including one that states "A true idea must correspond with its ideate or object," Spinoza unfolded his picture of the world in the form of demonstrations of propositions. When challenged as to how he knew this philosophy was the best, he replied, "I do not presume that I have found the best philosophy, I know that I understand the true philosophy. If you ask in what way I know it, I answer: In the same way as you know that the three angles of a triangle are equal to two right angles."[1]

The first book of the *Ethics* demonstratively develops his theory of substance "that which is in itself, and is conceived through itself," insisting first on its unity and simplicity. Then Spinoza established his startling conclusion that God or Nature is the only possible substance, and that everything in the world is an aspect of God, and can be conceived in terms of one of God's two knowable attributes, thought or extension. Wolfson has shown that Spinoza's pantheistic conclusion seems to be the result of pondering medieval discussions, especially Jewish, on whether there can be two Gods, and whether God is different from the world. Spinoza's argument is also like that offered by Orobio de Castro against the doctrine of the Trinity. Spinoza also followed the implications of Descartes' two kinds of substances, creative (God) and created (matter and mind), and found that only God can really be substantial and all else are just qualifications of Him.

If God or Nature is the only substance, everything else is understood in terms of Him, and is deducible from His essence. God acts solely by the laws of his own nature. In terms of this, the world is a logical order, following necessarily from God's nature, and nothing could be different than it is.

In the appendix to Book I, Spinoza spelled out what this meant. God is not a purposeful being. There are no goals being achieved. The teleological and evaluative interpretation of what is going on is just due to human fears and superstitions and leads to an unworthy conception of

God. He lacks nothing, needs nothing. He just is, and due to His being, everything happens, and happens of necessity.

Book II develops this view. Everything is in God. He is modified in terms of His two known attributes, thought and extension. The world of body and of mind are two aspects of God or Nature. "The order and connection of ideas is the same as the order and connection of things" (II prop. 8). The latter can be understood in terms of mathematical physics, the former in terms of logic and psychology, but both are ways of understanding the same substance, God. The mind and the body are essentially the same thing. The dualism of Descartes has been rejected, thereby supplying a new solution to the mind-body problem. The mind is the idea of the body. Roth[2] has suggested that Spinoza's monistic rejection of Cartesian dualism is similar to Maimonides' views, which influenced Spinoza.

For Spinoza the quest for knowledge starts with the confused experience, of which we have images through various physiological processes. The images are related mechanically rather than logically. Through the course of experience, we develop general ideas of what is going on, and through these a level of scientific understanding of the sequence of events taking place. From these we come to adequate ideas which give us a logical and causal understanding, and eliminate our previous confusion and lack of clarity. The highest form of knowledge would be to have complete understanding, to see everything as a logical system from the aspect of eternity. This intuitive knowledge is only completely and adequately possessed by God. Complete understanding would be to know the infinite idea of God, which we can only approach and thereby, to some extent, become God.

Spinoza's psychology then indicates the road toward achieving this goal. Starting from a Hobbesian view of man, we are driven toward self-preservation, constantly affected by the emotions in the form of pleasure and pain. On this level we are in human bondage, moved by causes which we do not understand, since we only have confused ideas of our experiences. As we reach understanding of what is going on in our lives, we achieve human freedom. We are no longer determined by external factors but by our own comprehension. Freedom for Spinoza consists not in being uncaused, but in being determined by oneself alone. The passions no longer control us because we are now guided by the laws of our own nature. When we understand why things are happening, and know they cannot be otherwise, we are liberated from bondage to emotion and ignorance, and are no longer driven aimlessly by feeling and events.

This understanding that gives us freedom is the highest good. We are no longer captives of external events and of the pain they cause. As our ideas become more adequate, and as we reach rational understanding, our ideas become part of the infinite idea of God. Our ultimate aim is the intellectual love of God which can give us the continuous supreme and unending happiness that was sought. Thus the philosophical goal of complete wisdom becomes man's salvation. The wise man rises above the ordinary experience and ordinary cares. In concentrating on God, the logical order of the universe, and in seeing everything as a necessary deducible aspect of God, the wise man achieves blessedness.

Spinoza's political theory, though deriving much from Hobbes, sees the aim of the good society as that of allowing rational men to think freely and achieve true knowledge. This requires civil peace which allows for free thought and discussion. A democracy ruled by men of property, like the Dutch Republic, is most likely to achieve this.

Traditional and popular religions, though not representing God adequately, can serve a useful purpose. For unenlightened, ignorant people, as Spinoza considered the ancient Hebrews to be, the conveying of moral teachings by stories, alleged prophecy, threats, and promises can have an important social effect of making people behave well and of making them obey the laws. The wise man needs only the religion of reason. When he sees the whole as a rational, necessary, scientific order he has arrived at the highest wisdom, morality, and insight.

Spinoza's totally rationalistic vision incorporates some basic Jewish themes: that of the existence and unity of God, of the dependence of everything on God, of the love of God being the highest good and the basis of morality. His view, however, is the first modern one to provide a metaphysical basis for rejecting any form of Judaism or Christianity portraying the human scene as a dramatic interplay of man and God. The denial of any distinction between God and the world, the denial of the possibility of any supernatural event or providential action, and the denial of the possibility of any revelatory knowledge, eliminated the basic ingredients of a Jewish or Christian cosmology, and reinterpreted the basic written and oral traditions so that they no longer provided any essential data about man's relationship to God. Wolfson has said that

Spinoza's uniqueness lies in being the first person in the Judeo-Christian world after Philo to construct a world view involving no axioms or principles based on revelation. Spinoza offered the basis for a thoroughly secular or naturalistic understanding of the universe. As Wolfson put it, "Benedictus is the first of the moderns; Baruch is the last of the medievals."

Though Spinoza has been described by Novalis as a "God-intoxicated man," he was also described by Bayle as a "systematic atheist." His theory provides the foundations for a kind of atheism in which the historical interrelationship of God and man is denied, and in which God has no personality whatsoever. Of all of the critics of Judaism and Christianity in the 16th and 17th centuries, Spinoza alone seems to have taken the radical and revolutionary steps of replacing religious tradition completely by rational, scientific reasoning, of making human religion a subject for scientific study, and of presenting a way of describing man and the universe totally apart from historical religious conceptions. Although Spinoza's views were immediately attacked, even by avant-garde thinkers like Bayle, he began to have an influence on biblical critics like Simon, on Deists, and on 18th-century French materialists and atheists. His more important modern influence began with the revival of his works in the German Enlightenment, first by Lessing, and then his adoption as a central thinker by the German Romantics. His ideas have since remained basic in naturalistic, atheistical thinking, and even been seen as precursors of Marxism. The image of Spinoza as one of the great heroes of free and modern thought, has become part of the hagiography of those who see a war between science and religion, in which the scientific side is the good one. Many modern Jewish thinkers have seen in him the basis for a more universalistic modern philosophical view. He has provided one of the fundamental ideologies for the secular world.

MOSES MENDELSSOHN

Mendelssohn was born in Dessau in 1729. As a child he suffered from a disease which left him with a curvature of the spine and permanently affected his nervous system. The son of a Torah scribe, Mendelssohn received a traditional Jewish education under the influence of David Fraenkel, who was then rabbi of Dessau. When the latter was appointed rabbi of Berlin in 1743, Mendelssohn followed him there in order to pursue his studies and to acquire a general education. He earned his livelihood with difficulty at the same time studying diligently and acquiring broad education. In addition to his fluent knowledge of German and Hebrew, he became familiar with Latin, Greek, English, French, and Italian. His teachers were young educated Jews. During this period he met the writer and dramatist G.E. Lessing and a deep and lifelong friendship developed between them. In 1750 he became a teacher in the house of the owner of a silk factory; in 1754, he was entrusted with the bookkeeping of the factory and eventually became a partner in the enterprise. During the whole of his lifetime he worked as a merchant, while carrying out his literary activities and widespread correspondence in his free time. Only in 1763 he was granted "right of residence" in Berlin by the king.

In 1754 Mendelssohn began to publish—at first with the assistance of Lessing—philosophical writings and later also literary reviews. In 1763, he was awarded the first prize of the Prussian Royal Academy of Sciences for his work *Abhandlung ueber die Evidenz in metaphysischen Wissenschaften* (On Evidence in the Metaphysical Sciences). However, when the academy elected him as member in 1771, his election was not ratified by King Frederick II. In 1769, he became embroiled in a dispute on the Jewish religion, and from then on, he confined most of his literary activity to the sphere of Judaism. He was also active on behalf of the Jews in practical affairs. He was as outstanding in his conversation as in his writing, and a circle of intellectuals gathered regularly at his home to discuss general and Jewish subjects. He was famous among both Jews and non-Jews for his wide knowledge, his sharp intellect and his moderate, patient, and modest character.

As a philosopher of religion Mendelssohn did not create an original system; he continued mainly in the tradition of classical rationalism current in the 17th and 18th centuries. His philosophy incorporates the dominant themes of Enlightenment philosophy; its emphasis on reason as the sole medium by which man acquires knowledge fulfillment; its notion that man is endowed with eternally valid innate ideas of absolute goodness and truth; its belief that all men are to be accounted by nature as equal; and its eudaemonistic orientation which sees the purpose of philosophy not in the discovery of truth but in the achievement of happiness by the individual and society through the perfection of man. The starting point of Mendelssohn's philosophy of religion is his theory of knowledge. With Locke, Shaftesbury, and, especially, Leibniz, he distinguishes between eternal truths *(vérités de raison)*, which are self-evident to reason, and historical or temporal truths *(vérités de fait)*, requiring the evidence of sense experience. Among the truths self-evident to reason are the belief in a wise and merciful God and the immortality of the human soul. These metaphysical truths, which are the essential elements of the religion of reason, are the themes of his two major religio-philosophical works, *Morgenstunden* (1785) and *Phaedon* (1767). In the former Mendelssohn seeks to demonstrate the rationality of the belief in the existence of God. In the latter he seeks to justify the doctrine of the immortality of the soul. He treats these subjects as principles of general metaphysics and man's universal religion of reason.

Mendelssohn's favorite proof for God's existence is a modification of the ontological[3] argument: Man finds the idea of a Supreme Being in his consciousness. Since this idea cannot have arisen out of man's limited and fragmented experiences—we have no direct knowledge of anything remotely resembling the idea of divine perfection—it is a priori and belongs to the category of concepts that precede all experience and enable us to comprehend the universe, including space, time, and causality. Although these concepts do not arise from experience, they are not subjective because they determine the character of universal experience. Further, there is a necessary connection between the concept of an absolutely perfect being and his existence, a being which is absolutely real, or perfect, must have existence among its attributes; otherwise, it would be lacking the full complement of its unconditioned possibility and hence less than perfect.

The question of the immortality of the soul is examined in Mendelssohn's chief philosophical work, *Phaedon* (1767)[4], modeled on Plato's dialogue of the same name. As early as 1760 Mendelssohn had expressed the wish to translate and rewrite Plato's text in the light of modern psychology. He was encouraged in this project by his correspondence with Thomas Abbt, a professor at the University of Frankfort, about the destiny of man and the soul and its fate after death. Mendelssohn develops his thesis along Leibnizian lines.[5] An infinite number of souls or monads constitutes the inner substance of the universe. Things that perish do not cease to exist; they are dissolved into their elements. The soul must be such an element or substance, rather than a compound, since it is the soul which imposes a unifying pattern on the diverse and changing elements of the body. Hence it is neither weakened by age nor destroyed by death. However, this line of argument demonstrates only that the soul is imperishable but not that it will retain its consciousness in a future state. That it will possess its consciousness is guaranteed by the goodness of God, who has implanted in man the idea that his soul is immortal. To assume that this notion is deceptive would be incompatible with God's goodness and justice. "If our souls were mortal, reason would be a dream. . . . We would be like animals destined only to seek food and to perish."

Mendelssohn's belief in the existence of God and the immortality of the soul, though developed as doctrines of the universal religion of reason, are in harmony with the dominant views of Jewish tradition. He differs from Jewish tradition, however, in his conception of free will. Inasmuch as every act of will must have a cause or motive, human freedom, if defined as an uncaused act, is logically impossible. Man's will can be free only in the sense that it is determined or aroused by a recognition of the good. But if man is not truly free, the sinner cannot be responsible for his misdeeds; why then should he be punished? Mendelssohn answers that divine punishment or retribution is not an end in itself; it is the means of purging the sinner to prepare him for life in the world to come. Divine justice is superseded by divine goodness, which never excludes man permanently from the bliss of eternal life. Mendelssohn's general philosophical position was soon challenged by Kant and his successors, whose critical idealism negated the presuppositions of the Enlightenment philosophy.

During the period in which his first philosophical writings appeared, Mendelssohn also began to publish critical articles. While his first reviews were mainly concerned with philosophical works, he also took up literary criticism. At this time German literature was struggling for recognition and a position in the cultural life of Germany which was dominated by Latin and French. Friedrich Nicolai, Lessing, J. G. Herder, and others accomplished a kind of cultural revolution by adopting German as the language in which to express their revolutionary ideas. Mendelssohn, the Jew, became a natural ally of these writers, who did not identify with the academic and intellectual establishment, which, in turn, looked upon them, "Nicolai's sect" with contempt and suspicion. Like them, Mendelssohn was not a member of the establishment; like them, he sought to renovate his spiritual world and was distinguished for his universal humanist aspirations; which, like them, he chose to express in German. Mendelssohn found himself so much at ease in this cultural milieu that he embarked upon an offensive war in support of the use of the German language, even venturing to criticize King Frederick II himself for the publication of a book of poems in French. "Will the Germans never be aware of their own value? Will they forever exchange their gold (i.e., their basic thinking) for their neighbors' tinsel?" (French literature). It is against this background that the personality of Mendelssohn and the cultural heritage which he handed down to future generations must be assessed. The aesthetic writings of Mendelssohn attest to the supreme value which he attributed to beauty and above all to poetry. Mendelssohn's philosophic style in German was recognized by all, including Lessing, Herder, and Kant, as one of the most excellent of his time, but his talent for poetic expression was limited, a fact which he admitted himself.

Although it was against his nature and his intentions, Mendelssohn was compelled publicly to defend his personal Judaism and the right of the independent existence of the Jewish religion before the society of his time. "I wanted to refute the world's derogatory opinion of the Jew by righteous living, not by pamphleteering," he said. During this period various Protestant circles sought the means to rescue Christianity from the onslaught of rationalism or even to unite the religion of reason and enlightenment with the traditional Christian religion. In this struggle, the integration of the Jews into the general society through conversion was to serve as a proof for the supremacy of Christianity. In line with these aspirations, John Casper Lavater, a talented Swiss clergyman given to irrational tendencies, publicly challenged the now-famous Mendelssohn to defend the superiority of Judaism to Christianity. As a young man, he had met Mendelssohn in Berlin (1763) and had been deeply impressed by his tolerant attitude toward Christianity, his appreciation of its moral value, and his general philosophic approach. In the summer of 1769, he translated into German a section of *La Palingénésie philosophique* by the Calvinist Charles Bonnet, professor of philosophy and psychology in Geneva, which was an apology for Christianity against deistic views and was based on contemporary rationalistic convictions and opinions. Lavater dedicated this translation to Mendelssohn, calling upon him "to do what wisdom, love of truth, and honor require, and what Socrates would have done had he read the treatise and found it irrefutable" or in other words, as Mendelssohn explained in his reply, "to abandon the religion of my fathers and to embrace the faith advocated by Bonnet." The astounded Mendelssohn was compelled to answer the attack in public, whcch he did in 1770 in a polite and restrained but definite style in a work entitled *Schreiben an den Herrn Diaconus Lavater zu Zuerich.*

From the very start, he based his counterargument on the personal question which had been asked of him, which he rejected as unbecoming from a personal, and unjustified from an objective point of view. His loyalty to Judaism, he claimed, was the consequence of a decision based on the studies, the inquiries, and the deliberations of his youth. He maintained that he refrained from entering into a polemic on religious questions for three reasons. First the Torah was given solely to the Jewish people who are therefore the only ones bound by it; all other men are only obliged to abide by the rules of natural religion—the religion of reason.[6] Also, Judaism is devoid of any missionary tendencies, discouraging those who seek to convert. This removes the need for a dispute on religious questions. Second, fundamental conceptions should not be subjected to debate, even if they are based on error, as long as they serve as the basis for the morality of society and do not infringe upon natural law. His third reason was a practical one: As a Jew in a country such as Prussia where the Jews enjoy only relative freedom, it is preferable to refrain from a dispute on the religion of the majority. "I am a member of an oppressed people," he said. Mendelssohn, thus, did not deal with the fundamental questions which Lavater had sought to pose; he did not publicly attack Christianity and did not justify his Judaism by means of fundamental proofs. He nevertheless gave vent to his thoughts on the subject in *Gegenbetrachtungen ueber Bonnets Palingénésie,* which was not published until the middle of the 19th century, and in letters, some of which were addressed to Bonnet himself. The polemic between Mendelssohn and Lavater persisted during the winter of 1769–70, but was brought to an end when Lavater, who also encountered the discontent of his Protestant colleagues, apologized. The above exchanges, however, gave rise to a general debate which continued until the beginning of 1771. A large number of booklets and pamphlets were published, the overwhelming majority of them attacking Mendelssohn. This controversy upset Mendelssohn to such an extent that for over seven years he suffered from a nervous disease which prevented him from pursuing his philosophic studies.

For Mendelssohn, these years proved to be a kind of catharsis. He came to realize that his Judaism committed him beyond the boundaries of his personal loyalty that was expressed in the observance of precepts, and that it conditioned his life not only in its external circumstances but also erected a barrier between himself and his enlightened colleagues and demanded of him a fundamental appraisal of his position in the two worlds: in Judaism and in his universal philosophic outlook. As a result of the crisis, Mendelssohn returned with greater vigor to the original sources of Judaism, especially to the Bible. From then on he considered it his obligation to attend to the betterment of the status and the condition of the Jews and he felt himself compelled to devote a place in his philosophic system for his belief in the Jewish religion. Among the results of this spiritual struggle was his work *Jerusalem,* which secured Mendelssohn's place in the history of Jewish thought.

Mendelssohn was sharply conscious of living in the Exile and being a man without a homeland. However, before the controversy with Lavater, he did not actively campaign for the improvement of the civic status of the Jews, but concentrated on maintaining the best possible relations with the authorities. From the 1770s, Mendelssohn became actively involved in the struggle for the protection and the civil rights of the Jews. He willingly replied to anyone who came to him for counsel or guidance, endeavoring to assist within the limits of his means any Jew who had been overtaken by misfortune or became embroiled with the authorities. He also came to the aid of Jewish communities throughout Europe involved in conflicts with the authorities, taking advantage of his recognized status in order to request help from various renowned personalities whom he had befriended.

Of decisive importance were the contributions which Mendelssohn brought to the debate on the question of the civic status of the Jews in the modern state. He expressed his views in his introduction to the German translation of the defense writ of Manasseh Ben Israel, *Vindiciae Judaeorum* (1782). In this first public argument on the subject of the civic status of the Jews, Mendelssohn set out with the fundamental optimism of the Enlightenment, expecting that the natural evolution of society would bring with it the solution to the Jewish question, stating that "it is a fortunate coincidence that the betterment of the situation of the Jews is identical with the progress of mankind." In this introduction, Mendelssohn emphasized that the character of the Jews and the categories of their occupations had been imposed on them, thus defending them against the contention that they should improve themselves. It was, however, not only incumbent upon the Christians to cease their humiliation and persecution of the Jews. The Jews on their part were also required to abandon those attitudes which were opposed to the freedom of man and particularly the freedom of thought.

Among the reactions to Mendelssohn's introduction to the German edition of Manasseh Ben Israel's *Vindicae Judaeorum* was the pamphlet, published anonymously in 1782, entitled *Das Forschen nach Licht und Recht in einem Schreiben an Herrn Moses Mendelssohn auf Veranlassung seiner merkwuerdigen Vorrede zu Menasseh Ben Israel* (The Searching for Light and Right in a letter to Herr Moses Mendelssohn occasioned on his remarkable Preface to Manasseh Ben Israel). Its author was Josef von Sonnenfels, an apostate who had secured a position for himself among the intellectuals of Vienna. The pamphlet accused Mendelssohn of having undermined the authority of traditional Jewish religion by arguing for the abolition of the *herem* (excommunication): "Clearly, ecclesiastical law armed with coercive power has always been one of the cornerstones of the Jewish religion of your fathers. How then can you, my dear Mr. Mendelssohn, continue to adhere to the faith of your fathers yet shake the entire structure by removing its very foundation since you deny the ecclesiastical law, given by Moses, which derives its authority from divine revelation?" On this occasion, Mendelssohn felt that it was his duty to provide an answer and explain and justify his stand, which he did in his *Jerusalem: oder, Ueber religioese Macht und Judenthum* (Jerusalem or, on Religious Power and Judaism) (1783). In this book he summarized and completed his thoughts, arguments, and notes of the previous 13 years.

During the course of his disputation with Mendelssohn, Lavater had already mentioned the problem of the former's attitude toward revelation and miracles upon which Christian dogma was based. In contrast, Sonnenfels, who did not believe in Christian dogma but accepted Christianity in the abstract attire of rationalist religion, was anxious to point out to Mendelssohn that since he had also ceased to believe in revelation it was incumbent upon him to abandon the traditional Jewish religion, which was no longer adapted to the present era, in order to embrace modern Christianity whose fundamentals were compatible with the religion of reason. This presentation of the problem exposed Mendelssohn to the following questions: if indeed he believed in revelation and the existence of miracles (a) why did he believe in the revelation at Sinai and not in the revelation of Jesus? (b) how can he reconcile belief in the revelation at Sinai with the universal religion of reason according to which every man can attain the truth through the power of his intellect and does not require its special revelation by God? (c) why does he reject religious coercion in Judaism if, in his opinion, the authority of the Torah is derived from God who revealed it to the Jews and compelled them to observe it? In contrast to his procedure at the time of the dispute with Lavater, Mendelssohn detached the problems from their personal context and dealt with them against the background of a general clarification of the roles of the Church and the state, and the relationship between them. He devoted the first chapter of *Jerusalem* to this question and the second to the place of Judaism within this framework.

According to the common understanding of the Enlightenment, the state's task is to provide for the welfare of its citizens by regulating their life on the ground of a contract. The church's task, on the other hand, is to take care of man's soul. The secular society, i.e., the state—Mendelssohn explains—deals with deeds while religion's sphere comprises men's convictions and their relationship to God, whereas, therefore, the first addressing itself to man's will, may use coercion, the second may only speak to man's mind and attempt to convince. Thus, the domain of religious thought and practice must be independent of any power of coercion, whether of the state or of the church. Mendelssohn, however, actually builds his image of the ideal society and his demand for toleration on grounds different from those of the Christian philosophers. Locke, he points out, claims that "the state as a state has no right to take notice of the differences between religions, because religion inherently has no bearing or influence on temporal affairs." But Mendelssohn's is the Jewish conception of the oneness of the world: true welfare in this life is one and the same as eternal bliss hereafter. Both are attained by fulfilling one's obligations in this world "the vestibule to the innermost chamber" as he says quoting *Avot* (4:16). The aim of state and church is one, only the state attains it through deeds, the church through conviction.

Following the approach of Enlightenment philosophy, he maintains that if the true doctrines of religion are based on reason, divine revelation is no longer needed as a source of truth, for revelation cannot disclose any ideas which cannot be discovered by man's reason. In taking this position, Mendelssohn divorces himself sharply from the views of earlier Jewish philosophers, especially Maimonides, for whom man's knowledge of truth is derived from both reason and revelation. For Maimonides too, the truth is essentially rational; it cannot contradict reason. Nevertheless, it requires the support of revelation in order to reach the masses of the common people who do not know philosophy and are unable to discover the truth by their own efforts. Mendelssohn rejects the notion that truth can be derived from two sources. It is superfluous and therefore illogical to assume that revelation can disclose a truth at which man can arrive by his own capacity to reason. Revelation cannot convince any man of the validity of something his reason cannot understand. Mendelssohn is aware that his rejection of revelation on philosophical grounds clashes with the classic self-image of Judaism which conceives itself as based on the Sinaitic covenant between God and Israel. If Judaism is revealed, it cannot be a religion for Mendelssohn or if it is a religion it cannot have been revealed.

Mendelssohn resolves this dilemma by defining Judaism not as a "revealed religion" but as "revealed law." The central religious tenets of Judaism—the existence and unity of God, divine providence, and the immortality of the soul—are not specific Jewish notions but doctrines of the general religion of reason, which require no proof or act of revelation to be intelligible. What distinguishes the Jew from the non-Jew is not his religion, which is the common property of all men of reason, but the unique laws, statutes and commandments that were disclosed at Sinai. That God spoke at Sinai is for Mendelssohn a *vérité de fait,* an established historical fact, because it was witnessed by the entire people of Israel with incontrovertible clarity. All people are destined to attain felicity, but Jews can attain it only by observing the Sinaitic laws. For him the God of reason and the God of Sinai are one and the same: the benevolent Creator and Sustainer of the world whom reason can affirm, and the King and Guardian of Israel who spoke at Sinai and ordained the laws that govern Jewish life. This "revealed legislation" has an additional function in that it prescribes rules of life that "guide the seeking mind to divine truths—partly eternal, partly historical—on which the religion of this [the Jewish] people was based." In emphasizing that the observance of the *mitzvot* constitutes Jewish particularity and is indispensable to Jewish existence, he adapts a theory previously formulated by the Chirstian theologian Faustus Socinus (1539–1604), who asserts that God can reveal to man laws but not metaphysical truths. Socinus, therefore, defines religion objectively as the giving of law and subjectively as its observance.

Mendelssohn argues that several conclusions follow logically from his definition of religion and revelation: (1) No miracle can validate the truth of any faith or doctrine that cannot be established by reason. Miracles can at most support or confirm rational truths, but they cannot establish them. (2) For the same reason Judaism does not possess dogmas. It addresses itself to man's will but does not attempt to control his thoughts. "Faith accepts no commands; it accepts only what comes to it by way of reasoned conviction." Judaism requires conformity in act but grants freedom in matters of doctrines. (3) If, as Mendelssohn firmly believed, a knowledge of truth is indispensable to the achievement of man's happiness, truth has to be accessible to all people without distinction of race or creed. No religion, not even his own Judaism, can be the sole instrument through which God discloses his truth. (4) Freedom of thought and doctrine requires equal respect for all religious ideas. "Let every man who does not disturb the public welfare, who obeys the law, acts righteously toward you and his fellow men be allowed to speak as he thinks, to pray to God after his own fashion or after that of his fathers, and to seek eternal salvation where he thinks he may find it."

Nevertheless Mendelssohn discusses the difference between the Jewish religion, which brings man closer to eternal truths through his daily conduct which is regulated by the Torah, and other ancient religions, which conceal the truth through idolatry. In ancient Judaism, in contrast to idolatry, there was a complete identification between religion and state. Thus a violation of the honor of God was a political crime and was chastised accordingly. This situation was brought to an end as a result of the destruction of the Temple. There is also no further validity in the punishments for those "political crimes," because they could only be applied as long as God was also the sovereign of the Jewish State. It was thus "Jerusalem"—that is, classic Judaism—which for Mendelssohn embodied the true religious might *("religioese Macht"),* united all contrasts, led to the eternal truths, and elevated the Jew toward felicity in this world and in the world to come.

There is no justification for the claim that there is no actual connection between the first and second parts of this world. The clarification of the relationship between church and state was required by Mendelssohn in order to justify the original unity between the universal God and the sovereign of the Jewish people, when in the ancient past, church and state were one. Furthermore, it was only on the basis of the limitation of the right of the state to interfere with the internal world of man that Mendelssohn could argue in favor of the right of the Jews to serve God after their own manner within the framework of the Christian states. The contradiction lay in the fact that the claim for the individual freedom of the religious man was voiced in the name of Judaism which, even in Mendelssohn's own view, was a coercive system. His supposedly historical explanation does not do away with the fundamental contradiction. Neither does his basic explanation remove the practical opposition between two compulsory constitutions: that of the state and that of Judaism. Critics of Mendelssohn's day were already aware of all these problems. It was to a lesser extent that they realized that Mendelssohn drew his view that the world was one and that there existed only one reality from the depths of Jewish thought, and that he was loyal to the conception of the unity of the world of the one God, even though he gave a rationalistic explanation to this.

Attitude to Christianity. Mendelssohn's views on Christianity were not expressed in concentrated form but are scattered throughout his notes, writings, and letters. He believed that Christianity is based on dogmas which are opposed to reason and natural religion, and he objects to its claim that only those who believe in Jesus and his miracles can perceive the truth and are worthy of eternal life. The Christian interpretations of the words of the Jewish prophets which supposedly herald the coming of Jesus are, in his opinion, completely unfounded. "The difference between the Old and the New Testament as I see it is therefore: the first harmonizes with my philosophical convictions or at least does not contradict them, the latter asks for a belief I am not able to provide." He regarded interpretations of the Christian intellectuals Bonnet and Sonnenfels as false and was vigorously opposed to any attempt to convert the Jews.

The Rebirth of Hebrew: One of the first literary activities of Mendelssohn was his anonymous collaboration with one of the first Jewish periodicals of Germany, the *Kohelet Musar* (its two issues appear to have been published during the middle 1750s), published in immaculate biblical Hebrew. Mendelssohn manifested zeal for Hebrew as for German, because, in his opinion, pure language was the basis of all culture, while he looked upon Yiddish with distaste, regarding it as a jargon, which fosters "immorality of the common man." *Kohelet Musar,* one of the first buddings of the Haskalah, was a forerunner of the well known Hebrew journal *Ha-me'assef* which Mendelssohn also had a hand in starting. Among Mendelssohn's other major publications in Hebrew was *Millot ha-Higgayon* (1761), an explanation on the logic of Maimonides, giving men the opportunity to deal with a rational subject based on a Hebrew text independent of the discussion about religion. In 1770 he published a commentary on Ecclesiastes. As early as 1770, in a letter to Michaelis, he had mentioned the publication of a translation of Psalms into German (it was not published until 1783), which was to act as a counterbalance to the translations and commentaries written in the spirit of Christianity. The principal work among his biblical translations was, however, the translation of the Pentateuch with the *Biur* (Commentary) between 1780–83.[7] The German text was written, in accordance with the custom which prevailed among German Jews, in Hebrew characters, and the commentary, *Biur,* in Hebrew. The *Biur* was essentially based on traditional exegesis, although Mendelssohn introduced a number of modern conceptions and emphasized aesthetic aspects. The translation aroused the anger of such traditional rabbis as Raphael Kohen of Altona and Ezekiel Landau of Prague, and after the publication of a sample of the translation entitled *Alim li-Terufah* (1778), there were threats of a ban against the reading of it. The work became a primer in German for European Jewry. It was their first step towards encounter with non-Jewish culture. It was Mendelssohn's hope that Jews would remain Jews while coming into contact with the European culture of their own day.

Mendelssohn's friendship with Lessing became one of the cornerstones of his life. It was Lessing who secured Mendelssohn a place in the circle of intellectuals, and Mendelssohn affirms that he was accustomed to think of Lessing as a reader and a critic when he wrote his philosophical works. As is well known, the protagonist of Lessing's *Nathan the Wise* is regarded as a portrayal of Mendelssohn. While Mendelssohn and Lessing generally agreed on philosophical questions concerning religion and the problem of tolerance, Mendelssohn opposed certain views that Lessing advanced in his last work, *Die Erziehung des Menschenge-schlechts,* and argued against them in his *Jerusalem.* In his last work, Lessing affirmed that the spirit of man was dependent on evolution. Reason was, therefore, no longer the primary comprehensive and static factor, which was given to every man in every period in the same measure, as was the opinion of the Enlightenment, but was revealed to man and took form in a gradual process. This invalidated Mendelssohn's conception of a single historic revelation. On this occasion Mendelssohn, however, still refrained from engaging in a fundamental argument with Lessing. He was unable to do so when the question of Lessing's attitude toward Spinoza was raised. While Mendelssohn recognized the importance of Spinoza, he objected to his radical conclusions with regard to religion in general and Judaism in particular. He thus developed a "refined Spinozism" which he professed first in his *Philosophische Gespraeche* (1755) and which he again propounded in his last work *Morgenstunden.*

According to Mendelssohn, the world is to be regarded as detached from God, in addition to its immanent existence within God—according to the pantheistic outlook of Spinoza. This enables Mendelssohn to uphold the concept of the creation of the world by God and divine providence which metes out reward and punishment—which Mendelssohn regarded to be the basis of moral conduct. Mendelssohn was compelled to dissociate himself from Spinoza's attitude toward Judaism as expressed in the latter's *Tractatus Theologico-Politicus.* Both Mendelssohn and Spinoza defined the powers of the state and religion in order to assure freedom of religion. However, whereas Spinoza essentially sought to liberate religion from the coercive measures employed by the state, Mendelssohn also called for the avoidance of coercive measures within the domain of religion itself. Mendelssohn also challenged Spinoza's appraisal of the revelation at Sinai. Both shared the opinion that revelation of a religious truth was an impossibility, but Spinoza characterized Judaism as being based on the revelation of a political constitution which created a theocracy and which had lost its practical validity with the destruction of the Temple, while Mendelssohn maintained that it had retained its validity and that the ancient Jewish state was a unique phenomenon that cannot be characterized by such general conceptions. It was because Mendelssohn was very close to Spinoza in point of departure and approach that he had to keep his distance and dissociate himself from that which was condemned as his "atheism."

At the time of the publication of his *Morgenstunden,* Mendelssohn was attacked for his divided attitude to Spinoza. F. H. Jacobi, in his *Lehre des Spinoza in Briefen an den Herrn Moses Mendelssohn* (On Spinoza's System, in letters to Moses Mendelssohn), claimed Lessing had admitted to him during the last years of his life that he had been a Spinozist. This attack struck at the very foundation on which Mendelssohn had established himself: he was publicly confronted with the conflict on the doctrine of Spinoza, while it was said that Lessing, the philosophical mentor, had deserted their common struggle and Lessing, the friend, had deceived him. Mendelssohn attempted to refute all three arguments in his work *An die Freunde Lessing* (To Lessing's Friends) (1786), and thus extricate himself from the ruinous conclusions of the claim of Jacobi.

Mendelssohn became a legend even during his own lifetime, and he was regarded as the embodiment of the humanist ideal. He was a charismatic personality whose influence withstood the changes of the time, even though his philosophical position did not withstand the undermining of its foundation by Kant—a fact which Mendelssohn recognized toward the end of his life. Moreover, he, the great defender of Judaism, actually undermined it because he subjected it to the test of the searching rationalism of the Enlightenment, although he sought to prove that it could withstand this test. The strength of the rationalism upon which he had based himself was, however, incapable of spanning the gulf between traditional Judaism, from which he had emerged, and the world of rationalistic thought, in which he had grown; between his inferior civic status as a Jew and his emancipated status in the circle of intellectuals; between his Jewish pride and his violent criticism of the social and cultural character of the Jews of his time: between his loyalty to *halakhah* and the cultural treasury of Judaism, on the one hand, and his despair over the prospect that the Jewish people would not find its place in a gradually changing world, on the other. His life became a testimony of the basic conflict of the emancipation—the conflict between assimilation and the safeguarding of the singularity of Jewish life, between equality of civic and individual right and the minority status, the conflict of the modern

A medal struck in honor of Moses Mendelssohn, c. 1774, by the Jewish medalist
Jacob Abraham and his son Abraham.

Jew in the Diaspora, who seeks integration while at the same time de-
siring to preserve his Jewish identity. Mendelssohn's personal solution
was made possible because of his personal qualities and the specific spiritual climate of the German intellectual society.

Those non-Jews who challenged his system were either those who had
developed an emotional culture of Christian romanticism, or rationalists
such as Kant. Both exploited Mendelssohn's argument that Judaism
was a revealed legislation in order to abuse it as a "ceremonial law," a
fossil of an ancient era which had become obsolete—a claim which Kant
bequeathed to German philosophy. Indeed, Jewish thinkers of the 19th
century were also compelled to dissociate themselves from Mendelssohn's views and to seek a new spiritual basis for Judaism. The hidden
ambivalence of Mendelssohn's position was matched by the open ambivalence of his non-Jewish admirers in their attitude toward him. This was
the case with not only Kant himself but also J.G. Hamann, who wrote
a whole book against *Jerusalem,* Herder, Lavater, and even Jacobi. On
the other hand, among the Jews in the course of time, the basic conflict
of Mendelssohn's position erupted into an open conflict when various
and contradictory trends of Judaism all claimed to find support in his
image and in his words. It was also Mendelssohn who set the example
for the deep identification of German Jewry with the German culture and
language and the aversion to Yiddish and the culture of Eastern European
Jewry. It was, however, the latter which developed modern thinking
through the Haskalah. Even during his own time, Mendelssohn was not
the only one among the Jews of Germany to contribute to the Enlightenment, but his personality and his life seem to have embraced all the
factors of the transition period of the emancipation, and has become the
symbol of that era.

THE EARLY 19TH CENTURY

The two most important general philosophic influences on 19th-century and (to a certain extent) 20th-century Jewish thought were the critical philosophy of Kant and the idealistic philosophies of Schelling and Hegel. Kant was important for his denial of speculative metaphysics; for his sharp distinction between theoretical and practical (moral) philosophy; for making God, freedom, and immortality postulates of practical reason; for his account of duty, the categorical imperative, and the autonomy of the will; and for closely connecting ethics and religion. The idealist philosophers were important for affirming the spiritual nature of all reality and for their notion that history presents the progressive self-realization of spirit. Jewish philosophers used these philosophies in varying ways and combinations, holding that Judaism is the best embodiment of the religion of reason (Kant) or the religion of spirit (idealists).

SOLOMON FORMSTECHER

Solomon Formstecher (1808–1889), rabbi and leader of the Reform movement, developed his philosophy in *Die Religion des Geistes* (The Religion of the Spirit; 1841), a work combining idealist philosophy with a special concern for ethics. From Schelling he accepted the notion of a world soul which is manifest in the phenomena of nature; but, whereas for Schelling the world soul was bound to nature, Formstecher emphasized its transcendence and identified it with God. However, there is another manifestation of the world soul and that is spirit, whose main characteristics are self-consciousness and freedom. When spirit becomes

162

conscious of nature it produces physics; when it becomes conscious of itself it produces logic. There exists an ideal for spirit in each realm: aesthetic contemplation in nature; moral action in the realm of spirit. Corresponding to the two realms there are two forms of religion: the religion of nature which considers the world as containing divine forces or which identifies nature with God; the religion of the spirit which considers God as transcendent. There are also two corresponding goals for human life: for religion of nature it is to become one with God; for religion of the spirit it is to become like Him through moral actions. Historically, paganism embodied the religion of nature, Judaism, the religion of spirit. There exist two kinds of revelation: prehistoric revelation which consists of the ideal that spirit can attain, and historical revelation which is the gradual attainment of this ideal. Historical revelation occurs in natural religion as well as in the religion of the spirit; but in natural religion it comes to an end with the cognition of a God bound to nature, while in spiritual religion it tends toward the cognition of the transcendent God.

The religion of the spirit is identical with absolute truth. (Formstecher does not succeed too well in harmonizing the idealist notion that man's final goal is understanding with his emphasis on ethics.) The religion of the spirit is the religion of the Jews, but it had a historical development. Since Judaism developed in a pagan world, the religion of the spirit had to be the religion of a specific people. However, as Judaism progressed from objectivity to subjectivity (which consisted in the spirit's becoming more and more conscious of itself) it gained greater universalism. This occurred at first through the destruction of Jewish national life. However, since the world was still hostile, Judaism had to maintain its identity, but now as a theocracy of law rather than as a political reality. Formstecher maintained that the process of becoming more and more universal was about to come to an end in the modern world which was marked by the emancipation of the Jews, and the absolute truth of spiritual religion was about to emerge.

But spiritual religion also had to penetrate natural (pagan) religion and this occurred through Christianity and Islam. Since Christianity addressed itself to the pagan world, it combined the religion of the spirit with the thought of paganism. The history of Christianity is the struggle between Jewish and pagan elements. As Christianity developed historically it freed itself more and more from its pagan elements. Since

Christianity, even in the modern world, has not completely freed itself from these accretions there is still room for Judaism as a separate religion. However, both religions strive toward the realization of the religion of the spirit. Judaism can prepare itself by stripping itself of its particularistic elements and its ceremonial law.

SAMUEL HIRSCH

Samuel Hirsch (1815–1889), rabbi and Reform leader, presented his views in *Die Religionsphilosophie der Juden* (The Religious Philosophy of the Jews; 1842), a work influenced by Hegel. Hirsch considered it the task of philosophy to transform the content of religious consciousness into the content of spirit (mind), and for him religious and philosophic truth are identical. Central to Hirsch's thought is the notion of freedom. Man by understanding himself as an "I" standing over against nature becomes aware of his freedom. However, this freedom is abstract and must be given content. One such content is natural freedom, his ability to do whatever he desires. Hegel held that abstract and natural freedom were in conflict and he held that this conflict was ingrained in man. Not so Hirsch. He tried to preserve abstract freedom for man by holding that alternate courses of action are open to him. Man may sacrifice his freedom to nature, or he may control nature by means of his freedom. These courses of action have as their concomitants two kinds of awareness of God. According to both, God is the giver of freedom, but according to the first view nature becomes the divine principle; according to the second view God transcends nature. Understanding nature as divine produces paganism; understanding God as transcendental produces Judaism.

Hirsch now analyzes the history of religion in a manner reminiscent of Formstecher. But whereas for Formstecher, paganism, being the partial recognition of spirit, has some redeeming features, for Hirsch, it does not. Whatever development paganism has, it is only to show its nothingness. Judaism also had a development, but only because it originated in a pagan world (Abraham lived in that world); but once it had become free by recognizing that the true nature of religion is moral freedom, no further development was necessary. In early times Judaism required prophecy and miracles to show that God is master of nature;

but once the threat of paganism had passed these were no longer necessary. The only miracle still apparent is the continuous existence of the
Jewish people. There is, however, a kind of development in Judaism, for
once one has discovered the truth of ethical freedom oneself one wants
to spread it to others. This Judaism attains, not by missionizing but by
bearing witness to its faith. There existed, however, a tendency to bring
Jewish beliefs to the pagan world in an active fashion and Jesus made
this his task. Jesus still moved within the world of Judaism, but a break
came with Paul. When Paul formulated a doctrine of original sin and
redemption through Jesus, Christianity severed its ties with Judaism.
Only when the work of Paul is undone will Christianity be able to fulfill
its true mission. When Christianity reaches that stage it will be essentially identical with Judaism. However, even in messianic times, when Israel
will become one with all mankind, it will retain a structure of its own.

NACHMAN KROCHMAL

Krochmal was born in the town of Brody, Galicia. His father Shalom
Krochmalnik maintained contact with Haskalah (Enlightenment) circles
in Germany, including Moses Mendelssohn, and Krochmal himself
attracted the luminaries of the Haskalah to the town of Zolkiew in Galicia, where he spent most of his life. He returned to Brody after his
wife's death in 1836 and later settled in Tarnapol, where he died after a
long illness.

Krochmal acquired his extensive education completely on his own.
He devoted himself largely to philosophy and history. His chief inspiration in Jewish thought came from Maimonides and Abraham ibn Ezra,
and in general philosophy from Kant, Schelling, and Hegel. His interest
in philosophy and history, however, was subservient to the central
preoccupation of Krochmal's life, namely, the understanding of Judaism
in its historical manifestation. This was summed up in his Hebrew *Moreh
Nevukhei ha-Zeman* ("Guide of the Perplexed of the Time"), which was
published posthumously in 1851.[8] Krochmal believed that his chief
contribution should be made through teaching and discussion. Through
verbal communication he exerted a decisive influence on his associates,
and it was only at the insistence of his friends that he set down his views
in writing.

Krochmal's lifework, *Moreh Nevukhei ha-Zeman,* was only partially devoted to pure philosophic speculation. Consisting of 17 chapters, the work may be divided into four sections: chapters 1–7 deal with issues in philosophy of religion and philosophy of history; chapters 8–11 provide a summary of Jewish history; chapters 12–15 contain an analysis of Hebrew literature by means of the critical-historical method; and chapters 16–17 present the nucleus of Krochmal's philosophy, which was never fully developed. Despite the absence of a systematic philosophical presentation, the direction of Krochmal's thought is evident. He belonged to the school of idealist philosophers (Schelling, Hegel), who regarded philosophic speculation as the proper vehicle for the final understanding of the nature of reality.

Following Hegel, he defined reality in itself as "the Absolute Spirit," which in his opinion, corresponded to the concept of God in religious tradition. Krochmal speaks of the Absolute Being as "a power equal to every latent and potential form within itself," and this being he identifies with God. This definition reflects the tendency of post-Kantian idealistic philosophy to identify the Absolute Being with total acting power, whose essential nature is pure, unqualified cognition. The transition from the Absolute Reality to the generated reality of finite things, which for Krochmal corresponds to the religious concept of the creation of the world out of nothing, is explained by him as an infinite process of God's self-confinement, which must be described as a voluntary contingent act. Krochmal's exposition reflects the kabbalistic notion that the world is created by divine self-confinement, and by identifying the "nothing" out of which the world was created with God, as did the Kabbalists,[9] Krochmal draws the conclusion that God created the world out of Himself.

In contrast to the major idealist philosophers Schelling and Hegel, Krochmal was not content with accounting for the overall derivation of finite reality from the Absolute. He concentrated on determining the relationship of religion and philosophy in respect to their relationship to the Absolute Spirit. Krochmal based his religious philosophy on the premise that the Absolute Spirit is the exclusive subject of human knowledge. Religion by its very nature is knowledge, no less than philosophic knowledge. Therefore, the difference between philosophy and religion is not one of essence but merely of form or degree. Religious belief and philosophic understanding are different degrees of comprehending the Spirit. The first is the level of "ideas of incipient thought," or the under-

standing of reality by means of images, whereas the second is the level
of the "ideas of mind and intellect," or the understanding of reality by
means of concepts and ideas. Since the intellectual understanding is
more general than that of images, philosophy imparts to religion (religious belief) a greater and more complete value. Krochmal assumed
that in presenting philosophy as the higher means of understanding
religious truth, he was continuing the view accepted by medieval philosophers, especially Maimonides, that the Torah encourages philosophic speculation, and contains within itself, at least potentially,
philosophic truth. All religious faith is based upon the Spirit, and thus
there is no essential difference between the various faiths. Nevertheless
the biblical faith is unique in its purity and the universality of its imagery.

Krochmal's philosophy of history is based on the assumption that
history, like all products of human civilization, depends upon its spiritual content. Each nation has its own spiritual principle which is the
foundation of its existence, and its life and continuity is determined by
the extent to which it directs itself toward that principle. In order to
understand the internal, concrete structure of the history of nations,
Krochmal turned to the evolutionary method of the philosophy of
history of Vico and Herder, according to which the history of every nation can be divided into three periods: growth and development, vigor
and enterprise, and decline and annihilation. The various factors—
economic, intellectual, and cultural—determining the life of a nation
must be analyzed in the light of these periods. However, Krochmal being
an idealist and greatly influenced by Hegel, subjects these factors—
without adequate clarification—to the metaphysical principle of the
Spirit: "The substance of a nation lies not in its being a nation, but in
the substance of the Spirit therein."

Krochmal attempted, by thorough historical analysis, to establish as
an empirical fact that the history of the people of Israel has the same
threefold structure as that of other peoples. The Jewish people differs
from all other nations, whose existences are transitory, in being eternal.
Krochmal explains that this eternity is caused by a special relation existing between the Jewish people and God, the Absolute Spirit, and that
this is lacking in the case of other nations. This relation was at its
strongest in the revelation on Mt. Sinai and in Israelite prophecy. In
spite of its special character, Krochmal does not believe that the people
of Israel transcends history; its eternity is assured by a continuous re-

newal of national life. With this concept of the earthly and metaphysical elements of Israel and the belief in the necessity of renewing the creative national forces following a period of spiritual stagnation, Krochmal became the forerunner of modern nationalist-Zionist philosophy of history.

Krochmal was one of the first scholars investigating Judaism to propose the method of historical investigation "for the purpose of recognizing our essence and our nature." With this he helped to lay the foundation of "the science of Judaism." While his method differed from that of the historical school represented by L. Zunz, A. Geiger, and H. Graetz, because he maintained that only philosophy can reveal the "ultimate purpose" of history, he also insisted that historical analysis must apply the evolutionary method in studying Judaism.

Krochmal's particular, and perhaps most important, contribution lies in his application of the analytic and historical method to the study of Hebrew literature. Especially noteworthy is his study of *halakhah* (*Moreh,* ch. 13) and *aggadah.* In his study of *halakhah* Krochmal had two basic aims: the interpretation of the Oral Law by establishing its origin in antiquity and the description of its development from its beginnings until its codification and publication by the sages of the Talmud. In reference to the antiquity of the Oral Law, Krochmal's position held that the fact that the Law was given to an entire nation required that its specific laws and customs be expounded only in a general way. The central theme of the evolution of *halakhah* is interpretation, namely, the systematic and logical development of the content of the Written Law. This approach determined Krochmal's position on the overall nature of the *halakhah.* Since only the fundamental laws were given verbally to Moses on Mt. Sinai, there can be no essential difference between the subsequent three phases of *halakhah,* which are: the direct transmission of tradition from person to person, the deduction of new laws, and the formulation of ordinances, strictures, and customs. But despite the unity of the *halakhah,* it is nonetheless possible to discern the stages of its development.

Krochmal also applied the evolutionary method to his study of *aggadah,* although without the systematic approach of his study of *halakhah. Aggadah* grew out of the moral-didactic need to bring biblical ideas to the people. Its chief concern lies in the thought con-

Samuel David Luzzatto.

Tombstone of Nachman
Krochmal at Tarnopol.

tent of the Bible, but it does not attempt to interpret it conceptually. *Aggadah* is popular philosophy, and the parables that deal explicitly with God, the world, man, history, and Israel are its best exponents. The intellectual substructure of *aggadah,* not its stylistic exterior, reveals the essential ideas of Jewish philosophy, which, in turn, are nothing but the conceptual interpretation of the truths contained in the Torah. According to Krochmal, the development of Jewish thought from Philo to Mendelssohn is an integral process, a *philosophia perennis,* subdivided into various periods according to degree of conceptual purity.

Though Krochmal had no important disciples in the field of metaphysics, the whole of the "Wissenschaft des Judentums" was indebted to him for methodological, historical and analytic insights.

S.D. LUZZATTO

While Formstecher, Hirsch, and Krochmal attempted to harmonize idealism and Judaism, Samuel David Luzzatto (1800–1865), translator of the Bible into Italian and biblical commentator, was an outright opponent of philosophic speculation. He agreed with Mendelssohn that Judaism possesses no dogmas, but unlike Mendelssohn he affirmed that moral action leading to righteousness is the purpose of all (even the ritual) commandments. While he does not hold that Judaism lacks beliefs altogether, he considers it the function of religious beliefs to induce moral actions. It is conceivable to him that some religious beliefs may be false. Ethical activity, according to Luzzatto, springs from the feelings of honor and pity. In his *Yesodei ha-Torah* ("Foundations of the Torah," published posthumously in 1880) he enumerates three principles of Judaism: the feeling of pity, reward and punishment, and the election of Israel. The first of these is the basic principle; the other two have only an auxiliary function. A belief in reward and punishment is necessary because without it man would be governed by the evil part of his nature; the election of Israel is important for motivating Jews to higher and higher ethical practices. Luzzatto distinguishes between Judaism which aspires to moral action and "Atticism" which has understanding as its goal. He maintains that cognition of God lies beyond the capacities of man, but he also holds that the existence of God can be demonstrated philosophically.

S. L. STEINHEIM

Solomon Ludwig Steinheim (1789–1866), physician, poet, and philosopher, was also an outright opponent of philosophic rationalism. In his *Offenbarung nach dem Lehrbegriff der Synagogue* (Revelation according to the Doctrine of the Synagogue; 4 vols., 1835–65) he defended the thesis that religious truth is only given through revelation. This meant to him not only that reason is inferior to revelation, but that when reason examines the contradictions contained within its content it must recognize its own insufficiency. Revelation is not the product of human consciousness but comes from without, from God. (Steinheim does not deny that religion possesses cognitive content; but this content can only come through revelation, not through rational processes.) The truth of revelation is not confirmed by external signs but by reason, which clearly recognizes the superiority of revelation and also that revelation meets human needs better than philosophy. Philosophy differs from religion in that philosophy conceives of all reality in terms of necessity, while religion understands it in terms of freedom.

Corresponding to these approaches are two kinds of religion: natural religion which conceives of God as subject to the necessity of His own nature and as dependent on the matter on which he acts; revealed religion which understands God as the Creator Who, unbounded by necessity, creates the world freely and out of nothing. Creation, according to Steinheim, is the first principle of revelation; other principles are freedom, immortality of the soul, and (very likely) the unity of God. Steinheim applies the two conceptions of religion to the historical religions: paganism is the embodiment of natural (philosophical) religion; Judaism is the embodiment of revealed religion; and Christianity is a mixture of the two. As revealed religion, Judaism emphasizes, besides the cognitive principles mentioned before, human freedom and moral activity. Hence in his conclusions concerning the content of the Jewish religion, Steinheim differs little from Formstecher and Hirsch;

but whereas the latter two philosophers saw Judaism grounded in reason, Steinheim sees it grounded in revelation.

Moritz Lazarus and his wife, Nahida Ruth.

MORITZ LAZARUS

Moritz Lazarus (1824–1903), writer on psychology and philosophy, devoted *Die Ethik des Judentums* (*The Ethics of Judaism;* vol. I, 1898; vol. II, published posthumously, 1911) to the philosophic interpretation of Jewish ethics. The avowed purpose of the work is to use philosophy to give a structured account of Jewish ethics; but he also uses philosophic concepts to analyze its content. He derives his main notions from Kant, but he gives these notions a psychological interpretation. From Kant, Lazarus accepts the notion of the autonomy of ethics, but to Lazarus this only meant that the sphere of ethics is independent. Whereas for Kant the autonomy of ethics further implied that ethics is independent of the emotions, Lazarus maintained that ethics is grounded in the emotions of duty and obligation. Religious ethics differs from philosophical ethics in that it recognizes God as the author of ethical imperatives. However, if ethical imperatives are given by God, ethics is no longer autonomous but heteronomous. Lazarus tries to solve this difficulty by stating that God is also subject to ethical imperatives. What God commands is right, but not because He commands it: rather He commands it because it is right. Judaism is essentially religious ethics and even the ritual commandments have an ethical purpose. Jewish ethics is an ethics for the individual, but even more for society. Lazarus also interprets the idea of holiness. God is holy, not because He is mysterious or remote but because he represents moral perfection. Man becomes holy through ever increasing moral activity.

THE 20TH CENTURY

Though the influence of Kant and Hegel continued to be of great significance in Jewish philosophical circles in the 20th century, different and important influences were at work in Jewish thought which gave it a dynamic new direction. Most significantly, under the impetus provided by the radical and original elements in Hermann Cohen's philosophy of religion and philosophy of Judaism, Jewish thinkers began to strive for a re-assertion of the autonomy of Judaism and biblical revelation. A growing number of philosophers argued that religious truth need not subordinate itself to philosophical, especially Kantian and Hegelian, notions of religious truth and the sources of these truths. Religions and religious truths had a dynamic independence which operated distinctly from philosophical norms and categories. The existentialist school, under the influence of Soren Kierkegaard, the great Danish theologian, added support to this programmatic independence of religion and religious thinking by stressing the significance of personal existence against abstract philosophy and this provided Jewish thinkers, especially the two most influential—Franz Rosenzweig and Martin Buber—with a different vantage point from which to view and evaluate the relation of philosophy and religion. The stress on subjective and experimental factors and a renewed openess to Divine revelation, paradoxical in the face of the 20th century's secularity, created a climate in which the more personal and intimate God of the Bible once again become the focus of Jewish thinking.

HERMANN COHEN

Hermann Cohen was born in 1842 in Coswig, the son of a cantor. He studied at the Jewish Theological Seminary at Breslau, but gave up his initial plans to become a rabbi. He turned to philosophy, studying first at the University of Breslau and then at the University of Berlin. He received his doctorate from the University of Halle in 1865. In 1873 he was invited by F.A. Lange, the well-known author of the *History of Materialism*, to become a *Privatdozent* (lecturer) in philosophy at the University of Marburg. Appointed full professor after only three years, Cohen taught in Marburg until 1912. He spent the last years of his life (1915–1918) in Berlin where he taught at the Hochschule für die Wissenschaft des Judentums.

Cohen's early works were devoted to a critical evaluation of idealism as embodied in the thought of Plato and, particularly, of Kant. "Die platonische Ideenlehre"[10] appeared in 1866. It was followed by *Kants Theorie der Erfahrung* (Kant's Theory of Experience) (1871), *Kants Begruendung der Ethik* (Kant's Principles of Ethics) (1877), *Von Kants Einfluss auf die deutsche Kultur* (1883), and *Kants Begruendung der Aesthetik* (Kant's Principles of Aesthetics) (1889). These critical works brought Cohen to a new interpretation of Kant's philosophy which came to be known as the Marburg School of neo-Kantianism. This approach found its expression in his three systematic works: *Logik der reinen Erkenntnis* (The Logic of Pure Knowledge) (1902), *Die Ethik des reinen Willens* (The Ethics of the Pure Will) (1904), and *Die Aesthetik des reinen Gefuehls* (The Aesthetic of Pure Feeling) (1912). The titles of these works reflect Cohen's contention that philosophy is divisible into three branches—logic, ethics, and aesthetics—which investigate, respectively, the underlying assumptions of the three basic modes of consciousness—thinking, willing, and feeling.

The starting point of Cohen's philosophic system, like that of Kant's, is the existence of scientific knowledge, expressed mathematically, and, like Kant, Cohen believed that the task of the philosopher is to unfold the logical conditions underlying this type of knowledge. However, Cohen criticized Kant for according sensation a special role in the establishment of scientific knowledge. While Kant had maintained that the sense content of our knowledge is a "datum," which, once given, is organized and synthesized[11] by thought, Cohen put forth the extreme idealistic thesis that thought produces everything out of itself. According to his "principle of origin" objects are constructs of thought. Thus he opposed Kant's notion of the "thing-in-itself," according to which there lies behind the object that we know an object which can never be known as it really is. For Kant, the action of reason is confined to the creation of associations between sensations, which are given. For Cohen, sensation merely describes the problem posed to thought.

Describing the method of science, Cohen holds that the scientist posits certain basic principles which help him to determine the facts, but as his research progresses he is required to revise these underlying principles and to conceive new hypotheses, which, in turn, lead to the discovery of new facts. In accordance with this view our knowledge of reality at a given time is determined by the particular stage of this process, and since this process has no end, man can never have a final knowledge of reality.

Considering ethics and its relation to science, Cohen held that the freedom of man, which is the basis of ethics, is not contradictory to the law of causality in natural science, for freedom and causality are both only methodological presuppositions used in the construction of two different systems which can exist simultaneously. The dignity of man is central to Cohen's ethical thought. A proponent of humanistic socialism, he regarded a nation's treatment of its working classes as an index of its level of morality. While he called Marx "God's historical messenger," he rejected historical materialism as well as the atheistic trends prevalent in the workers' movement.

A short time after his appointment as professor at Marburg, Cohen was obliged to declare publicly his attitude to the Jewish question. When the historian Treitschke attacked the German Jews in his *Ein Wort ueber unser Judentum* (A Word on our Judaism) (1879), defining Judaism as the "national religion of an alien race," Cohen countered with his *Ein Bekenntnis zur Judenfrage* (A Confession on the Jewish Question) (1880), in which he professed the total integration of German Jewry into German society "without any double loyalty," yet demanding at the same time that the Jews take their religion seriously. In 1888, Cohen was called upon to testify in a lawsuit against an anti-Semitic public-school teacher who had claimed that according to the Talmud, the laws of the Torah apply only to relationships between fellow Jews, and not to relationships between Jews and gentiles, whom the Jews are permitted to rob and deceive. Cohen published his testimony in a pamphlet called "Die Naechstenliebe im Talmud" (Brotherly love in the Talmud) (1888), in which he set out to harmonize two apparently contradictory notions that are basic to Judaism: the

idea of Israel as the chosen people, and the idea of the messianic unity
of mankind. The connecting link is provided by the concept of God as a
protector of the alien. The vocation of Israel begins with the fact of its
chosenness, but since God is conceived from the outset as one who loves
the stranger, Israel's chosenness is directed primarily at the unity of
mankind. The function of history, as it is understood by Judaism, is to
fulfill this final aim, i.e., to bring about the unity of mankind and to
establish the kingdom of God on earth. The concept of man and of the
unity of mankind emerge in Judaism as the consequence of the idea of
the oneness of God who had created man in his image.

Although Cohen had maintained throughout his Marburg period
that religion was only a historical presupposition for ethics, and that
ethics was destined ultimately to absorb religion, the idea of God
played a central role in his ethics. Ethics provides mankind with an
eternal ideal, but natural science indicates that the world is nearing its
end. If mankind ceases to exist, there will be no possibility of achieving
the ethical ideal. It is here that Cohen introduces his concept of
God. It is the function of God to guarantee the eternity of the world,
and consequently, the possibility of the fulfillment of the moral ideal:
and Cohen refers in this connection to the covenant established
between God and man after the flood (Gen. 9:15). Cohen's God was,
however, at this time very different from the personal God of traditional
Judaism. God was for Cohen an idea, or concept, rather than an existent
being.

Cohen's move from Marburg to Berlin at the age of seventy, was more
than a change of place. His preoccupation with Jewish philosophy in the
wake of his preparations for his lectures in Berlin at the Hochschule, his
journey to meet Polish Jewry in 1914 in order to assist in the foundation
of an independent institute of higher learning for Jews who found it
difficult to be admitted to the universities, and his contact with the life of
the Jewish masses in Vilna and Warsaw, all brought about a revolution
in Cohen's philosophical outlook and in his attitude to Judaism.

The first indications of this change can be seen in his book *Der Begriff
der Religion im System der Philosophie* (The Concept of Religion
within the Philosophical System) (1915), whose very title bears witness
to the change. It was in this book that Cohen attempted to accord religion
an independent place within the system of philosophy. In this work Cohen
maintained that there are problems which ethics cannot explain. Ethics

is concerned with man in general, that is, with man as a type and not with individual men. It does not take into account the personal concerns of the individual. The individual, however, wants his voice to be heard. It is religion that "saves" the individual, and introduces the categories of sin, repentance, and salvation to deal with the individual's anguish and guilt. Cohen sees the roots of this concern for the individual in the Later Prophets Jeremiah and, especially, Ezekiel. The Earlier Prophets judged the world from the general ethical standpoint only.

Cohen's new attitude to religion finds its full expression in his work *Die Religion der Vernunft aus den Quellen des Judentums* (The Religion of Reason from the Sources of Judaism) which was published posthumously by his wife in 1919. This book shows that Cohen had discarded the Marburg system, although he did not admit it. According to the Marburg system reality is rooted in human reason, and culture is the product of the human mind. Even God is but a hypothesis, a logical postulate. According to Cohen's new position, reality is rooted in God, man's reason itself originating in God. Cohen had thus shifted from an anthropocentric to a theocentric system. In the former system "becoming" had been the prevailing concept; now "being" is the basic concept. God was no longer an idea, but a pure being: "I am, that I am," while the world is becoming. There is, therefore, a wide gulf between God and the world. Thus a question arises that had no place in the former system: how is it possible for the world which is becoming and, therefore, by its very nature incomplete, to exist beside God who is eternal being? Cohen answers this question with a new concept: "correlation." Being and becoming are connected to one another insofar as one concept logically requires the other. Becoming could not exist if there were no eternal existence to endow it with power and significance. On the other hand, being could not exist without becoming. The existence of God would have no meaning without creation. His starting point, therefore, is the basic duality of God and man, from which merge the other dualities of God and the world, and man and man.

The correlation between God and man is characterized by the holy spirit, *Ru'ah ha-Kodesh,* which is not an attribute of either God or man, but of their relation. Cohen criticized Christianity and Philo for positing the holy spirit as an independent being intermediate between God and man, and failing to realize that it is, in fact, only an attribute of the relationship between man and God. The holy spirit binds together man and God, but they still retain their distinctiveness. The correlation between man and God is manifest in man's attempt to imitate God, the model and source of holiness, and to become holy himself.

The correlation between man and God is also revealed in the collaboration between them. Judaism views man as a "co-worker in the work of creation." Man's specific creative responsibility is the establishment of a united mankind, i.e., the bringing about of the messianic era. Cohen conceived of the messianic era in terms of a philosophic socialism, and viewed the struggle for the messianic kingdom as a struggle for justice and the rights of the poor. Before the messianic era can be attained among mankind as a whole, individual communities of men living together in peace and harmony will have to be established to serve as models for mankind as a whole. The Jewish people is such a community.

Although Cohen held to a liberal interpretation of Judaism which emphasized its moral teachings, he vigorously affirmed the value of Jewish tradition and law. Following the Kantian doctrine of morality, according to which an action is moral only if it is performed from a sense of duty and is autonomous, Cohen interprets *mitzvah* to mean both "law" and "duty." The law originates in God, the sense of duty, in man. The law is at the same time duty; duty, at the same time, law. God issued commandments to man, and man, of his own free will, takes upon himself the "yoke of the commandments." With the "yoke of the commandments," man simultaneously accepts the "yoke of the kingdom of God." Thus, the law leads to the messianic ideal.

Cohen's account of religion in general and Judaism in particular as developed in his *Die Religion der Vernunft aus den Quellen des Judentums* emphasized a universal messianic ideal which Cohen believed to be at the center of prophetic Judaism. In this emphasis he surely sounded an authentic prophetic note, but he also manifests an indebtedness to his earlier and still lingering Idealism which emphasized the concept of universality in thought and morality. This universalist emphasis put Cohen into opposition to Zionism which he saw as a betrayal of prophetic Judaism's ethic. He expressed this criticism in an article published in 1916 entitled "Religion und Zionismus".[12] However one can already see in Cohen's earliest work the grounds of such a view. Cohen always held the view that Judaism, especially as represented by the German Jew, and German Idealism both represented the same essential doctrine of spirit and morality; both, in their own ways, teach the same ethical and metaphysical truths. This claimed parallelism rules out all forms of Jewish nationalism, especially the hope of a return to Zion, and the uprooting of the Jew from European, and especially German, culture.[13] This view was shared by, among others, Franz Rosenzweig who defended it however on the different metaphysical interpretation of Judaism's role in history (or rather, as he saw it, outside of history) and for this he was vigorously criticized by Buber who was a life-long, ardent Zionist.

Influence. Cohen's influence on the younger Jewish intellectuals of the day was enormous. His work marks the greatest synthesis of Judaism and Idealism as well as its overcoming. No Jewish Idealist matched Cohen's philosophical competence, complete mastery of, and creative insight into the thought of Kant and his predecessors. Yet Cohen came to see the limitations of Idealist thought, especially with regard to the abstractness of its God concept and its lack of room for an existing individual human person. He therefore transcended Idealism with a demand for a new, more positive and immediate awareness of the reality of God and the importance of individual life. These elements he found manifest in Judaism, and he argued that within Judaism one finds represented the correct understanding of the dynamic relationship between man and God.

This new appraisal of the relation of Judaism to philosophy, and Cohen's clear demand that religion was not to be subordinate to philosophical demands revolutionized Jewish thought. Franz Rosenzweig and Martin Buber were especially influenced by Cohen's later thought. Rosenzweig's "existentialism", as he was the first to acknowledge, owed its greatest debt to his teacher, Hermann Cohen. Rosenzweig wrote a moving "Introduction" to Cohen's collected *Jewish Writings* (Juedische Schriften) in 1924. Buber, though not so obviously influenced by Cohen, was, in fact, greatly in Cohen's debt and, among other things, Cohen's important concept of correlation is the source of much of Buber's thinking about dialogue and the relation of God and man. Buber, like Rosenzweig and the whole of modern Jewish thought, was indebted to Cohen for liberating Jewish thought from having to seek a synthesis between Judaism and Idealism, thereby allowing Judaism to assert its own independent claims to truth and value.

Drawing of Hermann Cohen
by Max Liebermann, 1912.

Leo Baeck.

LEO BAECK

Leo Baeck (1873–1956) served as rabbi in Berlin from 1912. From 1933, he was president of the Reichsvertretung, the representative body of German Jews, and devoted himself to defending the rights remaining for Jews under the Nazis. At Theresienstadt concentration camp, to which he was deported in 1943, he continued the work of encouraging his people. Thus, he became a "witness of his faith," a theme that had long occupied a central position in his writings. After the war, he moved to London, where he became chairman of the World Union for Progressive Judaism.

Baeck was a philosophical-theological thinker of wide general knowledge, a preacher, and an historian of religion. In 1901 he published a polemical article against *Wesen des Christentums* (The Essence of Christianity) by the Protestant theologian Adolf von Harnack (MGWJ, vol. 45). Four years later, in 1905, Baeck published his main work, *Wesen des Judentums* (The Essence of Judaism).[14] The apologetic character that dominated the first edition was considerably modified in the second and the extreme rationalism was eliminated. This transformation was the result of the influences of mysticism and Jewish nationalism. Baeck viewed the essence of Judaism as a dialectical polarity between "mystery" and "command." The commands, according to Baeck, do not necessarily form a system of commandments like the establised *halakhah*, which imposes a required and fixed way of life; rather, they appear from time to time in the form of instructions for action like flashes of lightning that break through the cloud covering the divine "mystery." Baeck adhered to Hermann Cohen's interpretation of Judaism as "ethical monotheism." He believed that piety is achieved by the fulfillment of the duties between man and man and that even ritual observances are directed toward this ethical aim. In this respect Baeck was a liberal Jew, but he was far from spiritual assimilation, because he maintained that ethics must be supported by faith in God.

Baeck sharply rejected Christianity and had a sympathetic, although critical, attitude toward Zionism. In Christianity he saw a "romantic" religion of the abstract spirit longing for redemption[15] as distinguished from Judaism, the "classical" religion of the concrete spirit working for the improvment of this world. Although not a political Zionist, he thought that the building of Palestine was a valuable prospect for embodying the spirit of Judaism, but not a guarantee that it would be realized. This, according to him, could succeed wherever there is a Jewish community that truly desires it.

ABRAHAM ISAAC KOOK

Rabbi Kook (1865–1935) was the leading Rabbinical authority and orthodox philosopher of the modern era and first Ashkenazi Chief Rabbi of modern Erez Israel. He developed a mystical Zionist philosophy which drew heavily on kabbalistic doctrines. The basic theme of his thought was that everything emanates from the Divine and is dependent for its existence on God. Thus, "What is" is in God and nothing in reality is separate from its Divine Source. The world and God are united in an indissoluble bond. What man senses and knows cognitively, i.e., the seeming multiplicity of things, is an illusion. This seeming fragmentary nature of reality can however be overcome by a mystical intuition which reveals the underlying unity of reality.

As everything is really part of the Divine there is nothing which is wholly worthless or profane, nothing in which a 'spark' of Divinity does not rest. Here Kook draws heavily on the kabbalistic doctrine of the "Divine Sparks" which hide in everything. The aim of life, in Kook's system, as in classical Kabbalah and Hasidic thought, is to re-unite these "sparks" with their source, i.e., God, and thus bring about a total and final re-unification which is equivalent in this system to redemption or messianism. These traditional doctrines are now re-defined in the light of an emanationist theory of reality and its goal.

Kook tries to synthesize this mystical doctrine with a type of Darwinian naturalism to which all nature is seen as evolving toward God, a process which is propelled by an inner purposeful, dynamic force pointing toward the goal of final reunification of things with their Source. Jews have a special role to play in this cosmic drama of reunification and they can only play their role in their own land (the root of Kook's religious Zionism). The uniqueness of the people, Israel, lies in its special dimension of holiness which surrounds it. This quality allows it to recognize and respond to the "sparks" of Divinity which lie dormant in all of creation. Israel builds the world's redemption through its work of redeeming the "sparks" and thus works toward the Messianic era.

Abraham Isaac Kook at the cornerstone laying of the Kenesset Israel quarter, Jerusalem, 1925.

Franz Rosenzweig.

FRANZ ROSENZWEIG

Born in Kassel in 1886, Rosenzweig was the son of cultured parents whose adherence to Judaism was minimal and largely motivated by reactions to anti-Semitism. Rosenzweig entered university in 1905, studying a variety of disciplines, in a number of cities. Eventually he concentrated on philosophy, history, and classics. Friedrich Meinecke the historian had a great personal and intellectual influence on Rosenzweig. During this period, several of Rosenzweig's friends and relatives converted to Christianity, and he too contemplated conversion, arguing that he and his friends were Jews in name only—culturally, they were already Christians. However, he refrained from converting, because like his parents, he regarded conversion as a socially cowardly act.

In 1912, in Leipzig, he ran into a distant relative, Eugen Rosenstock-Huessy, who was on his way to becoming an unconventional but significant Protestant theologian. Out of his own highly literate and passionate faith, Rosenstock urged Rosenzweig to defend his nominal Jewishness or convert. After an intensive discussion on the night of July 7, 1913, Rosenzweig decided to convert, making only the reservation that he would become a Christian not as "a pagan" but "as a Jew," i.e., not by rejecting his Jewish origin but by recapitulating the consummation of Judaism in Christianity. He enacted this resolution by attending High Holiday services in a small Orthodox synagogue in Berlin, and he came out of this experience reversing his decision: he now declared that he knew himself to be a Jew; that the Jew does not need to seek God, for he is already with God; and that he intended henceforth to recover Judaism for himself and, possibly, for others like him. The circumstances under which this "return" to Judaism occurred continued to influence Rosenzweig's life and religious views to the end. He conducted an erudite and lengthy correspondence on Judaism and Christianity with Rosenstock while the two were soldiers during World War I, stationed far away from one another.[16] Rosenstock-Huessy's fundamental notion, that revelation, the incursion of the divine into history, is the point around which men organize their world and experiences, not only became the chief thesis of Rosenzweig's first Jewish theological essay, *Atheistische Theologie* ("Atheistic Theology,"[17]) but also the cornerstone of his later theological magnum opus. The Jewish liturgy, the calendar of the Jewish year, etc., became the building blocks of his theological edifice. To intensify his knowledge of Judaism, Rosenzweig went to Berlin where he fell under the spell of Hermann Cohen, then teaching at the liberal rabbinical seminary, having retired from the University of Marburg. Here he also made his first acquaintance with, among others, Martin Buber, who was to become his close friend and colleague. In 1917 his *Das aelteste Systemprogramm des deutschen Idealismus* was published. In this work, Rosenzweig identifies as Schelling's a manuscript written in Hegel's hand, which constituted Schelling's only attempt to formulate a unified system of idealism. Out of his prewar doctoral dissertation grew the important two-volume study *Hegel und der Staat* (Hegel and the State), published in 1920. By this time, however, his interest in general philosophy and German history had taken second place to his Jewish concerns. As a soldier during the war he experienced some of the "Jewish authenticity" of the Eastern European Jewish populace; he studied a great deal and wrote essays about the needed reforms in general as well as Jewish education. During the war he contracted an illness which is believed to have been the cause of his eventual fatal desease. During these years a close personal and intellectual relationship developed between him and Hermann Cohen, although their philosophical positions were far apart—Cohen being a reformed classical neo-Kantian, and Rosenzweig being oriented toward "life-philosophy" and existentialism. Rosenzweig also differed sharply with Cohen's somewhat hyperbolic German patriotism.

The most important product of the war years was his major work *Der Stern der Erloesung* ("The Star of Redemption," 1921)[18] which he began to write on postcards sent home from his military stations in August 1918 and which he completed in February 1919 after his return. In this difficult work he tries to formulate a "new thinking"[19] to outline a history of culture, and to propose a philosophical theology of Judaism and Christianity. The three parts of the work can be summarized as follows:

BOOK 1. The experience of "the fear of death" is completely private and cannot be conceptualized; thus it destroys philosophy's pretension that it is able to unify the cosmos and all experience. Rosenzweig regards the world as manifold, as being constituted of three elements—man, the universe, and God—and he rejects philosophy's attempt to reduce these three elements to one basic element on the grounds that this reductionism does not conform to reality. While in the "pagan" world view these three elements are independent and unrelated, according to the biblical view they interact through the processes of creation, revelation, and redemption. Revelation—which becomes possible once philosophy has been assigned its limited place—is initiated by God as the process of relating, first God to man, and then man to God, and through his life man to the world. "Truth," then, is not any set of abstract principles. Following Rosenstock's emphasis on "subjectivity," Rosenzweig maintains that truth is subjective, is arrived at by the individual on the basis of his own personal existence, and can be verified only in the life of the individual.

BOOK 2. Revelation so understood is clearly not an historical event but the continuous entry into relationship with man on the part of God. Revelation is the fundamental fact upon which biblical and all true religion is built. It takes a verbal form, and its content is not any kind of addition to the previously existing stuff of the universe but simply God's identification of Himself to man in love. This divine love evokes a response of love in man, which is expressed also in man's relationships with his neighbor. This love relation creates ties between man-God-man-man which extricates man from his basic isolation and gives his life meaning and value. Following a Kantian distinction, Rosenzweig distinguishes between "laws" *(Gesetz)*, which are universal, and "commandments" *(Gebot)*, which are personal. Though revelation does not comprise laws, commandments addressed to the individual are born out of the love relationship, which when carried out, change life. In his later argument with Buber in "The Builders,"[20] Rosenzweig broadens this conception by holding that the Jew must open himself up to the *halakhah* as an at least potential channel of the love commandments. What a man "cannot yet" accept, may, in the course of time and with real effort, become possible and, therefore, incumbent upon him.

BOOK 3. Men's desire, in prayer, action, and hope, for the repetition and permanent reality of the revelatory experience in community is the search for the kingdom of God. The people of Israel entered into this kingdom of eternity from the outset through his covenantal relation with God. The Jew is naturally born a Jew, and the continuity of the Jewish people is biological—thus biology, in the spirit of Judah Halevi, is a theological value. The Jew lives eternity essentially through the religious calendar and liturgy. Israel is outside the stream of history, in which the nations of the world are still flowing toward "the end of days." It has no need of history which is the sphere of "becoming" for it already is with God from the beginning. It is the risky business of Christianity to carry its own members and the rest of mankind toward the consummation in which God will be "all in all." Christians are, therefore, always converts to Christianity, which is superimposed upon their pagan origin and base. The language of the world of redemption, attained or envisioned, is liturgical chorus. Judaism and Christianity are both partial truths in history equally valid for their respective communities (i.e., there are two covenants with God each representing a different function and way towards Him), and both will be superseded by the absolute truth in the "end of days."[21]

Settled again in civilian life, Rosenzweig determined to devote himself to the pedagogical task of turning himself and as many fellow-Jews as he could influence into real Jews. He moved to Frankfort on the Main, where, with the help of an intellectually and Jewishly variegated group of men, including the orthodox rabbi N. Nobel, Martin Buber, Eduard Strauss, Richard Koch, Erich Fromm, Ernst Simon, G. Scholem, N. Glatzer, and others—men who were to become immensely influential— he organized the Freies Juedisches Lehrhaus ("Free Jewish House of Learning"). This was conducted along the educational lines he had for- mulated in various essays: regardless of their respective levels of academic qualification, in Jewish studies teachers and students were tyros together, trying to move from the periphery of European culture where they found themselves toward the center of authentic Jewish sources. Thus an emphasis on the classic texts was combined with the empathy which existed among the self-consciously "homeless" Jewish intellectuals.

In 1921 progressive paralysis set in; he soon lost, almost completely, his mobility and his power of speech. After July 1922 he was confined to his home, but not only did he live for seven years, he even continued his intellectual and literary activities. His confinement contributed to his increasing observance of Jewish law. His colleagues and friends visited him at home and held services there. Rabbi Leo Baeck bestowed a rab- binical teacher's title on him. Rosenzweig's wife, with the help of a specially constructed machine, deciphered his thoughts and wishes. He concentrated on talmudic studies and listened to much recorded music, and he conducted an active and wide correspondence until his death.

The main literary products of Rosenzweig's years of confinement are translations from Hebrew into German. These are of value not only in literary terms but also for their philosophical and theological implications, which he often spelled out himself. Thus his German renderings of liturgical poems by Judah Halevi are accompanied not only by a lengthy introduction which deals with the philosophy and problems of translation but also by many, often extended, footnotes that discuss the religious and theological subject matter of individual poems.[22]

In 1924 Rosenzweig and Martin Buber began a new translation of the Bible. By the time of Rosenzweig's death they had reached the Book of Isaiah.[23] Buber completed the project in the 1950s in Israel. Essays which the two wrote in connection with this undertaking, dealing with the principles of their translation and specific problems encountered in it, were gathered and published in Berlin under the title *Die Schrift und ihre Verdeutschung* (1936). The chief principle underlying Rosenzweig's translating activity is the notion that all human languages, like all groupings of mankind, are diverse developments from one single source; it must be possible, therefore, by tracing languages sufficiently far back, to find a common etymological root which will supply the basis for the proper translation of any expression in one language into its counterpart in any other. The intentional result of this methodology is that the Bible translation reads like strongly Hebraized German, forcing the reader into shocked attention rather than pious passivity. The translators also tried to reproduce in German what they believed to be the originally intended and traditionally preserved oral quality of the biblical texts. In accordance with their theological doctrine that the God of the Bible enters into unpredictable relations with men and is encountered only in this fashion, they rendered His traditionally unpronounceable name in the pronominal form appropriate to the grammatical occurrence, "You," "He," etc.

In general Rosenzweig's views of the Bible must be regarded as "post-critical." Fully conversant with so-called Bible criticism, he held that the important question to be asked about the Bible is not concerned with its origins but with its fate, not what the authors had in mind but what the reader gets out of it; in other words, the Bible read as history in the synagogue is carried forward by the contemporary reader's understanding. He symbolized this view by suggesting that the "R" (redactor) of the Bible critics ought to be read as "(Moses) *rabbenu*" ("(Moses) our teacher"). Whereas in the critical reading, divine anthropomorphisms are primitive remnants, in his they are quasi-Platonic paradigms of human features.

Rosenzweig did not share the view of such contemporaries of his as Rav Kook, A. D. Gordon and his close friend Martin Buber, that Zionism was a creative manifestation of the deepest elements of Jewish spirituality and in its wake would create new avenues and expressions of the Hebraic spirit. Zionism in its active, political enterprise was interpreted by Rosenzweig in terms of political necessity and the need for the escape from physical extermination rather than in positive religious terms. Rosenzweig, however, was realist enough to appreciate the fact that the continued survival of Judaism depended on the physical survival of Jews and in this very practical sense he supported the activist program of the political Zionists while rejecting its ideology. However, Rosenzweig's view of the Jewish people as an entity outside history made his posture toward Zionism ambivalent. On the one hand, he favored the Zionist thrust toward self-authentication and self-extrication from European acculturation; on the other hand, the trend toward political Zionist activity and goals clashed with his belief that Jewish redemption could come about only with the eschatological dissolution of exile and alienation.

Influence. In Jewish religious circles Rosenzweig's thought has exerted a significant influence. One reason for this is that the men who were associated with him and who long survived him, carried his imprint through their own, often noteworthy, intellectual careers. Among them one can list men such as A. J. Heschel, S. H. Bergman, Ignaz Maybaum, Ernst Simon, and Nahum Glatzer. In the *Commentary Symposium* conducted in 1965, Rosenzweig was credited by the modern Jewish thinkers polled with being the most influential modern Jewish thinker, being much more influential within Jewish circles than his colleague Martin Buber. Probably the single most important reason for his influence is his suggestive approach to the *halakhah* which, while being more positive than that of Reform Judaism (or the anti- or meta-nomianism of Buber), still does not accept the *halakhah* as binding without question or personal committment. It is also probable that his "double covenant" theory of Judaism and Christianity will attract increasing attention over the years as will his thought in general, insofar as the central problems with which he wrestled in the early part of the 20th century, especially that of Jewish authenticity in the face of modern secularity, are still our problems today.

MARTIN BUBER

Born in Vienna in 1878, Buber as a child lived in Lemberg with his grandfather Solomon Buber, the noted Midrash scholar. From 1896 he studied at the universities of Vienna, Leipzig, and Zurich, and finally at the University of Berlin, where he was a pupil of the philosophers Wilhelm Dilthey and Georg Simmel. Having joined the Zionist movement in 1898, he was a delegate to the Third Zionist Congress in 1899 where he spoke on behalf of the Propaganda Committee. In this speech, which bore the influence of modern Hebrew and Yiddish writers, notably of Aḥad Ha-Am, Buber emphasized the importance of education as opposed to a program of propaganda. In 1901 he was appointed editor of the central weekly organ of the Zionist movement, *Die Welt,* in which he emphasized the need for a new Jewish cultural creativity. This emphasis on cultural rather than political activity led, at the Fifth Zionist Congress in 1901, to the formation of the Zionist Democratic Fraction which stood in opposition to Herzl. Buber, a member of this faction, resigned before the Congress as editor of *Die Welt.* Together with his friends, he founded the Juedischer Verlag in Berlin, which went on to publish (in German) books of literary quality.

At the age of 26 Buber took up the study of Ḥasidism. At first his interest was essentially aesthetic. After attempting to translate the tales of Rabbi Naḥman of Bratslav into German, he decided to retell them in German in the form of a free adaptation. Later Buber's interest turned from the aesthetic aspect of Ḥasidism to its content. Deeply stirred by the religious message of Ḥasidism, he considered it his duty to convey that message to the world. Among the books he later wrote on Ḥasidism are *Gog u-Magog* (1941; translated into English under the title *For the Sake of Heaven,* 1945), *Or ha-Ganuz* (1943), and *Pardes ha-Ḥasidut* (1945; translated into English in two volumes *Ḥasidism and Modern Man,* 1958, and *The Origin and Meaning of Hasidism,* 1960).

In 1909 Buber resumed an active role in public affairs. He delivered three addresses to the Prague student organization, Bar Kochba, in 1909, 1910, and 1911,[24] which had a great influence on Jewish youth in Central Europe, and also marked a turning point in Buber's own intellectual activity. With the outbreak of World War I Buber founded in Berlin the Jewish National Committee which worked throughout the war on behalf of the Jews in Eastern European countries under German occupation, and on behalf of the *yishuv* in Palestine. In 1916 he founded the monthly *Der Jude*, which for eight years was the most important organ of the Jewish renaissance movement in Central Europe. In the spring of 1920, at the convention of Ha-Po'el ha-Ẓa'ir-Ẓe'irei Ẓiyyon[25] in Prague, Buber defined his Zionist socialist position and his adherence to utopian socialism in an address which reflected his affinity to Aharon David Gordon and Gustav Landauer. He was opposed to the current concept of socialism which looked upon the state, and not upon a reaffirmation of life and of the relationship between man and man, as the means of realizing the socialist society. Buber envisaged the creation of *Gemeinschaften* in Palestine, communities in which people would live together in direct personal relationship. During the years following World War I Buber became the spokesman for what he called "Hebrew Humanism," according to which Zionism, described as the "holy way," a notion explained in *Der heilige Weg* (1919), was different from other nationalistic movements. Buber also emphasized that Zionism should address itself also to the needs of the Arabs and in a proposal to the Zionist Congress of 1921 stated that " . . . the Jewish people proclaims its desire to live in peace and brotherhood with the Arab people and to develop the common homeland into a republic in which both peoples will have the possibility of free development." In 1923 Buber published his *Ich und Du* (I and Thou),[26] which contains the basic formulation of his philosophy of dialogue. In 1925 the first volumes of the German translation of the Bible appeared as the combined effort of Buber and Franz Rosenzweig. In *Die Schrift und ihre Verdeutschung* (1936) the translators set forth the guiding principles of their translation: today's reader of the Bible has ceased to be a listener; but the Bible does not seek to be read, but to be listened to, as if its voice were being spoken today. The Bible has been divested of its direct impact. In the choice of words, in sentence-structure, and in rhythm, Buber and Rosenzweig attempted to preserve the original character of the Hebrew Bible. After Rosenzweig's death in 1929 Buber continued the work of translation alone.

In 1925 Buber began to lecture on Jewish religion and ethics at the University of Frankfort, and in 1930 he was appointed professor of religion there, a position he retained until 1933, when with the rise of the Nazis to power he was forced to leave the university. In 1932 Buber published his *Koenigtum Gottes* (Kingship of God)[27] which was to be the first volume of a series dealing with the origins of the messianic belief in Judaism. This work was never completed. During the beginning of the Nazi period Buber traveled throughout Germany lecturing, teaching, and encouraging his fellow Jews, and thus organized something of a spiritual resistance. In 1935 he was forbidden to speak at Jewish gatherings.

In 1938 Buber settled in Palestine and was appointed professor of social philosophy at the Hebrew University. In 1942 his first book written in Hebrew, *Torat ha-Nevi'im (The Prophetic Faith),*[28] was published. This book, a history of biblical faith, is based on the supposition that the mutuality of the covenant between God and Israel testifies that the existence of the Divine Will is as real as the existence of Israel. Another book born out of Buber's efforts to penetrate the essential meaning of the Bible is his *Moses* (1946). Buber in his later years remained very active in public affairs and in Jewish cultural endeavors. He was one of the leaders of Iḥud, formerly Berit Shalom, which advocated the establishment of a joint Arab-Israel state. Even after the outbreak of the Arab-Israel war, Buber called for a harnessing of nationalistic impulses and a solution based on compromise. Buber was the first president of the Israel Academy of Sciences and Humanities (1960–62). In the years following World War II Buber lectured extensively outside Israel, and became known throughout the world as one of the spiritual leaders of his generation, making a deep impact on Christian as well as Jewish thinkers.

Philosophy of Dialogue. The starting point of Buber's philosophy is not man in himself nor the world in itself but rather the relation between man and the world. In *Ich und Du (I–Thou)* Buber distinguished two basic forms of relation—the *I–Thou* and *I–It,* into which all man's relations, both with other men and with things in the world, can be divided. The *I–Thou* relation is characterized by mutuality, openness, directness, and presentness; the *I–It,* by the absence of these qualities. The *I–Thou* relation is a true dialogue in which both partners speak to one another as equals. The *I–It* relation is not a true dialogue in that the partners are not equals but one uses the other to achieve some end. It is impossible to sustain an *I–Thou* relationship indefinitely, and it is inevitable that every Thou will at times turn into an It. The *I–It* relation is not evil in itself, for it is only through the *I–It* relation that objective knowledge will be acquired, and technical advances achieved. In the healthy man and culture there is a dialectical interaction between the *I–Thou* and *I–It* relationships. As a result of this dialectical interaction *I–Thou* relationships become *I–It* relationships which find their expression in knowledge and art, and these relationships in turn contain within themselves the possibility of becoming once again *I–Thou* relationships.

In *The Knowledge of Man* (1965) Buber systematically develops his "dialogical theory of knowledge," an epistemology based on the *I–Thou* relation. While Buber, like Kant, maintains that we cannot have objective knowledge of the universe as it is in itself, and that we know the world only through the categories which are imposed upon it, he does hold that in *I–Thou* relationships we can have direct contact with objects in the world although we can never know them in themselves. Our sense perception is built on this direct contact, and the *I–Thou* relation is, therefore, the basis of all knowledge of the world and of all art.

Buber's analysis of the *I–Thou* relation among men leads him to his notion of God as the *Eternal Thou,* and to his description of the relation between man and God as an *I–Thou* relation. God, the *Eternal Thou,* is known not through cognitive propositions, or through metaphysical speculation, but through one's particular *I–Thou* relationships with persons, animals, nature, and works of art and of course with God Himself. The *Eternal Thou,* met in every finite Thou, is itself the very uniqueness and concreteness of each particular *I–Thou* meeting. It is these meetings with the *Eternal Thou* which, according to Buber, constitute revelation. Revelation is only another term for relation between God and man. Thus revelation is not only something that happened at particular moments in the past at Mount Sinai or the burning bush, but something that can happen in the present, throughout one's life, if one is open to receive it. Buber's understanding of revelation as relation is one of his most fundamental and radical claims. According to his philosophy revelation is not, as traditionally believed, the disclosure by God to man of some objective content in the form of norms or directives on which man must act and base his life. Revelation, argues Buber, is never of objective content. Rather, in revelation one comes "face to face" with the *Eternal Thou* and through this encounter one affirms the meaningfulness of one's life and of life in general. What is revealed to man is God's "Presence" alone.

Buber claimed in *Ich und Du,* and elsewhere throughout his works, that the revelations in the Bible are in accordance with this dialogical account of revelation. Biblical revelation differs in degree of intensity not in quality or kind from the personal revelations, possible in ordinary life, to contemporary men and women. For Buber the Bible is: "a record of the dialogical encounters between man and God."[29] Buber's view denies the possibility that God's revelation can ever take the form of law. This possibility is denied because Buber believed that if God's revelation contained law it would corrupt the dialogical situation and turn the God-man encounter into an *I–It* relation. Accordingly, he held that all biblical law is not the content of actual revelation, but the human response to revelation; the product of man's attempt to solidify the Divine Presence revealed to him in a form which is constant and objective.[30]

This view seems to undermine traditional Judaism and its entire halakhic structure. Buber was aware of this and entered into a famous correspondence on this issue with Franz Rosenzweig.[31] However Buber was not convinced by Rosenzweig's arguments and never altered his view. Many have suggested that Buber's view is antinomian, while some, like Nahum Glatzer,[32] have suggested that it is not antinomian but meta-nomian. However, a thorough logical analysis of Buber's account suggests that there is little room for denying that ultimately Buber's account of revelation does invalidate the *halakhah* and the entire understanding of traditional Judaism which is predicated on the assumption that God is a Lawgiver in principle and that He did, in fact, give Israel the laws of the Torah at Mount Sinai. Buber was committed to the view that the Hebrew Bible is not a dead book but living speech in which the *"Eternal Thou"* of the past becomes present again to the one who truly listens. In this belief Buber drew upon and shared the most profound sentiments of his people, even if his account of the mechanics of this biblical dynamism is highly problematic.[33]

Buber's Ḥasidism. Buber is responsible for transforming Ḥasidism from a little known pietistic-mystical Jewish sect into a religious phenomenon which has become part of the modern religious consciousness among Jews and non-Jews.[34] For more than 50 years Buber edited, translated and explained Ḥasidism to the western world. In Ḥasidism Buber believed that he had discovered the most authentic modern religious community in which the prophetic dialogue of biblical religion was renewed. Buber believed that Ḥasidism's message was crucially important for modern man who had lost the vision of holiness and relation which Buber thought was at the center of the ḥasidic doctrine. In the relation between the ḥasidic Ẓaddik (leader of the ḥasidic community) and his followers the Ḥasidim, Buber saw the paradigm of *I-Thou* relation and in ḥasidic communities the paradigm of community life based on dialogical foundations.

Ḥasidism, based on the doctrines of Lurianic Kabbalah, taught that in everything and everyone there was a "spark" of the Divine which needed to be liberated and restored to its rightful place. Buber interpreted this as meaning that everything in the world is potentially sacred and all that is required to sanctify things is human energy directed in an *I-Thou* fashion. The meaning of redemption and messianism are, therefore, not other-worldly doctrines but the concrete actions of transforming the given world of everyday existence in which the "sparks" of Divinity reside. Man fulfills his destiny and concurrently works on the Divinely appointed task "not by any special work, but by the intention with which he does all his works. It is the teaching of the hallowing of the everyday."[35]

This world-affirming doctrine has had very wide appeal. However it is a question of importance whether or not Buber rightly interprets Ḥasidism, and whether what he claims to be the essence of Ḥasidism is actually Ḥasidism or some image of Ḥasidism which Buber has created largely by reflecting his own *I-Thou* philosophy. In the most important article so far written on Buber's version of Ḥasidism, Gershom Scholem,[36] the world's outstanding authority on Jewish mysticism, has argued that Buber's version of Ḥasidism is not correct and that in many fundamental respects the teachings of Ḥasidism are opposed to the world-affirming dialogical "hallowing of the everyday" which Buber sees as the center of ḥasidic life and teaching.

Buber and Christianity. While Buber is far from saying that this dialogical situation is peculiar to Judaism, he does argue that there is no

Martin Buber.

other group that has invested this concept of God and man with so much spiritual force as the Jews. He stresses the gulf between Judaism and certain currents of Protestantism that emphasize the passivity that is demanded of man in his relationship to God, and argues against those Catholic theologians who maintain that Judaism is an activism unmindful of the grace of God. His concept of the life of faith as the life of dialogue between man and God has had a deep influence on contemporary Christian theology. This influence on Catholic theologians is discernible in the writings of Gabriel Marcel, Theodor Steinbuechel and Ernst Michel (the very title of Michel's book, *The Partner of God,* testifies to his proximity to Buber), and on Protestant thinkers, in the works of Paul Tillich, Wilhelm Michel, Walther Nigg, and J. H. Oldham.

Despite his widespread influence in Christian circles, and the many sympathetic things he has said about Jesus and Christianity, Buber was a critic of Christianity in general. In his full length work devoted to the question of Christianity, *Two Types of Faith,* Buber argues that Jesus was a good Jew who shared authentic Jewish faith which he calls *Emunah.* However, primarily because of Paul, the Church turned away from the authentic Jewish faith relation to God, and replaced it with an improper dogmatic faith in Christ which which Buber calls *Pistis.* The Messiah has not come as the unredeemedness of the world attests and all claims to the contrary are mistaken. Though this is close to the traditional view of Christianity by Jews and Judaism, Buber's views are marked out by their sensitive appreciation of the person of Jesus as a Jewish teacher, and their intimate familiarity with the New Testament and Christian scholarship.

MORDECAI MENAHEM KAPLAN

Mordecai Kaplan, U.S. rabbi and minister, founded the Reconstructionist movement (see below). Kaplan taught at the Jewish Theological Seminary for five decades and influenced generations of Conservative rabbis. As a student of the history of Jewish thought Kaplan has made significant contributions. He edited and translated *Mesillat Yesharim* by Moses Ḥayyim Luzzatto (1937, 1966), contributed a study of Hermann Cohen's philosophy, *The Meaning and Purpose of Jewish Existence* (1964), and described modern Jewish ideologies in *The Greater Judaism in the Making* (1960).

In formulating his philosophy of Reconstructionism, Kaplan drew upon traditional Jewish sources, Haskalah thinkers, and American philosophical pragmatism. He defined Judaism as an "evolving religious civilization," attempting thereby to aid in the adjustment of world Jewry to the social and intellectual conditions of the 20th century. He maintained that as a "civilization" the Jewish people possess all the characteristics of land, polity, and culture subsumed under that designation, but that in each aspect of civilization radical adjustments in Jewish social

Mordecai Menahem Kaplan.

theory and polity are essential. Therefore, while Kaplan has always been an ardent Zionist, he has equally insisted that the creative survival of the Jewish people in the Diaspora is both possible and desirable.

By "religious" Kaplan means that Jewish civilization expresses its genius best in clarifying the purposes and values of human existence, in wrestling with God (who is conceived in nonpersonal terms), and in the ritual of home, synagogue, and community. However, because Judaism is a civilization, the secular elements of culture are essential to Jewish spirituality; they curb the tendency of religion toward rigidity, uniformity, and worship of the past. Thus, Jewish religion embraces both the purpose and the unconscious product of the Jewish people's search for a meaningful existence for itself.

By "evolving" Kaplan means that Judaism should be considered from a pragmatic, historical point of view, rather than a metaphysical, revelational one. The focus of the content of Jewish life is the Jewish people, its needs, and its responses to challenge, rather than revealed texts or metaphysical constructions. Kaplan argues that the Jewish people will not accept a static theory of Judaism. Each Jew must solve life's perplexities for himself. Tradition can guide but must not dictate. Even Kaplan's own naturalistic approach can be only one option. Henceforth, Jews must learn to live with and cherish diversity.

Kaplan's religious naturalism and humanism challenge both the belief in historical revelation and those theologies grounded on metaphysical interpretations of revelation. He argues that the idea of God is correlative to the idea of man and that conceptions of God necessarily bear an organic relationship to man's understanding of himself and the world. Kaplan regards God as that power in the universe on which man must rely for the achievement of his destiny (or, in theological terms, his salvation). Kaplan's views undermine the accepted forms of worship, ritual, and religious authority. The major foundation of Kaplan's views is to be found in his *Judaism as a Civilization* (1934).

This account of Jewish philosophy concludes with thinkers who were active primarily before 1945,[37] mostly in Germany—a Jewish civilization now destroyed. The thought of major thinkers who have been active since 1945, and the issues they have been concerned with, are treated in Part Four of this work: 'Jewish Thought since 1945'.[38]

NOTES TO PART THREE

[1] Letter LXXIV to Burgh.

[2] See Leon Roth, *Spinoza, Descartes and Maimonides* (1924).

[3] This argument was first conceived by Anselm, Archbishop of Canterbury, in his *Proslogion* and later became the favorite proof of the 17th century naturalists Spinoza, Leibniz, and Descartes, to whom Mendelssohn was so indebted.

[4] The *Phaedon* was translated into English in 1784.

[5] For Leibniz's views see his *Monadology* and his *Theodicy*. Both are available in English translations.

[6] These are usually referred to in the Jewish tradition as the "Noachide Laws," i.e., the laws of natural justice and morality given (according to *Genesis* 9:1-17) to Noah as the laws which were to govern the relations of all men. See also the discussion in *Sanhedrin* 56-60; *Yad:* Melakhim, 8:10, 10:12.

[7] The *Be'ur* (1780-1783) was a revolutionary work. For more details of this and Mendelssohn's other Hebrew works see Shalom Spiegel, *Hebrew Reborn* 1930) and P. Sandler's Hebrew work *Ha-Be'ur le-Torah shel Moshe Mendelssohn* (1951). For additional works on Mendelssohn see the bibliography.

[8] *Moreh Nevukhei ha-Zeman,* originally published by Leopold Zunz (1851), was edited by Simon Rawidowicz in 1924. The revised critical edition of this work was published in the collected writings of Krochmal published in 1961, *Kitvei Rabbi Nahman Krochmal.*

[9] This is the doctrine referred to by the Kabbalists as *"Zimzum"*—the process whereby God contracts Himself in order to allow space for a world which then flows from His Being.

[10] "Die Platonische Ideenlehre" in the *Zeitschrift fur Voelkerpsychologie und Sprachwissenschaft* (1866).

[11] Ein Bekenntnis in der Judenfrage" (1880) in *Judische Schriften,* 2 (1924) pgs. 73-94.

[12] "Religion und Zionismus" in *Judische Schriften,* 2 (1924) pgs. 319-327.

[13] See his remarkably patriotic essay extolling the glories of German ideals and their similarity to Judaism entitled "Deutschtum und Judentum" (1915) in *Judische Schriften,* vol. 2 (1924) pgs. 237-301.

[14] *Wesen des Judentums* was translated into English as the *Essence of Judaism* in 1936. This work had 10 German printings and in addition to the English translation it was translated into Hebrew (1968) and Japanese.

[15] For Baeck's views on Christianity see his *Judaism and Christianity,* translated by W. Kaufman (1958). The essay on Christianity originally appeared in *Festschrift zum 50 jaehrigen Bestehen der Hochschule fur die Wissenschaft des Judentums* (1922) pgs. 1-48.

[16] This remarkable correspondence has now been published in an English translation as *Judaism Despite Christianity,* ed. by Harold Staehmer (1969). It originally appeared in German, see *Briefe,* ed. by E. Rosenzweig and E. Simon (1935).

[17] "Atheistische Theologie" in *Kleinere Schriften* (1937). See also the article by Goldy and Hoch in the *Canadian Journal of Theology,* 14 (1968) p. 79ff.

[18] *Der Stern der Erloesung* was first published in 1921 and re-issued in 1930 and 1954. It was translated into English by W. Hallo as *The Star of Redemption* (1971).

[19] "The New Thinking" ("Das Neue Denken") is the title of a famous essay written by Rosenzweig in which he summarizes his basic "existentialist" views and the reasons for his rejection of Idealism. He had set out these views at great length in his *magnum opus, The Star of Redemption.* See "Das neue Denken" in Rosenzweig's *Kleinere Schriften* (1937), pgs. 373–398. Part of this essay has been translated by Nahum Glatzer in his study of Rosenzweig entitled *Franz Rosenzweig* (1961), pgs. 190–208.

[20] For Rosenzweig's argument with Buber over Jewish Law and the nature of revelation see "The Builders" (English translation) in *On Jewish Education,* ed. Nahum Glatzer (1955) pgs. 72–92.

[21] Despite Rosenzweig's "two covenant theory" it appears that Sinai retains primacy in his thinking. See the essay by S. Schwarzschild in *Conservative Judaism,* 11 (1956–57) pgs. 41–58.

[22] Rosenzweig's translations and commentaries on Judah Halevi can be found in his *Sechzig Hymnen und Gedichte des Jehuda Halevi* (1924); *Zweiundneunzig Hymnen und Gedichte* (1927); *Zionslieder mit der Verdeutschung von F. Rosenzweig und Seinen Anmerkungen* (1933).

[23] *Die Schrift* translated by Buber and Rosenzweig, 10 vols. up to 1925.

[24] These essays were published in English in *At the Turning* (1952) and reissued in 1967 in *On Judaism* ed. N. Glatzer. See also the essay by S. H. Bergman in *Ha-Shilo'aḥ* 26 (1912) pgs. 549–556.

[25] The Labor Zionist group.

[26] *I and Thou* appeared in an English translation prepared by R. G. Smith in 1937. A new translation by Walter Kaufmann appeared in 1970.

[27] The third German edition (1956) of *Koenigtum Gottes* was translated into English in 1967 as *The Kingship of God.*

[28] *Torat ha-Nevi'im* was translated into English in 1949 as *The Prophetic Faith.*

[29] Quoted from Malcolm Diamond, *Martin Buber, Jewish Existentialist* (1960) p. 92.

[30] For a discussion of Buber's views on Revelation see E. Fackenheim's essay in the *Library of Living Philosophers* volume dedicated to Buber.

[31] See the correspondence in *On Jewish Education* ed. N. Glatzer (1955) pgs. 109–118.

[32] See N. Glatzer's introduction (p. 22) to *On Jewish Learning* (1955).

[33] For a critical appraisal of Buber's view of revelation and *halakhah* see A. Cohen's essay "Revelation and Law: Reflections on Martin Buber's View of Halachah", in *Judaism* I (July 1952) pgs. 250–256.

[34] For Martin Buber's works on Ḥasidism see bibliography.

[35] M. Buber, *The Origin and Meaning of Hasidism* p. 127.

[36] G. Scholem, "Martin Buber's Hasidism: A Critique" in *Commentary* (October 1961); reprinted in Scholem's *The Messianic Idea in Judaism and Other Essays* (1971). See also the important critical article by Rivka Shatz-Uffenheimer in the *Library of Living Philosophers* volume on Martin Buber.

[37] Of course, Buber was still active after 1945 in Israel as were Baeck and Kaplan in the U.S. However their most important work was done in the pre-war period and belongs to the influences and currents of that period.

[38] Mention should be made of a number of outstanding historians of Jewish philosophy whose work has been very valuable in elucidating and clarifying the nature, scope and value of Jewish thought. The most outstanding are: I. Husik; Julius Guttman; L. Strauss; A. Altmann; H.A. Wolfson; G. Vajda; S. Pines, and S. H. Bergman.

Part Four

JEWISH THOUGHT SINCE 1945

INTRODUCTION

Contemporary Jewish thought is most striking in its diversity and the plurality of its commitments. Today the historic bonds of family, Torah, and community—which were imbedded in an organic religious civilization and which classically provided the centripetal forces of Jewish social order and personal Jewish existence—have become increasingly brittle, in many places already being totally dissolved or on the way to total dissolution. The modern Jewish community, paradigmatically represented by its philosophers, theologians and literary personalities, is in quest of itself and its purpose.

Though Martin Buber and Franz Rosenzweig are unquestionably the two most influential thinkers on contemporary Jewish thought, even in areas where one would not expect it, the specific and varied application of their thought is so diverse—often being used to support diametrically antithetical positions—that one can safely argue that no one school of thought represents the current "orthodoxy." It would however be a correct generalization to assert that the majority of modern Jewish thinkers and the positions they advocate can be broadly described as belonging to the "existentialist" mood[1] which has dominated modern theology and European philosophy since World War II. The one outstanding exception to this generalization is Mordecai Kaplan's Reconstructionist position, which, already articulated clearly in the 1930's (his major work *Judaism as a Civilization* appeared in 1934) has been an influential position, at least in the U.S., since 1945.

The search for an "authentic contemporary Judaism" is not a uniquely contemporary problem. Someone familiar with Jewish intellectual history might even argue that it is as old as Judaism itself, that it is of the essence of the Prophets, of the Rabbinic tradition, of medieval Jewish thought, of Zionism, Neo-Orthodox and Reform Judaism. This past in part creates our present. However the actual situation addressed by and which addresses Jewish thinkers since 1945 has an unprecedented quality created by two overwhelming and transformative events in Jewish historical existence: the Holocaust and the rebirth of the State of Israel. Nazism and its aftermaths (one of which was the creation of the State of Israel) redefined the contemporary Jewish landscape. However anxious the pre-war Jew, however precarious the pre-war Jewish situation, however unsatisfactory and "inauthentic" the traditional answers seemed to many Jews before Hitler, everything has been qualitatively altered by Auschwitz and all that it symbolizes to the survivors (and every Jew is a "survivor"!). Now the Jewish thinker has to ask not only what it means to be a Jew in the modern world, but even more pointedly: "what does it mean to be a Jew after Auschwitz?" In partial answer at least he must deal with the "miracle" which is the State of Israel. Is God speaking to the survivors through her, and if so, how? What does national rebirth mean? What theological, philosophical, and some would even add "messianic," weight can she bear? And then again, is theodicy blasphemy in the face of the Ḥurban (the Holocaust)? Can we hear the voice of the living God in the testimony of the ruin and rubble of European Jewry and the exaltation and deliverance of Zion?

These two events have unquestionably and irrevocably altered Jewish history and Jewish destiny; they have also altered the character and tone of Jewish responses. If it is true that contemporary Jewish thought owes much, perhaps too much, to the existentialist and dialogical philosophies of Buber and Rosenzweig and other pre-war Jewish thinkers, it is also true that contemporary Jewish thought speaks with a new militancy about things Jewish, a militancy which was absent from all pre-war Jewish thinkers. It may be that Jews have learned that anti-Semitism will not go away if Jews "keep under cover"—the anti-Semites will pull the covers off!! Or it may be the rediscovered pride which comes from seeing President Shazar receiving the Pope in the sovereign State of Israel,[2] or the Israeli flag flying over Jerusalem; most probably it is a combination of all these. Whatever it is, Jews now seek the answers to their questions and investigate the sources of authenticity and the nature of meaning with a new sense that Judaism is not a "fossil"[3] and that it may have within its deepest structures the spiritual resources to address contemporary man. There is a new positiveness about Judaism and its vitality even before the actual enquiry begins, a new willingness to listen even before the address is spoken.

In what follows we shall explore various responses to the modern Jewish situation. We shall examine those thinkers and issues which have made the most profound impact.

ABRAHAM JOSHUA HESCHEL

Abraham Joshua Heschel (1907–72), one of the most influential modern philosophers of religion in the U.S., was born and studied in Europe, arriving in America in 1940; from 1945, he was professor of Jewish ethics and mysticism at the Jewish Theological Seminary of America.

As befits the scion of two great ḥasidic families, Heschel's work is united by a sense of the immediate and direct reality of God. Heschel does not work toward God's existence, he works from it: it is the presupposition of his *weltanschauung* which creates the possibility of his theology.[4] He argues that in the very givenness of the human situation man is aware that both his being and the meaning of his being are intelligible only against the backdrop of a more profound cause and purpose.

Drawing upon traditional Jewish sources, Heschel sees man's situation as a boundary situation in which man is called and sustained in being by God, and in which man's purpose and goal is found in meaningful relation with his Creator. This relational situation is the basic "religious" reality and Heschel's theology is an attempt to explicate it. Man and God are the two subjects of religious reality and the life of true religiosity is the record of their encounter and relation. *Man is not Alone* (1951), *Man's Quest for God* (1954), and *God in Search of Man* (1956), the titles of three of Heschel's major theological works, all reflect Heschel's vision of authentic religion as the dialectical interaction of man and God. Crucially significant in Heschel's phenomenology of encounter is his view, drawn from his study of biblical God-man relations and also clearly influenced by his intimate knowledge of kabbalistic-ḥasidic doctrines, that in such encounters God and man are both transformed by the power of the meeting. Religious relation is not one-sided; both the divine and human are affected by their intimacy. This is Heschel's "absolute pre-supposition" and it is this which forms the foundation of Heschel's vision.

For Heschel reality is always more than it appears. Through all things and all experience is suffused a divine-mysterious presence. Reality is a prism through which God is made manifest. In nature, in society, in history, all things point beyond themselves to their Divine origin; in all things men gain a glimpse of transcendence. The inherent quality of self-transcendence in experience gives men an intimation of the source of value and an assurance about the meaning and purpose of life. This spiritual dimension of reality is the ontological foundation of all that is. Yet despite its significance this dimension of reality is not knowable in any ordinary way, its very reality is not always apparent, its nature and existence are only obliquely recognized by men even at the most exalted of moments. Its very character requires that men refer to it by circumspection and call it "mystery" and "ineffable." It is at once the most important and elusive of things: "we have a certainty without knowledge: it is real without being expressible."[5]

Heschel does not argue for this understanding of things; he asserts it. Heschel possesses a powerful unitive vision of the interdependence of all reality and its supra-sensible, supra-empirical, foundation which can be intimated, addressed, responded to but never described in ordinary descriptive language or analyzed by logical or scientific means. For Heschel the religious man—potentially every man—shares this vision, senses the ineffable, and participates in the cosmic rhythm. Much to our detriment, however, modernity, with its technological and objective priorities, with its scientific and pragmatic concerns, de-sensitizes modern man to this transcendental dimension of human experience and to the "spiritual suggestiveness of reality."[6] We "see" things in terms of use and power, causal connectedness and results—not in terms of their self-transcendence, their spiritual grandeur or their power to reflect Divinity. Heschel's concern as a theologian is to break this circle of secular immanence and the chain of objectivity and liberate contemporary human spirituality and sensitivities.

Men do not "know" the dimension of reality we call the "mysterious" and the "ineffable"—they feel it. The "ineffable" is not a separate dimension of reality but a dimension of every reality. Accordingly, men can adopt three postures in their encounter with the world which might be described[7] as: (1) the political-technocratic; (2) the aesthetic;

(3) the religious. If we adopt the first we will attempt to exploit the world, if the second we will attempt to enjoy the world, if the third we will accept it with awe.[8] Ours is an age in which the first two responses dominate, in which the awareness of the world's sublimity has been all but lost. This loss is the source of contemporary societal and personal *anomie*, of the felt "absurdity" of modern existence and of the cruel face man sees in nature, history, and his neighbor. Contemporary man needs to re-discover the "awe-fulness" of reality, the transcendent dimension in the immanent, in order to revivify and re-direct his life.

To evoke the 'ineffable' in our own lives a mediating source and model of authentic spirituality is required and Heschel argues that this is found, paradigmatically, in Hebrew Scripture. Scripture is the record of an authentic human response to the Divine address, and as such an authoritative model. Biblical man sensed the Divine mystery and responded appropriately in wonder and awe.[9] A renewed recognition of the former and the lived response of the latter are the pressing needs of our generation.

Still more important however, biblical man discovered that the transcendental reality revealed in and through nature and history was a moral, personal, God, who was more appropriately alluded to as Father than as Being, Cause, or Intellect. Biblical man met and articulated the Mystery as "personal" rather than "impersonal" being, as concerned rather than indifferent reality. Above all else biblical religion is seen as God's loving concern for His creatures and men's loving concern for his God. The transitive concern of God and man's sympathetic response to the Divine are the two complementary axes of human life and meaning. The biblical witness does not reveal propositional truths about God-in-Himself; rather it reveals the ongoing diary of God's relations with Israel, of God's actions and Israel's reactions, of God's demands and man's responses. The Bible is not a metaphysical treatise, it is an epic love poem about the intimate affair of God and man.

The outstanding features of Heschel's biblical theology and exegesis was his understanding of the biblical God-idea and the related notion of prophetic consciousness. Beginning with his doctoral dissertation submitted to the University of Berlin in 1934 on the subject of prophecy and then more fully in a book published in Cracow in 1936 entitled *Die Prophetie*,[10] Heschel developed his doctrine of "Divine Pathos" and "Prophetic Sympathy"—the two individuating characteristics of Hebraic monotheism as he understood it. "Divine Pathos" is the term Heschel uses to characterize the openness of the Divine to human action. The Bible shows us a God who is a moral personality, authentically concerning himself with mankind, and especially Israel, and who is actually affected by His creation.[11] So the Bible repeatedly gives us an image of God and man and God and Israel in covenantal relations. Israel acts as it should and God is made happy; Israel sins and God is made angry and sad. God's personality and destiny no less than man's is shaped by human action. Heschel argues persuasively that: "this notion that God can be intimately affected, that he possesses not merely intelligence and will, but also feeling and pathos, basically defines the prophetic (i.e., biblical) consciousness of God."[12]

The human response to the Divine Pathos is "prophetic sympathy," that is, the prophet's recognition of his relation to and influence upon the Divine and the human situation thereby created. In this situation men, "sympathetically" disposed toward God, willingly desire to align themselves with God's purpose and actively work to realize God's will in order to fulfill creation and create a state of joyful Divine pathos. Aware of God's sensitivity to human action, the prophet calls men to do what is right by God. The prophet aligns himself with the Divine will so that the two co-mingle and become inseparable and God's task becomes man's. In *The Insecurity of Freedom,* one of his late works (1967), Heschel describes the prophetic consciousness as follows: "What is the essence of being a prophet? A prophet is a person who holds God and man in one thought at one time, at all times."[13]

Through the Bible man discovers that his being is rooted in that which transcends him and that his life is meaningfully lived only as response to the God he encounters. This response is understood by Heschel as requiring "a leap of action"—not "of faith." Man need respond to God, like the prophet of old, by making God's work his own. Heschel sees the essential imperative of the religious life in deed not word, action not thought.

Uniquely in Judaism, response to God finds its appropriate manifestation in the holy deed, in *mitzvot. Mitzvot* create the adequate conditions in the human soul so that it responds appropriately to God in the present and guarantees that man will respond appropriately in the future. The *halakhah,* demanding as it does the sanctification of all life and every

deed, heightens man's sense of transcendence and develops his power
to see beneath the flow of events and toward their source. The *halakhah*,
far from legalism or mechanical religion, is the mode through which
man sharpens his sensitivity to the ineffable dimension of the given
and the mysterious which remains in the midst of the known. With
his profound understanding of revelation and prophecy, and his dynamic
interpretation of *halakhah* and *mitzvot*, Heschel weds together and
renews with a fresh intensity the foundation elements of traditional
Judaism.[14]

What gives Heschel's work such authority is the fact that it grows
out of a profound understanding of classical and normative[15] Jewish
sources. He possesses a thorough grasp of the classical rabbinic sources
as well as the important but exceedingly difficult materials of medieval
Jewish philosophy and Jewish mysticism and in all these areas he has
made major contributions. Moreover, his studies in these areas are at
one with his more general theological outlook and reflect and illuminate
it.

In the area of rabbinics Heschel's major contribution is his 3-volume
Hebrew study of what might be appropriately called Talmudic
theology.[16] Entitled *Torah min-ha-Shamayim ba-aspaklaryah shel
ha-Dorot* ("Divine Revelation in the Light of the Generations") and sub-
titled in English "The Theology of Ancient Judaism," this work investigates the central category of revelation in rabbinic thought and the
complementary rabbinic notions of the "Written" and "Oral" Torah
(Torah she bi-khetav and *Torah she-be-al pe)*. The "Written" Torah is the
Divine revelation to Moses at Sinai found in the Torah; the "Oral"
Torah is the Divine instruction manifest in the teaching of the talmudic
sages claimed by tradition also to emanate from God through Moses
at Sinai.

Drawing upon his rabbinic erudition, Heschel scrutinized the whole
of the vast rabbinic literature on the relevant and related issues of
revelation. His study suggested to him that the thought of the Sages
was not monolithic; rather than giving us only one model for understanding the doctrine of *Torah min ha-Shamayim* ("Torah from heaven",
i.e., revelation), the talmudic literature gives us two: a rationalist-
naturalist[17] one and a non-rationalist (mystical)-supernaturalist one.
The former, which Heschel associates with the talmudic figure of Rabbi
Ishmael, seeks clarification of the holy texts through patient, pains-

taking analysis which is careful over every word, dares no more than is clearly seen to be right by all and recognizes a human element in the composition and transmission of the Torah; the latter which Heschel associates with Rabbi Akiva, argues that the essence of the Torah is found on a deeper mystical level of meaning which transcends a literal or rationalistic interpretation of the text and recognizes no human element in the composition or transmission of the Torah. With an extraordinary richness of examples and interpretations, Heschel paints a vital picture of these two ways of comprehending God's revelation. His point, moreover, is not made only for the sake of scholarship. Heschel wants to draw the following theological implication: according to the tradition of Rabbi Ishmael, to understand the written text of the Torah (the *Torah she-bi-khetav*) one must take account of the recipient as well as the revealer of the Torah. Accordingly, revelation is not understood as being analogous to God dictating onto a tape-recorder or handing down a finished record. Rather it is more akin to human dialogue in which the natures of the partners shape the meaning of what transpires between them. In such an understanding of *Torah min ha-Shamayim,* of Divine revelation, the Torah becomes a product of Divine-human encounter and as such, the human element and the whole issue of the composition, transmission, and interpretation of the Biblical record is transformed and the processes of the rabbinic "Oral Law" become vitally important in new ways.

In the area of medieval Jewish philosophy, in which Heschel was an acknowledged authority, he wrote a wide variety of penetrating studies of the major figures of medieval Jewry, especially Maimonides, Solomon Ibn Gabirol, Saadiah Gaon, and Isaac Abrabanel.[18] In interpreting the philosophical outlook of these thinkers Heschel departed from the then standard accounts of their thought and tried to portray them not as medieval rationalists but as deeply religious men whose philosophical enterprises were primarily intended to show the limits of reason and the validity of religious faith. He depicts these men as being aware of the fundamental mysteriousness of God which transcends and silences all philosophical investigation. His earliest and most sustained effort in this direction was his biographical study of *Maimonides.*[19] According to Heschel's account Maimonides, the Jewish contemplative man *par excellence,* comes to understand that godliness lies in prophet-like involvement with man rather than in and through removed and rarefied philosophical enquiry. Again, in his study of Saadiah Gaon, an even more obvious rationalist than Maimonides, Heschel is not content to allow the rationalist-interpretation of Saadiah's Jewish Kalām philosophy to stand unchallenged. Instead, Saadiah is interpreted as a profoundly religious man who, despite his adaptation and use of Kalamic argument and method, "did not surrender completely to rationalism."[20]

Heschel's studies of medieval Jewish philosophy reveal a fundamental unity of outlook. In each there is a plea for existential commitment as the focus of authentic Jewish thought, a commitment which must translate itself into action. The great medieval Jewish thinkers are seen as possessing and supporting this "prophetic" stance. In his Hebrew essay on "Inspiration in the Middle Ages," Heschel reminds modern students that the medieval sage did not make any sharp disjunction between Divine Inspiration and human cognition; "human thought itself is touched by Divine concern, the *ruah ha-kodesh* (Holy Spirit) hovers over the reason of man."

As one would expect from someone with Heschel's family background, Heschel was a profound student and interpreter of Ḥasidism. His entire religious outlook was intimately shaped by his ḥasidic roots, and his vision of God's need of man is unquestionably a product of ḥasidic influence. In *The Earth is the Lord's: The Inner Life of the Jew in East Europe* (1963), and again in more specialized biographies and studies of ḥasidic figures, Heschel paints one of the most moving images of the intense spirituality of ḥasidic life.[21]

Building upon his historical researches, Heschel made a valuable contribution to the interpretation of Ḥasidism. In a number of wonderfully rich studies of the individual ḥasidic masters who belonged to the immediate circle of the Baal Shem Tov, Heschel has provided one of the most profound images of the character of the ḥasidic movement in its earliest and most important phase. Through a series of biographical investigations of the great men of this original phase, Heschel illuminates the meaning of Ḥasidism and the nature of the Baal Shem Tov's message. Heschel had hoped that all his studies on Ḥasidism would culminate in a definitive study of the Baal Shem Tov; unfortunately this was not to be. However in his last work on Menahem Mendel of Kotsk and in his earlier studies he provided the groundwork for this project.

Abraham Joshua Heschel.

Joseph Dov Soloveitchik.

Of all the post World War II Jewish thinkers Heschel has been the most productive and influential, and his stature and importance seem likely to increase with the passage of time. In addition to his own philosophical contribution, his studies in the various branches of Jewish thought have been among the ablest and most suggestive contributions made in these areas. This rare combination of sound scholarship and philosophical vision gives Heschel's work an authenticity and authority possessed by few other contemporary Jewish theologians.

JOSEPH SOLOVEITCHIK

Today most Jews live outside the teachings of the *halakhah*. Jewish philosophy and theology reflect this situation with their various existentialist approaches to Judaism and their recasting of the traditional notions of revelation and Torah. Today the majority of Jews seek to move into the circle of faith rather than speaking naturally from within it. This was not always the case, nor even nearly always the case. For the greatest part of Jewish history all Jews lived within the halakhic circumference, whether they lived in ancient Alexandria or Pumbedita, medieval Spain, Renaissance Italy, 17th and 18th century Poland, or 19th and 20th century Russia. In fact, both Jews and non-Jews defined the status of a Jew through religious (halakhic) norms and a Jew who wanted to be free of the *halakhah* had to become a Moslem or Christian. It was religiously, socially and legally impossible to be a Jew without the *halakhah*. Slowly over the last 200 years this has changed; today the notion of a secular, cultural, or Reform Jew strikes no one as odd or in any sense paradoxical.

As a result of this transformation, however, questions regarding the norms and criteria of Judaism and Jewishness have become paramount and with respect to Jewish philosophy and Jewish theology one has seriously to ask what makes a philosophy or theology Jewish. What position must modern man take up in relation to the halakhic tradition to justify calling him a Jew, and a Jewish thinker? This question is the most vexatious in modern Jewish thought, for most Jews and most Jewish thinkers are proud of their "Jewishness" and see it as their greatest treasure and yet they by no means share a common understanding of what constitutes Jewishness and Judaism, nor very often do they possess any profound understanding of traditional Judaism and the sources of Jewish tradition which would allow them to grapple with this question in a sustained and rigorous manner. Much that passes for Jewish thought today is little more than personal biography or Protestant theology sprinkled with a few Talmudic quotations or ḥasidic tales drawn from English anthologies.

This prologomenon is necessary in order to understand the work and position of Rabbi Joseph Soloveitchik, the head of the Theological Seminary at Yeshiva University and chairman of its Rabbinic Council *Halakhah* Commission. Almost unique among modern Jewish thinkers, Soloveitchik speaks from within the classical halakhic tradition. His rabbinic learning, which is unsurpassed in the modern generation and which makes him the world's pre-eminent contemporary halakhist, coupled with his interest in modern theological issues, puts his work in a special category, vis-a-vis both the Jewish tradition and contemporary Judaism. Though his religious position is not shared by most contemporary Jews, and most will not be able to accept his views because of their own secular and modernist particularity, Soloveitchik speaks with a certain authority unmatched by other contemporary Jewish thinkers. Above all, he possesses control and understanding of the halakhic sources which have defined Judaism over the centuries and he therefore has an unequivocal norm of Jewishness and Judaism. In speaking from the perspective of the *halakhah* he faces modernity from the perspective of the mainstream of the Jewish tradition.

What makes Soloveitchik a modern Jewish thinker, rather than only a great traditional halakhist, is that he is sensitive to modern issues both religious and philosophical and his outlook has been influenced not only by classical Jewish sources but also by the major figures in the western philosophical tradition from Plato to Kant and their more recent heirs, Kierkegaard and the contemporary existentialists. Soloveitchik's thought shows the deep imprint of both of the two most influential schools in modern continental thought, neo-Kantianism and Existentialism. These influences are seen most clearly in his general metaphysical schema and most particularly in his religious anthropology (view of the human condition).[22]

Though the influence of the existentialists is more obvious in certain readily apparent features of his thinking, Soloveitchik's thought is as equally, if not more profoundly, influenced by Kant and the neo-Kantian

"Marburg" school of Hermann Cohen, on whose thought Soloveitchik wrote his doctoral dissertation in 1931. The Kantian influence appears most markedly in Soloveitchik's basic metaphysical account which posits a Kantian-like dichotomy in the order of things. There is a natural order regulated by spatio-temporal categories and causal connection in which every event, i.e., every natural and scientific event, is subject to these categories and intelligible in their terms. Complementing the spatio-temporal order, there is a realm of "freedom" in which events and entities are not governed by the rules of spatial location, temporal successiveness, and causal connection. This is the world of morality, creations of the spirit, and religion. Kant called these the phenomenal and the noumenal realms which are appropriately studied by "pure reason," i.e., metaphysical, scientific and mathematical reasoning and procedures, and "practical reason," i.e., moral and religious, rather than scientific reasoning.

Soloveitchik, though using a different language to describe reality, gives a Kantian picture of the ontological structure of reality. In an idiom more appropriate to Jewish life, Soloveitchik finds in the two Genesis creation accounts a parallel image to that of Kant's. Using the two accounts of Adam given in Genesis 1 and 2, Soloveitchik draws two different images of man and his world. These two accounts give two different "types" of men. The first (Genesis 1) refers to man as "created in the image of God." It portrays man as a majestic creature whose purpose in creation is to understand and master the world he inhabits. This Adam is directed to subdue nature, to make progress in technology and science and to discover the laws of the natural order so that he might exploit them for his purposes and gain. The Adam of Genesis 1 asks "How does the cosmos function?", i.e., the objective-scientific question, not "Why does the cosmos function at all?"[23] i.e., the metaphysical question concerned with origins and purpose. The aims of the technological Adam are pragmatic and limited.

Adam II, described in Genesis 2, is a different creature and reflects a different order of existence. As compared to the natural, majestic man described above he is concerned not with the subjugation of nature and its practical manipulation but rather with the source of nature and nature's (and his) ultimate ground and destiny. Adam II asks the metaphysical questions; he wants to know "why the universe is" not "how the universe is." In order to pursue the metaphysical questions

Adam II does not require the mathematical, scientific and qualitative constructs of technological Adam. His world is the world as it is; he is open to the wonder of nature and the awe-fulness of existence which have no functional value, or pragmatic import; nor is it governed by the iron-clad laws of causality and space-time. This second Adam is concerned with the source of the world, not the world itself. He seeks to commune with the God who is the ground of nature, rather than interrogate nature itself.[24]

Soloveitchik employs the double Adam account to describe two distinct types of human being who reflect the two dimensions of reality. For the sake of simplicity, we might call these two dimensions (a) the objective-scientific and (b) the subjective-religious. Each type of reality has a corresponding type of human personality which inhabits it. Soloveitchik does not intend to suggest that there are actual men who are either Adam I or Adam II; these are abstract analytic categories and norms which provide us with tools for interpreting the nature and condition of actual man. It might be helpful to think of them as philosophical ideals. In reality men are a combination of both these types. Actual man, like biblical Adam, is two-sided; he possesses within his one reality both technological and metaphysical man. He manifests in his life both technological and metaphysical aims and desires. He moves in both the world of nature and causality and the world of spirit and freedom.

Adam I (technological man) and Adam II (religious man) have so far been used as Judaic analogues to the Kantian categories of phenomenal and noumenal reality. However, there is another level to Soloveitchik's analysis of the human situation which transcends the metaphysics and corollary anthropology of Kant and the neo-Kantians and draws heavily on Kierkegaard and the modern existentialists, and it is on this level that Soloveitchik is most profound and original. He examines the existential implications of the two sorts of existence open to men, and in and through this analysis he illuminates the human condition in general and the Jewish situation with its normative-halakhic structure, in particular.

Soloveitchik enriches the already given skeleton of man's situation through the following analysis. Technical man (Adam I) seeks as the goal of his existence dignity and majesty commensurate with his power over nature. These categories Soloveitchik defines as social rather than existential ones.[25] "Dignity" in this sense is achieved by impressing others with one's majesty and influence, it is the reward for convincing others of one's worth. As such Adam I requires society and thus God creates Eve so that he should not be alone and bereft of these categories of meaning. Adam I (the type) continues to require society to function and therefore he enters into social interaction with other men in order to further his own ends, to secure his biological and natural needs and to create the conditions for the expression of his pragmatic-techno-logical concerns. Alternatively, Adam II (religious man) does not live to be dignified, but to be redeemed.[26] In this, Adam II manifests an ontological dimension as compared to the social dimension of Adam I. This ontological dimension reaches to the very essence of the human personality and brings him face to face with God. Adam I seeks dignity through power over nature; Adam II seeks redemption through being overpowered by God. Redemption is a solitary rather than a social phenomena. The man who experiences God's redemptive love experiences it as a "singular being," as an "isolated I."[27] The profoundest level of human personality is experienced in solitude and crisis. Moreover, in redemptive solitude, man discovers that the authentic human condition is not social but singular, not communal but isolated and alone. Man becomes aware that he is neither "naturally" at home with other men nor with nature as a whole. "Each great redemptive step forward in man's quest for humanity entails the ever-growing tragic awareness of his aloneness and only-ness and consequently of his loneliness and insecurity."[28] Though not unique to modern man, Soloveitchik sees this analysis of man's loneliness as especially applicable to modern man who is not only lonely by "nature" but whose loneliness is re-enforced by the increasing technocracy of contemporary life which compounds the source of man's anxiety. Actual men, modern men, carry within themselves this tension of social and solitary being; they seek redemption from the absurdity of existence and they find it in faithful relation to God. In man's existential situation he lives between the worlds of the two Adams; he is both Adam I and Adam II in his unique individuality.

Adam II, "The Lonely Man of Faith," discovers his isolation and the source of his redemption, God, at one and the same time. Moreover, Adam II appreciates the need to make his redemptiveness manifest in action and therefore he, too, seeks social interaction and community. But the community he seeks is different from that of Adam I. Adam II seeks existential community.[29] This is the community founded by two isolated individuals who come together through a shared commitment to the God who has redeemed them both. Thus this existential community becomes the "covenantal community," in which there are three, rather than two, partners: I, Thou, and God. All relationships are similarly triadic rather than two-sided. In this covenantal community of shared commitment the Divine Himself becomes an equal and ever-present covenantal partner.[30] Through covenantal community God reveals Himself to men and men reveal themselves to God and to each other. In this revelatory situation man overcomes his solitariness. In the covenantal community man and God address each other "face to face." In the covenantal relationship each partner freely assumes obligations and commitments.[31] Prophecy and prayer are the two vehicles of this communication; through prophecy God addresses man, through prayer man addresses God.[32] Both are acts of revelation through which man's isolation is overcome.

Soloveitchik's metaphysical and anthropological diagnosis of existence sets the stage for traditional Judaism and halakhic man to be the authentic representatives of such covenantal encounter with God. According to Soloveitchik the mutual obligations and commitments of the covenantal partners require that the encounter between God and man in covenantal relation "be crystalized and objectified in a normative ethico-moral message."[33] Subjective religious emotion and dialogical relation have to be translated into deeds and moral actions. The *halakhah* is the vehicle for the translation and its application. Furthermore and accordingly, Soloveitchik asserts the primacy of content in revelation, i.e., God's actual revelation of given norms and Divine teaching against all existentialist and liberal theologies. Covenantal prophetic revelation is not to be reduced to mystical experience; rather it is the revelation of Divine instruction, and it is through the medium of revealed instruction that God participates in the covenantal community. The God of the covenant is "the teacher *par excellence*."[34] Without such instruction the covenantal faith community, according to Soloveitchik, would be impossible. Through the *halakhah* the halakhic man becomes the only authentic covenantal partner of God, for it is only he who is willing to submit himself totally to the Divine, making God present in each action and directing each moment toward God through the *halakhah*. Individually as halakhic men and collectively as a halakhic community, Israel brings to full realization the Divine imperative and manifests the ever-present relation of God to man.

The *halakhah* understood as Divine Revelation is thus the means for overcoming the existential anxiety which the Adam II in each of us senses. Through it we confront the Divine and order our lives accordingly, witnessing to God as the source of meaning and of redemption. In this process, through the *halakhah,* man's purpose and goal become parallel with God's, and man and God share in a unitive existence and a common purpose and will.[35] This overcoming of existential solitude is never final, even for a true man of faith, for the world of Adam I, of majesty, of technology, constantly summons man and man must respond.[36] Indeed, paradoxically, from within the halakhic-covenantal circle covenantal man, by the very nature of the covenant, is commanded to go into the world of Adam I and to unify the worlds of Adam I and Adam II, i.e., God must be proclaimed in the whole of man's life.[37] The *halakhah* recognizes this imperative and thus embraces every aspect of the totality of man's life, no matter how seemingly trivial, providing the means for turning everything towards God's will and purpose. Through the *halakhah* the Jew witnesses to his God in every action. The *halakhah* provides for the immediate and concrete manifestation of man's concern for God and God's concern for man.

Soloveitchik's difficult yet profound account of the existential situation and the unique role and purpose of the *halakhah* attempts to account for modern man's alienation from his own nature and from society in general and to prescribe a means for overcoming it. It stresses above all the Divine imperative in human life and the need for man's submission to the transcendent will of the Almighty. Alone among major modern thinkers[38] Soloveitchik thus argues for religious heteronomy and religious positivity, interpreting the revelation at Sinai and the halakhic process in a strictly traditional fashion. Though Soloveitchik does not claim to be able to verify his view to the person who does not share his faith, indeed he claims that no such proof could ever be forthcoming, he attempts to give convincing witness to his beliefs through the personal confession of his faith and through his life. Only if one experiences in one's own life the faith commitment of a Soloveitchik will everything become "verified." Nonetheless listening to Soloveitchik one realizes that Jewish theology, if it is to answer the needs of modern Jews, will have to renew its intimacy with the halakhic tradition in some way.

FAITH AFTER THE HOLOCAUST

Jewish life and thought have been radically transformed by the Holocaust. However one copes with the Holocaust, and many possible interpretative schemas have been suggested, one must bear with a recognition that it is now one of the defining elements of Jewish experience, an inescapable "datum" for all Jewish thought which must be given some weight in all Jewish accounts of the meaning and nature of convenantal relation and of the encounter between God and man.

The tragic immensity of the Holocaust left Jewish thinkers numb. In any case, what energies they had were needed to help the survivors, especially to create a refuge in the State of Israel; the cry of the living demanded precedence over the sacred duty of remembering the dead. It was just as well, for the horror of it all had been too great to understand, too unbelievable to fashion into any coherent form, too seemingly impossible to allow of any meaning. That this is still the case may well be true. Moreover, who could speak with authority on Auschwitz? Of those who were there, few were still able to speak; of those who were there, even the survivors knew not what to say; of those who were not there, could they speak without blasphemy and with justification, could they even understand the issues involved? And yet, if only to remember and to make others remember, Jewish thinkers had to begin to talk about Auschwitz. Of course, once the conversation began it was clear it could not stop, nor could it be avoided: it called into question God, Torah, and Israel—the three coefficients of Judaism.

There are several common responses to the Holocaust and combinations and variations of them. (1) The Holocaust is like other tragedies and raises again the question of theodicy and the "problem of evil," but it does not significantly alter the problem nor contribute anything new to it. (2) The Holocaust is retribution for sin; Israel was guilty and Auschwitz is its just retribution. This is the application to Auschwitz

222

of the classical Jewish doctrine of *mi-penei ḥataeinu* "because of our sins we were punished." (3) The Holocaust is the ultimate in vicarious atonement. Israel is the "suffering servant"—it suffers for the sins of others. (4) The Holocaust is a modern *Akedah* (sacrifice of Isaac)—it is a test of our faith. (5) The Holocaust is an instance of the "Eclipse of God"—there are times when God is absent from history. (6) The Holocaust is the maximization of human evil, the price we have to pay for human freedom. The Nazis were men not gods; Auschwitz reflects ignominiously on men, it leaves God untouched. (7) The Holocaust issues a call for Jewish affirmation, from Auschwitz issues a command: Jews survive! (8) The Holocaust is proof that "God is dead"—if there were a God He would have prevented Auschwitz; if He did not then He does not exist. (9) The Holocaust is inscrutable mystery; like all of God's ways it transcends human understanding and demands faith and silence.

There are probably other ways of fitting together the pieces: these have been the most common ones. One can safely say that none has become "normative." Many essays and monographs have been written on these themes and many more will undoubtedly follow. Four major statements each representing a different response and drawing on one or more of the themes outlined are represented by the best known contributors to the discussion, Richard Rubenstein, Emil Fackenheim, Ignaz Maybaum, and Eliezer Berkovits.[39]

RICHARD RUBENSTEIN

Richard Rubenstein has been a man of our times. Coming to the Hebrew Union College Reform seminary in 1942 and sharing its optimistic vision of man and its liberal ideal of human progress, he has been converted by the Holocaust into holding a Jewish "Death of God" theology. His sensivity to the reality of evil witnessed by the death camps has forced him to call into question the very foundations of Judaism. "The one preeminent measure of the adequacy of all contemporary Jewish theology," Rubenstein writes, "is the seriousness with which they deal with this supreme problem (the Holocaust) of Jewish history."[40] No one has taken the problem more seriously and no Jewish theologian has drawn more radical conclusions regarding it.

The theological problem raised by the Nazi extermination of Jews is simple to describe: if God is the God of History and Israel is His chosen people what responsibility does God bear for Auschwitz? Did God use the Nazis, as He used Assyria of old, as "the rod of His anger?" If He did not, how could such a thing happen in the face of the living God? It is the ancient "Problem of evil" to which men of faith have responded with countless theodicies; now it is raised with maximum vigor, clarity, and urgency. In Germany, in August 1961, Rubenstein was confronted by a well-meaning Protestant clergyman with the affirmation that God had indeed used the Nazis as the instrument of His will.[41] This affirmation shocked Rubenstein; it was, he tells us, "a theological point of no return."[42] The consequences seemed clear and Rubenstein felt compelled to reject the presence of God at Auschwitz rather than believe that Hitler was God's instrument: "If I believed in God as the omnipotent author of the historical drama and Israel as His Chosen People, I had to accept Dean Grueber's conclusion that it was God's will that Hitler committed six million Jews to slaughter. I could not possibly believe in such a God nor could I believe in Israel as the chosen people of God after Auschwitz."[43] Rubenstein was driven to the conclusion of the talmudic heretic Elisha ben Avuyah, *Let din ve-let-dayyan* ("There is neither judgment nor judge").[44]

In Rubenstein's view the only honest response to the death camps is the rejection of God, "God is dead," and the open recognition of the meaninglessness of existence. Our life is neither planned nor purposeful, there is no Divine Will nor does the world reflect Divine concern. The world is indifferent to men. Man must now reject his illusions, and along with his fellow men, recognize the existential truth, that life is not intrinsically valuable, that the human condition reflects no transcendental purpose, history reveals no providence. The theological account of Auschwitz which sees it as retribution, which re-echoes one side of the ancient theology of Judaism that Israel's suffering is "because of our sins" is to blaspheme against both God and man. What crime could Israel have committed, what sin could have been so great as to justify such retribution? What God could have looked out on His chosen ones and meted them such justice? All such "rationalizations" of Auschwitz pale before its enormity, and for Rubenstein, the only response that is worthy is the rejection of the entire Jewish theological framework: there is no God and no covenant with Israel.

. Man must turn away from illusions and face his actual existential situation. Drawing heavily upon the atheistic existentialists, Rubenstein interprets this to mean that in the face of the world's nihilism man must assert value; in response to history's meaninglessness men must create and project meaning; against the objective fact that human life has no purpose, man must subjectively, yet meaningfully, act as if there were purpose. All men have/are themselves and each other: Auschwitz has taught that life itself is the great value, there is no need to see life as valuable only because of its reflection of transcendental values or metahistorical meanings. What worth there will be will be of one's own creation. This radical thesis is not new, but it is new in a Jewish theological context.[45]

Had Rubenstein merely asserted the denial of God, his would not be a Jewish theology. What makes it "Jewish" are the implications he draws from his radical negation with respect to the people of Israel. It might be expected that denial of God's covenantal relation with Israel would entail the end of Judaism and so the end of the Jewish people. From the perspective of traditional Jewish theology this would certainly be the case. Rubenstein, however, again inverts our ordinary perception and argues that with the "death of God," the existence of "people-hood," of the community of Israel, is all the more important. Now that there is nowhere else to turn for meaning, men need each other all the more to create meaning: "it is precisely because human existence is tragic, ultimately hopeless, and without meaning that we treasure our religious community."[46] Though Judaism has to be "demythologized," i.e., it has to recognize the renunciation of the normative historic claims to a unique "chosen status,"[47] at the same time it paradoxically gains heightened importance in the process. Now that "God is dead" religious community is all the more important!

"It is precisely the ultimate hopelessness and gratuity of our human situation which calls forth our strongest need for religious community. If all we have is one another, then assuredly we need one another more than ever."[48]

The Jew after Auschwitz, despite his recognition of the now transcended "mythic" structure of historic Jewish experience, is still a Jew and as such carries within him the "shared vicissitudes of history, culture and psychological perspective"[49] that define a Jew. Jews, like all men, are rooted in concrete life-situations. For Jewish man only Jewish experience can be authentic. It is in the traditional forms of life that we best express all our aspiration and ideals, and participate in a "community of shared predicament and ultimate concern."[50]

In many of his writings Rubenstein has carried on a re-examination of classical Jewish values for the modern, post-Holocaust Jew. Through the use of psychoanalytic categories[51] he has tried to re-interpret the meaning of classical aspects of Judaism while advocating their retention. He has been especially concerned to make out a case for the retention of religious ritual and symbolism. Though these forms of religious life have lost their traditional justification, they can and do have profound psychological implications and are to be retained on psychological grounds. Thus, Bar Mitzvah is valuable as a *rite de passage,* a ritual in which the community formally recognizes the new sexual maturity of the boy and confirms publicly his new masculine role.[52] This is psychologically valuable for both the boy and society. Again the synagogue retains a central role in Jewish life, if only as a psychological clinic. Rubenstein has extended this psychoanalytic interpretation of Judaism to the rabbinic material in his book, *The Religious Imagination* (1968),[53] and to Paul, whom he sees as one of the "greatest Jewish theologians," in his book on Paul entitled *My Brother Paul* (1972).

Coupled to this psychoanalytic model of interpretation is a mystical paganism[54] in which the Jew is urged to forgo history and return to the cosmic rhythms of natural existence.[55] The modern Jew must recognize the priorities of nature. So, for example, he must come to understand that the real meaning of messianism is "the proclamation of the end of history and the return to nature and nature's cyclical repetitiveness."[56] The future and final redemption is not to be the conquest of nature by history as traditionally conceived in the Jewish tradition, but rather the conquest of history by nature and the return of all things to their natural origins. Man has to rediscover the sanctity of his natural life and reject forever the delusions of overcoming it; he must submit and enjoy his body and his nature—not try to transform or transcend them. Rubenstein sees the renewal of Zion, and the rebuilding of the land with its return to the soil by the Jew, as a harbinger of this return to nature on the part of the Jew who has been removed from the soil (symbolic of nature) by theology and necessity for almost two thousand years. The return to the earth points toward the final escape of the Jew from the negativity of history to the vitality and promise of self-liberation through nature.

Rubenstein's account is meant not only as interpretation of what has been, but of what ought to be. It is intended as a program for Jewish renewal and spiritual re-integration. Among the aims of this program is the eradication of those elements which create the explosive mix which produces a Holocaust. One of the most significant lessons, we are told, to be drawn from the "demythologization" of Jewish history, and its rejection of history in favor of nature, is its overcoming of the root-cause of anti-Semitism. Rubenstein argues that anti-Semitism is a product of the mythic structures of Jewish and Christian theology. The contributing Jewish myth is its claim to be a "chosen people." This created a "specialness" about Jews which has been disastrous. The contributing Christian myth was predicated on its acceptance of the antecedent Jewish one—the Church accepted the "chosenness of Israel" and was therefore able to see it only in theological terms; para-doxically it saw Israel as providing "both the incarnate Deity and His murderers."[57] The most potent of all Christian myths—the Crucifixion—is indissolubly linked to the deicidal activity of the "chosen people"—the Jews. Everywhere the Christian story is retold, a powerful anti-Semitic seed is planted. In order, therefore, once and for all to put an end to anti-Semitism, it is necessary for the Jew to renounce his mythic self-image as a "chosen people" so that his relation to his Christian neighbor may be normalized and the Christian will be able to see him in the same light as other men. This process needs to be paralleled in Christianity; it too has to correspondingly "demythologize" its image of the Jew. Yet to do this is to rupture historic incarnational theology and its claims for Jesus as the promised Christ coming out of the body of historic Israel. This is to ask a great deal of Christianity, but, Ruben-stein argues, unless it occurs there will be future tragedy.

An integral part of this mythic relation between Judaism and Chris-tianity, Rubenstein claims, is an urge toward vicarious atonement and the role of the sacrificial victim. This element arises, in Freudian fashion, from man's deepest wish, which is to kill God. Through deicide, men would be liberated from restraint and from the commands of morality and virtue. The Crucifixion is the most powerful human symbol of deicide. However, the nature of the tale allows the Christian to deflect his own guilty desires of deicide onto the Jew who is objectified as the

"Christ-Killer." The Christian therefore can find a "legitimate" outlet for his murderous instinctual desires by deflecting his instincts against the Jew. Thus whether the Jew is conceived in the mind of the Christian as Jesus or as Judas, his end is the same: ritual slaughter as sacrificial victim.[58]

Rubenstein has given us a powerful image of what it means to draw the extreme conclusion from Auschwitz: "God is Dead." Yet his is not the only nor the final word.

EMIL FACKENHEIM

No philosopher or theologian has written as extensively or as feelingly about the Holocaust as Emil Fackenheim. Himself a survivor of the camps,[59] Fackenheim, seemingly out of a sense of compulsion, has tried to grapple with the overwhelming events of the death camps in order to draw some meaning from them for post-Holocaust Jewry. In a series of essays, and especially and most clearly in his *God's Presence in History*, Fackenheim has tried to find a way to avoid both the absolute faith of the pious who do not see any special problem in the Holocaust and those like Rubenstein who argue that the only reasonable conclusion to be drawn from Auschwitz is the "Death of God" and the ultimate absurdity of history.[60] The former alternative blasphemes against Hitler's victims, the latter blasphemes against the God of the victims. Both victims and God have to be held together in dialectical tension after Auschwitz; neither can be devalued without resulting distortion and loss of truth.

To keep God and Israel together is the demand of Jewish theology; to do so after the Holocaust is still the demand; how to do so is the problem. If Rubenstein's Jewish communal existence without the God of historic Judaism is no answer, what is? Fackenheim's reply is both subtle and difficult. He is adamant in his refusal to allow any theological explanation of the Holocaust to be given. In no sense, he argues, can any particular theodicy be propounded in which God's goodness can be vindicated and Auschwitz seen as part of a rational cosmic pattern whose interpretation men can understand. In this sense the Holocaust is devoid of explanation and meaning. Thus, like Rubenstein, any account which interprets Auschwitz in terms of *mi-penei ḥataeinu* "because of our sins"—is to be rejected totally. The various attempts to explain the horrible events in terms of vicarious suffering or martyr-dom achieve no more lasting result. For Fackenheim the enormity of the tragedy transcends all the classical explanations of suffering and evil. In his staunch rejection of explanations Fackenheim resembles Rubenstein and like him he realizes that which is called into question is nothing less than the God of history Himself.

Yet despite the implications, despite the absolute failure of theodicy, despite the seeming absurdity, Fackenheim calls men to believe. Ruben-stein becomes an atheist because he cannot and will not accept God as in any sense the author of Auschwitz; Fackenheim, in opposition, insists that this is what we must do. It is the presence of God in con-temporary Jewish history, even at Auschwitz, that Fackenheim would have us find. Fackenheim insists that we do not and cannot understand what God was doing at Auschwitz, or why He allowed Auschwitz, but we must and do insist that He was there. For Fackenheim, unlike Rubenstein, the Holocaust does not prove that "God is dead." From Auschwitz as from Sinai[61] God addresses Israel.

How does this voice address Israel and what does it say? In order fully to understand Fackenheim's views on this we have to turn away from his direct writings on the Holocaust and come to an understanding of his theological position in general. In his own biographical odyssey he has moved slowly but perceptibly from a liberal to a neo-orthodox[62] understanding of Judaism. Involved in and affected by the Nazi on-slaught Fackenheim, like most of his generation, felt the need to re-appraise the nature and status of Judaism. In this re-appraisal the generally held liberal position with its dogmatic belief in the perfectability of man and the translation of the commanding God of the Bible into a moral Ideal was seen to be untrue to Judaism's deepest insights and superficial[63] in its analysis of the human situation.[64]

Judaism is not Deism or moral Idealism; it has its foundation and its continuance in the meeting with the Living God of the Bible, who is continually present in history. For Fackenheim Judaism can only be understood as the dynamic response to the present address of the Divine. Fackenheim's espousal of this existential supernaturalism, with its central emphasis on the reality of God and His incursion into history which calls man to deeds is due to the influence of Buber and Rosenzweig. It was they who had "sought nothing less than a modern presence of the ancient God."[65] In working out the implications of this rediscovered supernaturalism Fackenheim has been especially influenced by Buber's dialogical philosophy of I and Thou. Fackenheim accepts, in its general specifications, the Buberian doctrine of *I-Thou*[66] encounter as the proper model for Jewish openness to the reality of the living God. Thus he does not begin with any proof for the existence of God but rather with the presumption that God exists. God cannot be proven, but He can (and must) be met.[67] Only from within the circle of faith can one "hear" the Divine and respond. Like Buber, Fackenheim insists that God reveals Himself in history in personal encounters with Jews and Israel. Revelation understood as the encounter of God and man happens everywhere and at all times. Yet the experience cannot be verified by any objective criteria, it cannot show itself decisively to those who would not "hear" the voice. The I-Thou encounter has its own rhythm, and any attempt to force it into improper (I-It to use Buber's terminology) categories destroys its character and silences its message.[68] The Fackenheim who hears a "commanding voice from Auschwitz" is the Fackenheim who stands within the covenantal affirmation.[69]

Buber applies his concept of revelation to Israel's history and sees God's address in the overwhelming events of Israel's life.[70] Building upon Buber's work, Fackenheim develops his own account of Jewish history. For him Jewish history is a series of overwhelming events but not all the events are of the same character. The most powerful events, such as those connected with the Exodus from Egypt and the giving of the Torah at Sinai, actually created the religious identity of the Jewish people. These creative extra-ordinary historical happenings Fackenheim calls "root experiences."[71] "Root experiences" are historical events of such a formative character that they continue to influence all future "presents" of the people, they are of such a power that these past events legislate to every future era.[72] In addition, "root experiences" are public, historical events. They belong to the history of the people and continue to claim the allegiance of the people. Thus, for example, the miracle at the Red Sea is an historical event which is re-enacted at every Passover Seder and whose power affects each subsequent generation and continually reveals the saving activity of God to each age. Third, and most importantly, "root experiences" provide the accessibility of Divine Presence here and now[73]; past events are lived through as "present reality" and thus one is "assured that the past saving God saves still."[74]

Not all the great events in Israel's history however meet these criteria. There is a second category of events whose function is different. Fackenheim calls these events "epochmaking events."[75] These are events which, unlike "root experiences" are not formative, they do not create the essentials of Jewish faith, but rather they are historical experiences which challenge the "root experiences" through new situations, which test the resiliency and generality of "root experiences" to answer to new and unprecedented historical conditions and realities. For example, the destruction of the First and Second Temples severely tested whether or not the commanding and saving Presence of God could be maintained. The Sages of the talmudic era, who lived through the destruction of the Second Temple and the Prophets who lived through the first, were able to respond to these crisis situations with both realism and faith in the "root experiences" of Israel. Jeremiah sees Nebuchadnezzar as the "rod of God's anger" (Jer. 25:9, 27:6, 43:10) and the Sages saw the Second Destruction and subsequent Exile as nothing less than God's own exile with His people, allowing for the dispersion and yet holding fast to God's presence in all history at all times and places. And such a God, present in all history, would redeem Israel in the future as He had in the past.[76] The faith was severely tested by experience, but a way—admittedly fragmentary and contradictory[77]—was found to hold both together. In other times and other places the "root experiences" have again and again been tested, indeed the history of Israel in diaspora from one culture to another, from one era to another, is a series of "epochmaking events" which try and try again the foundations of Jewish faith in the God of History. Yet, through it all, the midrashic framework has held fast: God and History are not divorced; Israel and God are not torn asunder. Each trial brings new strength and new affirmation of the saving and commanding God first revealed at the Red Sea and Sinai. But what of Auschwitz? Can it too be assimilated to the traditional pattern of midrashic response? Is Auschwitz another testing, another epochal event; or more drastically is it perhaps a "root experience" which is formative for Jewish faith but in an ultimately negative and destructive sense.

Fackenheim argues that Auschwitz is an "epochmaking event" in Jewish history, that it calls into question the historical presence of God in a uniquely powerful way. Yet according to Fackenheim the Jew must still affirm the continued existence of God in Jewish history—

even at Auschwitz—and he must re-affirm the present reality of the people's "root experience" of a commanding God (of Sinai), now commanding Israel from within the Holocaust itself. This radical reply to the unprecedented crisis of faith is Fackenheim's response to Auschwitz. The Jew cannot, dare not, must not, reject God. Auschwitz is revelation! In the gas-chambers and crematoria we must, we do experience God. Fackenheim dares to affirm what drives others to atheism or silence. Like Job, Fackenheim gives expression to a great faith: "Though you slay me, I shall believe in Thee."

The commanding word that Fackenheim hears from Auschwitz is: "Jews are forbidden to hand Hitler posthumous victories;"[78] Jews are under a sacred obligation to survive; after Auschwitz Jewish existence is itself a holy act; Jews are under a sacred obligation to remember the martyrs; Jews are, as Jews, forbidden to despair of redemption, or to become cynical about the world and man, for to submit to cynicism is to abdicate responsibility for the world and to deliver the world into the hands of the forces of Auschwitz. And above all, Jews are "forbidden to despair of the God of Israel, lest Judaism perish."[79] Hitler's demonic passion was to eradicate Jews and Judaism from history, for the Jew to despair of the God of Israel as a result of Hitler's monstrous actions would be, ironically, to do Hitler's work and to aid in the accomplishments of Hitler's goal. The voice that speaks from Auschwitz above all demands that Hitler win no posthumous victories, that no Jew do what Hitler could not do. The Jewish will for survival is natural enough, but Fackenheim invests it with transcendental significance. Precisely because others would eradicate Jews from the earth, Jews are commanded to resist annihilation. Paradoxically, Hitler makes Judaism after Auschwitz a necessity. To say the "no" to Hitler is to say the "yes" to the commanding voice of the God of Sinai; to say "no" to the God of Sinai is to say the "yes" to Hitler.

Since 1945 every Jew who has remained a Jew has, from Fackenheim's perspective, responded affirmatively to the commanding voice of Auschwitz.

The God of biblical faith is both a commanding and a saving God. The crossing of the Red Sea is as much a part of Jewish history as is the revelation at Sinai: both are "root experiences." Fackenheim is sensitive to this. He has made much of the commanding voice of Auschwitz, but where is the saving God of the Exodus? Without the crossing of the Red Sea there can be no Sinai. Fackenheim knows this. He also knows that to talk of a saving God, no matter how softly, no matter how tentatively, after the Holocaust is problematical when God did not work His salvation there and then. Even to whisper about salvation after Auschwitz is already to speak as a man of faith, not as a seeker, and even then one can only whisper. The continued existence of the people of Israel however, and most specifically the establishment and maintainance of the State of Israel, forces Fackenheim to risk speaking of hope and the possibility of redemption. Auschwitz and the State of Israel are inseparably tied together; what the former seems to deny the latter, at least tentatively, affirms. For Fackenheim, the State of Israel is living testimony to God's continued saving presence in history, and through it the modern Jew witnesses a re-affirmation of the "root experience" of salvation essential to the survival of Jewish faith.[80]

IGNAZ MAYBAUM

Ignaz Maybaum, a distinguished English Reform rabbi, seeks the meaning of the Holocaust from within the traditional Jewish responses to suffering. For him, unlike Rubenstein or Fackenheim, Auschwitz is not a unique event in Jewish history, but a reappearance of a classic and sanctified event. A disciple of Franz Rosenzweig, Maybaum affirms the dynamic relation of God and Israel. He believes in the reality of the transcendent God of the Bible and the movement of this God into covenantal relation with Israel. Israel is unique among the nations, and its history bears witness to its uniqueness. Within its historical experience it bears witness to its God and His purpose as well; its historic experience reveals a pattern and the Holocaust fits this pattern.

The pattern of Jewish history is one in which Israel's role is to be a nation among other nations and in which it is non-Jews who are the prime movers of events. Israel's destiny is not isolated from its historical interdependence with the nations of the world, and its covenantal purpose is only revealed in and through this intercourse. From its very beginnings in the Exodus-Sinai events, Israel's history is played out in relation to other peoples, first Egypt, then later Assyria, Babylonia, and Rome and the empires of Christendom and Islam. Therefore the categories of Jewish history have to be categories intelligible to non-

Jews. Fackenheim introduces two categories to explain the structure of Jewish historic experience, "root experiences" and "epoch-making events." In the latter class he places such events as the destruction of the First and Second Temples. Maybaum, conscious of Israel's relation to the gentiles, goes one step further in his analysis of Jewish history. He subdivides what Fackenheim calls "epoch-making events" into two classes, that of *Hurban* and that of *Gezerah*. *Hurban* (="destruction") are events, like the destruction of the First and Second Temples, which "make an end to an old era and create a new era."[81] *Gezerah* (plural 'Gezerot' = evil decree) are those events, such as the expulsion from Spain in 1492 and the Chmelniecki massacres in 17th century Poland, which although cataclysmic do not usher in a new era. According to this classification, Maybaum sees the Holocaust as a *Hurban*, i.e., an event which signals the end of one era and the beginning of another in Jewish and world history. Moreover a *Gezerah* can be averted. As has been said for generations on the Day of Atonement: *Teshuvah u-Tefillah u-Zedakah ma'averin et roa ha-Gezerah* ("Penitence, Prayer, and Charity annul the evil decree"). A *Hurban* however, cannot be averted; its meaning goes beyond the parameters of Israel's own history, effects world history, and most importantly, is an intercession of God in history which is irreversible.

Maybaum goes further still in explicating the meaning of *Hurban*,— *Hurban* implies progress.[82] There is positive value in destruction; Auschwitz as *Hurban* has world historical significance in man's striving for advancement. In Jewish history the term *Hurban* has been applied twice previously, the first time to the destruction of the First Temple (586 B.C.E.) and the second time to the destruction of the Second Temple (70 C.E.). In each case Maybaum sees the advancement of humanity as a result of the catastrophe. The first destruction created the Jewish diaspora, and through the diaspora Judaism went out among the other nations to spread God's word and do God's work: this was progress. The destruction of the Second Temple saw the establishment of the synagogue, and in the synagogue the world saw a form of religious piety in which no sacrifices were performed, no blood was shed, and religious life was "elevated" to a higher spiritual level than hitherto. The Holocaust is the third *Hurban*, and like the earlier two Maybaum sees it as helping in human advancement; it is the medium of spiritual development.

To understand Maybaum's view one added feature of his perspective, already mentioned, needs to be more sharply brought into focus. The historical inter-relation of Israel among the nations, in which the prime movers of the historical order are the non-Jews, requires that Judaism conform to non-Jewish motifs in order to make its presence as God's agent among the gentiles felt. With a profound insight into the relative world-views of Judaism and Christianity, Maybaum argues that for Judaism the central motif is the *Akedah* (the sacrifice of Isaac, [Gen. 22]), whereas for Christianity the central motif is the enormously powerful image of the Crucifixion. The *Akedah* is a sacrifice which never happened. Isaac can grow to maturity, marry, have children, die normally. According to Maybaum there is no heroic tragedy in the *Akedah,* its message is: there can be progress without martyrdom and without death. The Crucifixion is a sacrifice that did happen. Jesus' life is foreshortened, no time to marry, to have children, to die normally. Here is the stuff of heroic tragedy, its message is: martyrdom is required that others may live, vicarious death is needed so that the world may go forward. "The cross contradicts the *Akedah:* Isaac is sacrified."[83] As Maybaum understands it, the message of the Crucifixion is: "somebody had to die that others may live."[84] With the Crucifixion as its model of Divine activity in history the Christian world is unable to grasp the higher religious meaning of the *Akedah.* Tragic as this may be, for Judaism to speak to Christians it must speak in a language they understand—the language of the Cross. Thus the modern Jew collectively, as the single Jew of two millenia ago, must mount the Cross (undergo persecution, suffering and death) in order to arouse the conscience of the gentile world.

So powerful is the hold on western consciousness of the image of the Crucifixion that progress can only be made when framed in terms assimilable to this pattern. The third *Ḥurban* (the Holocaust), like the earlier two, is a divine event which is meant to bring about humanity's advancement. It is framed in the shape of Auschwitz, an overwhelming reliving by the entire Jewish people of the Crucifixion of one Jew, in order to be able to address the deepest sensitivities of modern Christian civilization: "In Auschwitz Jews suffered vicarious atonement for the sins of mankind."[85] Pushing this interpretation of Jewish history to the utmost, Maybaum writes:

"The Golgotha of modern mankind is Auschwitz. The cross, the Roman gallows, was replaced by the gas chamber. The gentiles, it seems, must first be terrified by the blood of the sacrificed scapegoat to have the mercy of God revealed to them and become converted, become baptized gentiles, become Christians."[86]

Crucially important to Maybaum's entire schemata is his contention that Ḥurban means both destruction and progress. What progress then comes through Auschwitz? Have we not since Nazism seen the Congo, Biafra, and Vietnam? Has the State of Israel not been involved in four wars? Maybaum's conception of progress very much reflects his perspective as a Reform Jew. He is aware that Hitler's defeat was not the defeat of all evil, but he does see the destruction of Nazism as the final destruction of the remnants of the medieval period in human history. Though the medieval period seems to have been long transcended as an historical epoch, Maybaum sees Nazism as the final manifestation of the medieval world view and the cataclysmic event—Ḥurban—as the means whereby the world moved with finality from medievalism to modernity. This movement from past to present is symbolized in the destruction of Eastern European Jewry, for it was they who still lived according to the pattern of medieval Jewry, i.e., centered in ghettoes, cut off from their neighbors, focusing all activity within a strict halakhic framework. Their destruction in the Holocaust represents the passing of the medieval historic time which generated this pattern of Jewish existence. As a Reform Jew, who still shares the optimistic vision of classical Reform, and its unflattering opinion of traditional Jewish observance, Maybaum is able to interpret the end of the shtetl and the destruction of Eastern European Jewry, even if through the means of a Hitler, as progress. After Auschwitz world Jewry lives almost exclusively in modern western cultures, America, Israel, Western Europe, and Russia, and this, according to Maybaum, is progress. In these cultures the Jew is free from the halakhah,[87] and free to engage the possibilities open to him through Enlightenment and political emancipation. Repeating the humanistic version of messianism espoused by classical Reform, with its belief in progress and humanity's perfectibility, Maybaum invests the post-Holocaust era with at least the veneer of messianic redemption: "The Jewish people, is, here and now, mankind at its goal. We have arrived. We are the first fruits of God's Harvest."[88] One cannot but hear in Maybaum's enthusiasm for the post-Holocaust era an echo of the hope that 19th century Reform Jews expressed at the original promise of emancipation.

In the Christian world the transcendence of medievalism is manifested in the new ecumenicism of the Catholic Church, most clearly expressed in the spirit of Vatican II which recognized, at least in small measure, the spiritual legitimacy of other religious traditions, and removed from its liturgy and teaching such "medieval" elements as the *perfidiis Judaeis* ("perfidious Jew") phrase from its Easter rite. As the playwright Hochhuth, in his play *The Deputy* noted: "The S.S. were the Dominicans of the technical age," and the Fuehrer-principle was a Nazi version of papal infallibility; indeed the entire tragedy of the Holocaust was the medieval Inquisition repeated in modern dress. All these are elements of a best forgotten Middle Ages. After Auschwitz, both Jew and Christian can go beyond the historic postures of their medieval period through progressive reform more suitable to a post-Holocaust future. Auschwitz makes possible the transcendence of the medieval church and the medieval ghetto.

Maybaum, like Rubenstein and Fackenheim, is sensitive to the essential issue of God's presence in history as raised by the Holocaust. Like Fackenheim, Maybaum is a man of faith, but more than Fackenheim and more than almost all other Jewish thinkers, he is willing to draw the conclusion that others will not draw: Hitler is God's agent. Maybaum follows the logic of his commitment to God's presence in History further and more radically than do the others. Outrageous as this entailment appears, to credit God with being the all-powerful God of history seems logically to require seeing God as the agent behind Auschwitz who works His will through Auschwitz. Though others, who would find God in history, even at Auschwitz, recoil from this final attribution, Maybaum does not. As the prophet Jeremiah saw Nebuchadnezzar, the destroyer of Jerusalem, as the "servant of God" (Jer. 27:6) so Maybaum consciously parallels Jeremiah's phrase and gives expression to the awful paradox: "Hitler, My servant!"[89] Maybaum does not shy away from the full meaning of this expression: "Hitler was an instrument. . . . . God used this instrument to cleanse, to purify, to punish a sinful world; the six million Jews, they died an innocent death; they died because of the sins of others."[90]

Maybaum is a man of great faith, only so can he affirm what he has affirmed. Calling upon Isaiah's image of the remnant,[91] the *she'ar yashuv,* Maybaum affirms that though one-third of world Jewry was destroyed in the death camps, two-thirds survived and in this salvation is a miracle

Emil Fackenheim.

Eliezer Berkovits.

no less great than that at the Red Sea; it too is redemption. Maybaum here sees the picture in a more traditional way and calls us to do the same. Look at the salvation of the majority, not the death of a large and sacred minority. See in and through the Nazi Holocaust the saving face of God and none other.

ELIEZER BERKOVITS

Eliezer Berkovits has been a keen student of contemporary Jewish philosophy and has made an especial contribution to the creative discussion of the nature and purpose of the *halakhah* in modern orthodox Judaism. In his work entitled *Faith After the Holocaust* (1973) he gives a more traditional response to the Holocaust than any of the other thinkers already mentioned and points out important elements that need to be considered in any response to Auschwitz.

Berkovits begins his discussion by calling attention to the history of Christian anti-Semitism, which cannot be forgotten or undervalued in any account of Nazi anti-Semitism. This is perhaps the most difficult issue to face after the Holocaust. Berkovits however does not run away from this issue or deflect it; he faces it and requires others to face it if both Jew and Christian want to understand the past and make sure that it does not repeat itself in the future.

Having made clear the historic anti-Semitic background to Auschwitz Berkovits, a learned rabbinic scholar, explores, as did Fackenheim in his *God's Presence in History,* the various traditional historic responses to suffering in the Jewish tradition. Martyrdom is not new in Judaism and Berkovits explores the tradition to see what, if anything, can be taken from it that would be applicable to our response to the death camps. The first response and the most important in historical terms is that known as *Kiddush Ha-Shem*—death for the sanctification of the Divine Name (of God), i.e., death which honors rather than dishonors God and bears witness to His truth. In religious circles this has always been the most frequently given answer to Jewish martyrdom: martyrdom is the ultimate act of resignation and trust in God; it is a testing and a response of faithfulness; it is the climactic act of religious heroism. During the Holocaust there were many who were unable to face the horror of their existence and their end with faith, yet there were many others who, like Rabbi Akiba of old, went to their death in joy that they could give their life for God. One example:[92] the Ostrovzer Rebbe, Rabbi Yehezkiel Halevi Hastuk, went out to meet his Nazi executioners wearing his *tallit* and *kittel,* and before he was shot he announced: "For some time now I have anticipated this *zekhut* [special merit] (of Kiddush ha-Shem). I am prepared."[93] Berkovits knows that such acts do not prove anything conclusive about the ultimate questions relevantly raised about Auschwitz, but he asks that in all discussions of Auschwitz this data too be considered. Berkovits pointedly asks the valid question: if Nazi barbarism speaks for the absence of God, what is to be said about the piety, moral grandeur, and saintliness of many of the victims?

Berkovits' account proceeds from this point as if he, at least, is satisfied that there is more to the issue of "Faith after the Holocaust" than a Richard Rubenstein is aware of. What is required above all else, Berkovits argues, is to provide an adequate Jewish self-understanding of its history and religion so that the events of contemporary history can be properly appraised. Only against such a background can one even begin to argue about the theological relevance of the Holocaust. Critical of many other recent attempts to deal with the "data" of Auschwitz, Berkovits argues that these other attempts "suffer from one serious shortcoming: they deal with the Holocaust in isolation, as if there had been nothing else in Jewish history but this Holocaust."[94] This theme re-appears throughout Berkovits' treatment, not only as critique but as grounds for positive affirmation.

On the basis of this, Berkovits makes the important declaration, which in one sense at least puts him close to Maybaum, that in the framework of world Jewish history Auschwitz is unique in the magnitude of its horror but not in the problem it presents to religious faith. "From the point of view of the problem, we have had innumerable Auschwitz's."[95] With this declaration Berkovits states the basic presupposition of his entire response to the Holocaust. For in declaring it not unique as a problem for faith, he radically dissociates himself from, for example, Fackenheim and Rubenstein, who rest their entire positions on the Holocaust's uniqueness and its forcing Judaism into new and unprecedented responses. If Auschwitz is only the repetition of an ancient pattern, then the entire nature of the problem of response to Auschwitz is altered. The theological problem, as Berkovits sees it, is the same whether one Jew or six million are slaughtered. Each raises the question: How could God let it happen? How does this square with God's providential presence and moral perfection?

If, then, our problem is not unique what have other generations of Jews, after previous Holocausts, made of Jewish martyrdom? Berkovits rejects outright, as do all the other major Jewish thinkers who deal with the Holocaust, the simplistic response that the death camps are *mi-penei ḥataeinu* ("because of our sins"). He acknowledges that the Holocaust was "an injustice absolute."[96] Moreover, with great honesty he adds, "It was an injustice countenanced by God."[97] Yet, Berkovits' concern is to make room for Auschwitz in the Divine scheme despite the fact that it is an unmitigated moral outrage. He calls our attention to a more significant and sophisticated response to evil already stated in the Bible, the notion of *hester panim* ("The Hiding Face of God"). *Hester panim* is the view that at times God, mysteriously and inexplicably, and without any obvious human cause such as sin, hides from man.[98] In response to their martyrdoms previous generations have had those who answered the "problem of evil" with unbelief. Judaism as a whole, however, has rejected the skeptical response and formulated the doctrine of *hester panim* in order to hold on to God's presence despite His hiddenness. In some mysterious way, God's hiddenness and God's redemptiveness are both seen as necessary features of His unfathomable being.

Moreover Berkovits argues that God's hiddenness is required for man to be a moral creature. God's hiddenness creates the possibility for human action. God allows man freedom by "absenting" Himself from history. Thus man can exercise his moral will, he can become good or evil. For good and evil to be real possibilities, God has to respect man's decisions and be bound by them. God has to abstain from reacting to human moral evil if human action is to possess value. Moral humanity requires freedom and freedom is always open to abuse. Berkovits here re-asserts the classic view of the necessity of "free will" to morality. God is long suffering with an evil humanity, yet this results in suffering to some while God waits for the sinner. Thus "while He shows forbearance with the wicked, he must turn a deaf ear to the anguished cries of the violated."[99] The paradoxical implication of this situation is this: humanity is impossible if God is strictly just; if God is loving beyond the requirements of strict justice there must be human suffering and evil.

For Berkovits this is the correct way to view the problem of theodicy in order to be able to continue to believe despite Auschwitz.

God must absent Himself for man to be, but God must also be present in order that ultimately meaninglessness does not gain final victory. Thus God's presence in history must be sensed as hiddenness, and His hiddenness must be understood as the sign of His presence. God reveals His power in history by curbing His power so that man too might be powerful. The only enduring witness to God's ultimate power over history is the history and fate of the Jewish people. In its history, Berkovits declares, we see both attributes of God. The continued existence of Israel despite its long history of suffering is the greatest single proof that God is present in history despite His hiddenness.[100] Israel is the witness to God's presence in history. Nazism, in its satanic power, understood this fact of Jewish history and their slaughter of Jews was an attempt to slaughter the God of history. They understood, even as Israel sometimes fails to understand, that God's presence in history is necessarily linked to the fate of the Jewish people. The nature of Jewish existence stands as prophetic testimony against the moral degeneracy of men and nations; it is a mocking proclamation in the face of all human idolatry, and it witnesses to the final judgment and redemption of history by a moral God.

Berkovits forces his readers to consider whether the Holocaust is a sign of the "death of God" or whether it is a sign of God's too great mercy and long suffering with sinners.

Berkovits forces us back to have another look at Jewish history and see Auschwitz in the long context of Jewish historical experience. The Jew is forbidden to treat Auschwitz as if it were all he knew of God's relation to Israel. Auschwitz is not the only, or even the ultimate Jewish experience.[101] The Jew who today witnesses the absence of God is the descendant of those who at Sinai and the Red Sea saw the Divine "face to face." More important still, the Jew who today talks of Auschwitz also knows the joy of a rebuilt Zion and an "ingathering of the exiles" in its ancient homeland. Jewish survival after Auschwitz proclaims that Auschwitz is not absolute. This does not answer the agonizing questions of theodicy though it gives hope that they will be answered in God's future redemptive acts.

The final element in Berkovits' analysis of contemporary Jewish faith after the Holocaust is his passionate Zionism. Of all the thinkers discussed Berkovits is the one most committed to Zionism and draws most heavily on the theological implications of the rebirth of the State of Israel. Fackenheim and Maybaum certainly value it and indeed, Fackenheim has become increasingly ardent in his attitude to Zionism, yet it is Berkovits above all others who gives it a theological significance and pride of place in the renewal of the possibility of Jewish faith after Auschwitz. The rebirth of the State of Israel is contemporary revelation; it is the voice of God speaking forth from history. The events of 1967 especially have an "inescapable revelation quality."[102] The return to the land must be understood in both historical and eschatalogical terms. "The return is the counterpart in history to the resolution in faith that this world is to be established as the Kingdom of God."[103] The return to Zion is the ultimate vindication of God's presence in history and His providential governance of man and the world. If at Auschwitz and all previous Auschwitz's we have witnessed "The Hiding Face of God," in the rebirth of the State of Israel and its success "we have seen a smile on the face of God. It is enough."[104]

CONCLUSION

Several responses to the Holocaust have now been considered. Each has seen the events of the Nazi era from a different perspective and with differing faith commitments. In conclusion, it should be noted that each of the responses considered, and others which have been suggested, all represent, at best, partial descriptions and solutions to the major questions raised by Auschwitz. Given the nature of the Holocaust this is not surprising; each response can at best be partial and fragmentary in the face of the reality, quality and quantity of evil witnessed in our time. Those who speak to the issue of "Faith after the Holocaust" render service in the authenticity with which they wrestle with the issues and prod others to do likewise, even more than in the nature of their results.

OTHER CONTEMPORARY VOICES

WILL HERBERG

After Heschel and Soloveitchik, Will Herberg (1909–   ) has been the most influential thinker in American Judaism since the end of World War II. Herberg turned to the study of Judaism after his romance with Marxism ended.[105] Rather than trusting in a materialist dialectic, Herberg came to hold that the ethical ends he (and the Marxists) sought could only be produced by a religious existentialism that "would give full recognition to the transcendent aspects of man's nature and destiny."[106]

Herberg's understanding of religion is largely influenced by the Christian neo-orthodoxy of Karl Barth and especially its leading American proponent, Reinhold Niebuhr.[107] As such, it was religion reacting to the naive liberalism which had dominated Protestant "social Gospel" theology, and Reform and Reconstructionist Judaism alike. In contrast to the optimism and innocence of such theology, Herberg, like Niebuhr before him, argued for a more complex and less optimistic image of man, a greater recognition of human sinfulness and human limitations, and a more radical awareness of the demanding Word of the Living God in one's life. The Nazi era seemed to Herberg to have destroyed the foundations of Protestant Liberalism and Reform Judaism, and a new, more passionate, and difficult neo-orthodox religious existentialism was required to meet the post-war situation. Herberg's work is thoroughly infused with these emphases. In addition, Herberg, in trying to find a model for the Jewish affirmation of this position, and especially for a viable model of Divine revelation acceptable to Judaism, was led to and deeply influenced by the dialogical *I-Thou* philosophy of Buber and Rosenzweig, and his account of Divine-human relation is framed in Buberian terms. The clearest and most detailed expression of these concerns is found in Herberg's important, though derivative work,

Judaism and Modern Man.[108] Since the appearance of this work Herberg's thought has increasingly matured and overcome some of the narrowness imposed upon it by its original neo-orthodoxy. In his later work there has especially been a more profound understanding of Judaism and the relation of Jewish thought and reality to history.

In addition to his theological work, Herberg has written a minor classic in the field of American religious sociology entitled *Protestant, Catholic and Jew.*[109] Herberg here gives a penetrating analysis of the peculiarities and unique features of American religiosity in terms of its sociological determinants. According to his account it is religion rather than class or ethnic background which is the social determinant in American society. One must be a member of a religious community in order "to belong" in American society. Thus religion becomes a matter of institutional loyalties created by social pressures rather than religious faith. Furthermore, institutional religion is understood as being part of the "American ideal" which is the actual religion of most Americans. The growth of synagogues in post-war suburbia is a monumental (in both senses) testimony to it. Such "affiliation Judaism" has serious consequences for Judaism; it threatens especially the rich personal-religious life of the Jew which traditionally has been the central focus of Judaism and Jewish life.[110]

RECONSTRUCTIONIST THOUGHT

Though Mordecai Kaplan, the father of Reconstructionism, has been discussed[111] in terms of the major figures of the pre-war era in Jewish life, his thought has had a substantial impact in post-war American Jewish thought and he has continued to contribute seminal works to the Jewish community since 1945.[112] In addition, his thought has been institutionalized into a separate movement within modern Judaism with its own Reconstructionist seminary, its own publication, *The Reconstructionist,* and its own liturgy and ceremony.

The leading second generation spokesmen for the Reconstructionist position have been Milton Steinberg, Ira Eisenstein, Jack Cohen and the younger Alan Miller. Steinberg (1903–1950) has been the most eloquent and persuasive popularizer of Kaplan's views. As a member of the editorial committee of *The Reconstructionist* and in a series of popular books, such as *A Partisan Guide to the Jewish Problem* and *Basic Judaism,* Steinberg attempted to show the power of the Reconstructionist position to meet the needs of modern man. Steinberg, however, became increasingly critical of Kaplan's position for what he saw as its failure to provide an adequate philosophical rationale for its theology. In a series of vigorous essays, most of which can be found in his collection entitled *The Anatomy of Faith* (1960), he began to point out the inherent philosophical inadequacy of Kaplan's views. In this criticism Steinberg was anticipating the major struggle in which Reconstructionism has been engaged since 1945, namely, the struggle to maintain its theological credibility to the modern generation.[113]

The vigorous debate, first anticipated by Jacob Agus and then Steinberg, was sparked by a long critique of Kaplan's views by the orthodox theologian Eliezer Berkovits.[114] In his critique Berkovits, in an intense philosophic polemic, argues that Kaplan's view cannot do justice to the basic Jewish theological realities of "God," "man" and "world" and that it is wedded to and dependent upon an outmoded optimistic evolutionary schema which is bad science, bad metaphysics, and bad Judaism. The inescapable point of Berkovits' critique is that Kaplan's naturalism is inadequate for theology, and Reconstructionism needs to make an alliance with "some metaphysical and supernaturalist philosophy."[115] Berkovits' critique was followed by another, this time by Emil Fackenheim.[116] Fackenheim accepted Berkovits' critique as definitive in showing the inadequacy of Reconstructionist thought. However, Fackenheim held that Berkovits had not adequately stressed the issue of immanence versus supernaturalism, and in line with Fackenheim's own maturing supernaturalism he argued that the greatest weakness of Kaplan's position, and the one most deleterious to a renewal of Judaism, was its desire to be rid of supernaturalism.

Berkovits' and Fackenheim's criticisms did not go unchallenged. Ira Eisenstein, Kaplan's successor as the active head of the Reconstructionist movement, replied to their critique.[117] His reply reasserted Kaplan's views, especially regarding the correctness of his naturalism and immanentism. Eisenstein's reply however was more by way of assertion than argument and advanced the discussion little, if at all, from where it stood in the confrontation of Kaplan and his critics. The case for Reconstructionism has been stated more rigorously by Jack J. Cohen[118] who has argued for the Reconstructionist position

on pragmatic and psychological grounds. Those who object to reductionism for philosophical and theological reasons however will not
find Cohen's discussion persuasive, for it too is unable to provide a
basis for "value" which is grounded in anything other than psychological
need. The debate has continued in and out of the pages of the *Reconstructionist* and other journals. In 1970 the discussion over Reconstructionism was again joined with new vigor due to a lengthy exposition
and critique of the movement by Charles Liebman, an orthodox American social scientist now teaching at Bar-Ilan University in Israel.
Liebman's study, which appeared in the *American Jewish Yearbook*
for 1970, is the most comprehensive and wide-ranging study of Reconstructionism to date and covers the theology, as well as the history
and general organization of the movement. Liebman again questions
the philosophical correctness of Kaplan's thought, finding his "God-
Idea," his approach to evil, and his ability to do justice to prayer, ritual
and Jewish tradition, among other issues, inadequate. Ira Eisenstein
has attempted to reply to Liebman's criticisms. In a series of 3 articles
in the *Reconstructionist* entitled "A Critique of a Critique,"[119] he
takes up Liebman's position in considerable detail. However, as in his
earlier dialogue with Fackenheim (and Berkovits) his reply is primarily
re-statement and paraphrase of Kaplan and little new light is shed.

Most recently, Alan Miller, a Reconstructionist Rabbi, has tried
again to make a case for Kaplan's position in a work entitled *"The
God of Daniel S."* (1969). In addition, Kaplan and Arthur Cohen
have published their discussions of the nature and weaknesses of the
Reconstructionist position[120] and its relevance to modern Jewish
life. Throughout this period, and despite all that has happened, one
of the extraordinary features of Reconstructionist thought in general
and of Kaplan's thought in particular is how little it has changed since
Kaplan first gave it its classic expression in the 1930's.

CONSERVATIVE THOUGHT

Conservative Judaism has been a center of theological discussion
since 1945. Trying to find a middle way between rejection of the *halakhah*
and domination by the *halakhah,* many Conservative thinkers have attempted to mediate a creative approach to tradition. Among them, the

most significant are Jacob Agus, Robert Gordis, and Arthur Cohen. The English scholar, Louis Jacobs, though orthodox in his training and observance and the Rabbi of an orthodox synagogue, has also published views which belong under the rubric "Conservative."

Jacob Agus (1911–   ), a rabbi and an outstanding historian of Jewish philosophy and the author of, among other works, *Modern Philosophies of Judaism, The Evolution of Jewish Thought,* and *Banner of Jerusalem* (a study of Rav Kook), has been active in all phases of the modern discussions within Jewish thought, i.e., the nature and role of Zionism; the character and purpose of Jewish-Christian dialogue; the character of the *halakhah* in modern Jewish life, and the discussion of faith after Auschwitz. He has also had a long dialogue with Arnold Toynbee on the place of Israel in history and his correspondance and critique of Toynbee's harsh early judgment of modern Judaism as a "fossil" is printed in volume 12 of Toynbee's *Study of History* (1961) entitled, appropriately, "Reconsiderations."

All of Agus' views on these diverse subjects reflect a basic humanistic optimism, belief in progress, and a belief that Judaism is not a monolithic faith with only one right way. He has been critical of Zionism because he holds that there is a conflict between spiritual-prophetic Judaism, which he sees as a Judaism of universal ethical monotheism, and the nationalism and particularism he sees inherent in Zionism. For a similar reason he has advocated a re-definition of the concept of Israel as the "Chosen People," arguing that Israel is only "unique" insofar as every nation and people are unique.[121] Agus has also been one of the leading Jewish figures in Jewish-Christian dialogue, and has contributed a volume on Judaism to the Catholic Theological Encyclopedia. In his view, the time has come for Jews to end that insularity which has separated them from their Christian neighbors and for both to go forward into a better future together.[122] Finally, he is a liberal interpreter of the *halakhah* and the role that man must play in interpreting and applying the tradition. He holds that "all religion is man-made"[123] and open to human error and distortion, Judaism being no exception. The halakhic tradition is the human response to God's revelation; it is human in character and open to change.

Robert Gordis (1908–   ), primarily noted as a Bible scholar and interpreter of the Book of *Job*[124] and *Koheleth,*[125] and an active participant in inter-faith discussion, has also been a significant interpreter of Judaism to his generation. In several works, among them, *A Faith For Moderns*,[126] *Root and the Branch*,[127] and *Judaism in a Christian World*,[128] he has attempted to mediate between Judaism and modernity and between Judaism and a non-Jewish world. He has stressed the existential nature of Judaism and the legitimacy of contemporary doubt in religious matters. He argues against reducing Judaism to other contemporary branches of knowledge but he makes a good case for taking all forms of knowledge seriously, and for the importance of relating Judaism to other areas of contemporary concern. In the *Root and the Branch* he applies this outlook by evaluating the relation of international politics, law and ethics to Judaism. Gordis has been an able interpreter of the Conservative views on the *halakhah* and its importance to modern man. In his *Judaism for the Modern Age* he makes a persuasive case for *"Torah min-ha-Shamayim,"* which he understands to mean "The Torah as a revelation of God,"[129] as the foundation of all authentic Judaism. Gordis however argues that this need not be taken to mean that every word of the Torah was "dictated" by God. Judaism recognizes the legitimacy of human involvement in revelation and the need for a doctrine of "progressive and growing revelation"[130] to meet new situations in each age.

Louis Jacobs (1920–   ), perhaps the most outstanding contemporary British Jewish scholar, has made major contributions to a variety of subjects. He has been a significant spokesman for a very traditionalist conservatism in which the *halakhah* is binding in all its detail but which at the same times allows for an intellectual openness to new archeological, philosophical, literary, and historical studies about the genesis and transmission of biblical and other ancient texts and a willingness to face honestly the findings of sound scholarship. Thus Jacobs, in his controversial book, *We Have Reason to Believe* (1957), and in subsequent works such as *Jewish Values* (1965), *The Principles of the Jewish Faith* (1964, a study of Maimonides' "Thirteen Articles of Faith"), and *A Jewish Theology* (1974) has been willing to acknowledge the results of biblical criticism and to recognize a human element in the transcription and composition of the Torah. This acknowledgment is Jacobs' major deviation from traditional Rabbinic theology.

Another figure who shares the Conservative outlook and who has made important contributions to modern thought is Arthur A. Cohen

(1928–   ). He is the author of an interesting, if idiosyncratic, history of modern Jewish thought entitled *The Natural and the Supernatural Jew*. In addition he has written a work denying the reality of the "Judeo-Christian tradition" entitled *The Myth of the Judeo-Christian Tradition*, and has edited an interesting collection of essays on modern Jewish thought in the aftermath of the Holocaust entitled *Arguments and Doctrines*. He has described himself as a non-Zionist, supernaturalist Jew.

ORTHODOX THINKERS

Modern Orthodoxy, as one would expect, has been the movement least subject to change, or to discussions about possible change. Guided by the traditional halakhic norms, and continuing largely in the halakhic mould in which halakhic (legal) discussions are the essential intellectual arena, Orthodox Judaism has, for the most part, been timid about engaging in philosophy or philosophical theology. The authoritative voice of Rabbi Soloveitchik and the views of the great 19th century orthodox Rabbi Samson Raphael Hirsch have been the accepted norms of almost all discussions within modern American orthodoxy. However, there are a number of other spokesmen of importance. We have already reviewed Eliezer Berkovits' position on the Holocaust. In addition, Berkovits, who is Chairman of the Department of Jewish Philosophy at the Hebrew Theological College in Skokie, Illinois, has been an active spokesman for religious Zionism and a student of the relations between religious and secular Zionism. His work, *Towards Historic Judaism* (1943) is devoted to this theme. He has also been interested in re-interpreting the halakhic tradition in order to emphasize its dynamic qualities and value for modern man. He has dealt with these issues at length in journal articles and a monograph entitled *God, Man and History* (1959). Berkovits' concern with *halakhah,* though strictly traditional, shows the influence of existentialist thought, especially that of Rosenzweig and Buber.

Other orthodox thinkers of note who have also worked towards interpreting traditional Judaism to modern man include Samuel Belkin, Emanuel Rackman, Leon Stitskin, Norman Lamm, Aaron Lichtenstein, Shubert Spero, David Shapiro, Marvin Fox, and Michael

Wyschograd. Though the work of this group of scholars is not widely known it has not been without interest and importance, especially in applying the halakhic tradition to contemporary issues, and in re-assessing, while strictly maintaining, the meaning of the halakhic norm. Samuel Belkin's *In His Image* (1960) is especially noteworthy in this respect. Belkin, president of Yeshiva University and the author of a valuable work on Philo, does not offer any radical suggestions about the meaning of the Torah and *halakhah,* but he shows how the halakhic tradition operates in practice and gives a valuable exegesis of traditional Jewish categories, such as the character and purpose of *teshuvah* (repentance), the meaning of *mitzvot,* and the nature of the Jewish community, from a halakhic perspective. Norman Lamm's *Faith and Doubt* (1971) does much the same sort of thing in respect of different problems and with more sympathy for modern "unbelief" than Belkin shows. Lamm tries to meet some of the doubts which seem to prevent widespread modern acceptance of the halakhic tradition and to show the relevance of halakhic thought and practice to important issues in contemporary life.

In addition, these modern Orthodox thinkers have individually and collectively served as important critics of non-traditional re-formulations of Judaism, constantly reminding all who are concerned that there is more to Judaism than sincerity, biography, emotion, philosophy or even Jewish studies, and that the halakhic tradition is the essential manifestation of Judaism which all meaningful Jewish philosophy and Jewish theology needs to engage. Berkovits and Fox, the latter for many years professor of philosophy at Ohio State University and then professor of Jewish philosophy at Brandeis University, have played especially valuable roles in this respect.

REFORM JUDAISM

Reform Jewish thinkers, traditionally the most radical in modern Jewish thought, have, since World War II, been in a transition period of uncertainty, trying to re-define their relation to the essential features of traditional Jewish life, most especially their relation to the *halakhah.*

Among the leaders of the Reform re-appraisal of the *halakhah* has been Jacob Petuchowski (1925–   ), professor of rabbinics at Hebrew

Union College in Cincinnati. Petuchowski has made a major theological effort to re-establish a viable reform approach to *halakhah*. The basis of Petuchowski's labors is a Rosenzweigian[131] doctrine of revelation, with its distinction between Law and Commandment, in which the Torah and the Rabbinic tradition represent an admixture of God's address and man's response. This tradition is not binding if it does not speak to each man in his particular situation; however, if approached in sincerity some or all of the Divine address embodied in this traditional literature may strike a responsive chord in modern man. There are no absolutes, only invitations. Petuchowski puts it this way: "The modern Jew. . . . will want to 'try out' those practices and observances which *might* contain God's commandments to *him*."[132] Linked to this revelatory schema is an evolutionary account of Torah and *halakhah* which recognizes frankly its historical development. However Petuchowski argues for a Divine inspiration working in and through this historical process so that, on no account, is it reducible to a merely human phenomena.[133] In such an account the danger of subjectivism is always real and always present. However, Petuchowski holds that the communal nature of Judaism is a check against excess subjectivism. The strengths and weaknesses of this view are the strengths and weaknesses of Rosenzweig's (and Buber's) doctrine of revelation.

It should also be mentioned that Petuchowski has become increasingly sympathetic toward Zionism and in this he is representative of Reform Judaism as a whole which has moved steadily from extreme anti-Zionism to an active endorsement of Zionism. He is also the author of several important studies on liturgy and the history of changes in the Reform ritual and prayerbook.

Another Reform theologian of significance is Eugene Borowitz. Borowitz, professor of education at Hebrew Union College (N.Y. Division), has been especially active in trying to explore and frame the conditions necessary for there to be a workable Jewish theology. In a series of essays and monographs, such as *A New Jewish Theology in the Making* (1968) and *How can a Jew speak of Faith Today?* (1968), he has explored some of the relevant issues. Like Petuchowski, Borowitz is unable to accept a Judaism based on heteronomy and absolute halakhic authority, and yet he appreciates the need for a substantive doctrine of revelation which will provide the ground for a realizable and meaningful Judaism. His still tentative beginning to meet this demand is an argument in favor of the need for a passionate openness to Judaism which makes faith in one's Judaism primary and prior to all other values. In this way the modern liberal Jew can confront the whole of the Jewish tradition and respond to it according to his own unique and individual sensitivities. Again, as with Petuchowski, a Buber-Rosenzweig account of revelation is influential in Borowitz's program for the renewal of Liberal Judaism.

A third Reform Rabbi who belongs to the same camp as Borowitz and Petuchowski and who shares their views on dialogical revelation and affirms the reality of God's covenant with Israel is W. Gunther Plaut. Plaut is the author of a two-volume study[134] of the history of Reform Judaism and of a work dealing specifically with the meaning of Israel as the 'Chosen People' entitled *The Case for the Chosen People* (1965). A fourth person who should also be mentioned in this group is Lou Silberman, professor of Jewish studies at Vanderbilt University, who has been active in the discussion of the meaning of revelation and tradition in the contemporary situation.

Two older scholars of the Reform movement who made significant contributions to Jewish thought both before and after 1945 and are included here because of their work and influence since 1945 are Abba Hillel Silver (1893–1963) and Samuel S. Cohon (1888–1959). Silver, a life-long Zionist and one of the leading figures in the history of American Zionism, and the man, who as chairman of the American section of the Jewish Agency, argued the case for the establishment of Israel before the United Nation's General Assembly on May 8, 1947, was also a scholar of significance. The author of many works, especially important among his early works being a study of Jewish messianism published in 1927,[135] Silver contributed one of the most widely discussed books of the post war era, *Where Judaism Differed* in 1957. In it Silver argued vigorously for the uniqueness of Judaism, being especially concerned to show the theological *differences* between Judaism and Christianity in comparison to the more usual approach which attempts to highlight their similarities. Though much of the work is polemical in tone, a good deal of what Silver has to say is important and needs to be said, for a close examination of Judaism and Christianity does reveal basic and uncompromisable points of theological difference. Samuel S. Cohon, professor of theology at the Hebrew Union College, Cincinnati, though not a widely known figure, was important in moving

Reform Judaism toward a more positive view of Jewish tradition, halakhic observance, and the value of Zionism and Jewish peoplehood. His theological views are most fully expounded in a work published posthumously, entitled *Jewish Theology* (2 vols, 1971) and also in an earlier work entitled *Judaism: A Way of Life* (1965).

Reform Judaism is also represented by thinkers of a very different persuasion from the existentialism of Petuchowski and Borowitz. One thinks in particular of Levi Olan (1903–) and Roland Gittelsohn (1910–) who have pushed out in Kaplan's direction of religious naturalism and beyond. Levi Olan, a Reform Rabbi in Dallas and Roland Gittelsohn, a Reform Rabbi in Boston, have both tried to pursue an extreme Jewish rationalism based on science, nature, and logic. Olan, though recognizing the "faith" element even in his scientific version of Reform Judaism, sees the task of the Reform theologian today as one of purging Judaism of supernaturalism and of replacing it with the immanentist findings of science which, in their increasingly powerful explanatory force, make a transcendent God unnecessary. Gittelsohn, perhaps an even more ardent rationalist and advocate of the application of scientific techniques and findings to religion, has wedded his naturalism to contemporary "Process Philosophy" (deriving from the thought of A.N. Whitehead and Charles Hartshorne). The traditional transcendent referents of Judaism, e.g., God and Torah, are re-defined in immanentist naturalistic terms which translate, for example, the term "God" from meaning "the transcendent Creator of the world" to a natural process within the universe: "God is to nature what energy is to matter. He is *within* nature. He is not supernatural."[136] Both Olan and Gittelsohn have difficulty accounting for value, especially 'moral' value in their systems. In addition, their faith in science has been criticized as naive.

CONCLUSION

As our review has shown, there has been a substantial amount of Jewish theological activity in the past thirty years. Much of it will not stand the test of time; some of it might. Whatever the judgment of history on particular views, it will however have to acknowledge that ours is, and has been, a period of intense energy and effort in which theologians and philosophers have tried to grapple with the new con-

ditions (themselves contradictory and problematical) of our age and
the new realities of Jewish life after Auschwitz in both the Diaspora
and the reborn and flourishing State of Israel. Throughout all the
work there runs a new pride and a new vigor in respect of one's Jewishness and things Jewish. Perhaps the most outstanding feature of the
entire period, and the major contribution to future Jewish thought, is
the transcendence of the 19th century apologetic stance and the affirmation of Jewishness per se, without need of apologia or embarrassment.

From within the current debate six issues stand out as most pressing.
The first is the "problem of revelation." The word "problem" is used
advisedly for, as we have seen, all authentic modern Jewish thought
has to come to terms with the Torah and halakhic tradition, and this
requires an understanding of traditional conceptions of God's revelatory
acts as well as a means of making the concept of revelation viable to
modern man. Those who do not accept the traditional orthodox position
(the majority of contemporary theologians) yet wish to make a meaningful contribution to Jewish thought, have to be able to give a coherent
account of God's relation to man and the way God makes His will
known, if indeed He does. For an alternative account of revelation
most modern thinkers depend on the dialogical thought of Buber and
Rosenzweig, whose influence is evident in almost every non-traditional
version of Jewish theology. However it can be held that for a variety
of philosophical and theological reasons the existentialist version of
revelation as "presence" is unable to fulfill all the conditions required
of revelation. More important still, it undermines the whole dimension
of Jewish covenantal community which it was intended to maintain,
making *mitzvot,* ethics, and Torah, at best, subjective and personally
appropriable by individuals. Such an account makes for the dissolution
of a dynamic and meaningful concept of Divine activity in human
history. To provide a more adequate understanding of revelation
therefore remains the most pressing single need in contemporary Jewish
thought.

Related to a more adequate understanding of revelation is the need
for modern Jewish theologians to become more competent in halakhic
matters. This is an intellectual if not a religious requirement. The
halakhah has been the main expression of Jewish spirituality over the
centuries and its study and development has historically been the major
vehicle of and for Jewish theology. Most modern Jewish theologians

are less than competent halakhists and thus their thought does not grow out of or take adequate account of the major element in the Jewish theological tradition.

A third pressing issue for modern Jewish theology is that it become more sophisticated in its understanding of logic and language. The existentialist influence on modern Jewish thought has had a deleterious side effect: it has created the impression that theologians could talk in "paradoxes" and write in grand, vague generalizations and still communicate what they wished to. This is a serious mistake. What are "paradoxes" to the man who utters them are usually just illogical and contradictory statements to the people who hear them. In order for theology to be a public enterprise open to rational discussion and debate, the rules of logic and the nature of language must be understood and respected by theologians, as they are by everyone else. Otherwise theology is reduced to the making of statements which have little cognitive content, and serve more as personal biographical utterances than meaningful theological statements which tell us something about the world and God's relation to men. Furthermore, Jewish theologians have to consider the whole related area of theological and philosophical epistemology in order to come to a better understanding of just what the proper function of language and logic is to a Jewish theology, and what method or methods are best suited for Jewish theology.

Fourth, modern theologians will have to continue to face the issue of the Holocaust. In the last 10 years this issue has moved increasingly into the center of Jewish theological debate. We have examined the major responses to it, and it is clear that none are completely convincing. This is not surprising and is due to the very nature of the Holocaust itself. Nevertheless, Jewish thinkers will have to continue to wrestle with the Holocaust and continue to try to make some "sense" of it in light of and in relation to the other claims of Judaism and the Jewish understanding of God and His relation to men.

The fifth and sixth issues are related to the re-creation of the State of Israel. The existence of a Jewish State in Erez Israel (the Land of Israel) makes a re-examination of the notions "religious" and "secular" a pressing need. The very existence and maintainance of the State clearly has religious value—just how and how much are still unclarified theological issues. However it is clear that the notion of religiosity and the meaning of religious life which were and are appropriate to

Galut (Exile) need to be reviewed, at least in terms of the State of Israel.

Finally, the State of Israel renews an ancient debate in Jewish theology: What is the meaning of Zion in Judaism and the proper relation between Zion and the Diaspora? Though much has been written on these issues, no major theoretical understanding has emerged that can provide a truly persuasive account of all the factors at work in the contemporary situation.

The future success or failure of Jewish theology will depend largely on its ability to deal adequately, intelligently, and creatively with these six issues.

[1] Hermann Cohen and Leo Baeck have had only limited influence on postwar thinkers. Interestingly, where this has occurred, they have also been interpreted, incorrectly, as at least marginal or pioneering existentialists.

[2] Compare the role of the Jew in the traditional coronation ceremony of the Popes in the medieval world. See for example, the description given by Joachim Prinz in his *Popes from the Ghetto* (p. 149), (1968). For further details see Prinz's sources listed in his Bibliography.

[3] As it was characterized by Arnold Toynbee—later to be retracted!

[4] In *God in Search of Man*, Heschel implicitly calls attention to this by calling the existence of God his "ontological presupposition." See chapter 11, pgs. 114–124. See also Ch. 12 on "About the meaning of God."

[5] *Man is not Alone*, p. 22.

[6] *Man is not Alone*, p. 22.

[7] These designations are not Heschel's.

[8] These three responses are Heschel's. In *God in Search of Man* (pgs. 33–34) he writes: "There are three aspects of nature that command our attention: its power its beauty, and its grandeur. Accordingly, there are three ways in which we may relate ourselves to the world—we may exploit it, we may enjoy it, we may accept it in awe."

[9] See *God in Search of Man*, p. 33.

[10] An English edition entitled *The Prophets* appeared in 1962. See also Heschel's essay "The Hebrew Prophet in relation to God and Man" (in Hebrew) in *Old Testament Conceptions of God, Man and the World* ed. by Zevi Adar, 1957, pgs. 215–224.

[11] This reflects both biblical and kabbalistic doctrines.

[12] *Die Prophetie*, p. 131.

[13] *The Insecurity of Freedom*, p. 93.

[14] There are deep problems in Heschel's account of *halakhah* which go beyond the scope of this essay. However, among contemporary Jewish thinkers Heschel's attempt to do justice to the halakhic tradition, while not adopting a totally "orthodox" stance, is the most profound and far more subtle and sophisticated than, say, Rosenzweig's, Buber's, or Kaplan's.

[15] The word "normative" is used here to suggest those texts which every Jewish thinker of whatever theological persuasion must come to grips with, even if ultimately he takes a critical or negative stand towards them. Outstanding among such texts, next to the Bible, are the Talmudic and Rabbinic materials.

[16] Vols. 1 and 2 were published in 1962 and 1965, and Vol. 3 is being published posthumously.

[17] Of modern halakhic giants, the theology of Joseph Soloveitchik might be

thought to represent this school, while that of the Rav Kook, might be seen as representing the non-rationalist (mystical)-supernaturalist orientation.

[18] His published works on these thinkers are: *Maimonides: Eine Biographie,* Berlin: Erich Reiss Verlag, 1935; "Did Maimonides Strive for Prophetic Inspiration?" in Louis Ginzberg Jubilee Volume (in Hebrew), N.Y.: The American Academy of Jewish Research, 1945, pgs. 159–188. A small part of his views on Maimonides can be found in an English translation of Ch. 25 of his book on Maimonides entitled, "The Last Years of Maimonides" in the *National Jewish Monthly,* vol. 69 No. 10 June 1955. In connection with Maimonides' view of prophecy and whether or not Maimonides thought of himself as possessing prophetic inspiration see also Heschel's essay "Inspiration (ruach ha-Kodesh) in the Middle Ages" (in Hebrew), in *Alexander Marx Jubilee Volume* (Hebrew section), N.Y.: The Jewish Theological Seminary of America, 1950, pgs. 175–208. His views on Solomon Ibn Gabirol are presented in the following essays:

"Der Begriff der Einheit in der Philosophie Gabirols," in *Monatsschrift für die Geschichte und Wissenschaft des Judentums,* Vol. 82 (1938), pgs. 89–111. "Das Wesen der Dinge nach der Lehre Gabirols," in *Hebrew Union College Annual,* Vol. 14 (1939), pgs. 359–385.

"Der Begriff des Seins in der Philosophie Gabirols," in *Festschrift Jakob Freimann* zum 70. 1937, pgs. 67–77.

An abridged English translation of this last essay appeared in the memorial issue of *Conservative Judaism* Vol. 28, No. 1, Fall 1972 as "The Concept of Beings in the Philosophy of Ibn Gabirol" trans. by D.W. Silverman. Heschel's views on Saadiah were published as *The Quest for Certainty in Saadiah's Philosophy,* 1944. For his understanding of the life and thought of Don Isaac Abravanel see his *Don Jizchak Abrananel* (in German: 1937).

[19] *Maimonides: Eine Biographie* (1935). Published in French in 1936.

[20] *The Quest for Certainty in Saadia's Philosophy,* p. 55.

[21] Heschel's specialized studies on ḥasidic and related themes (in the Jewish mystical literature) include: "A Cabbalistic Commentary on the Prayerbook" (in Hebrew) in *Studies in Memory of Moses Schorr,* ed. by L. Ginzberg and A. Weiss, (1944) pgs. 113–126: "The Eastern European Era in Jewish History" in *Yivo Annual of Jewish Social Science,* vol. I, (1946) pgs. 86–106: "Rabbi Phineas of Koretz" (in Hebrew) in *Alei Ayin: The Salman Schocken Jubilee Volume,* (1948–52) pgs. 213–244: "The Mystical Element in Judaism" in *The Jews: Their History, Culture and Religion,* ed. Louis Finkelstein, (1949) Vol. I, pp. 602–623. This work was reprinted in 3 volumes as a paperback by Schocken Books in 1970. Heschel's essay is in vol. 2: "Rabbi Gershon of Kuty" (in Hebrew) in *Hebrew Union College Annual,* vol. 23 (1950–51) part II, pp. 17–71: "Rabbi Mendel mi-Kotzk" (in Hebrew) in

Hadoar, vol. 39 No. 28, (June 5, 1959) pgs. 519–521: "Rabbi Naḥman of Kossov, Companion of the Baal Shem" (in Hebrew) in *The Harry A. Wolfson Jubilee Volume* ed. by Saul Lieberman et al., (1965) pgs. 113–141.

22 Of all the thinkers of the modern period, Soloveitchik is the most difficult to fully understand and his views are very hard to summarize and transmit because he has published so little. The paucity of sources for his views makes all statements about his views tentative, though based on a thorough study of the small amount of material that has been published.

23 These questions are framed by Soloveitchik in his paper "The Lonely Man of Faith" in *Tradition* vol. 7 #2 (1965) p. 12.

24 On Adam II see *Ibid.,* pgs. 16–18.

25 *Ibid.,* p. 19 ff.

26 *Ibid.,* p. 23 ff.

27 Both these terms are Soloveitchik's. See *Ibid.,* p. 24. They clearly reflect Kierkegaard's analysis of the religious man as "The Single One." Compare, for a very different view of the human situation, Buber's dialogical account as presented in his *I and Thou.*

28 *Ibid.,* p. 25.

29 Soloveitchik's term, *Ibid.,* p. 28.

30 For Soloveitchik's full discussion of the nature of the covenantal community see *Ibid.,* p. 28 ff.

31 *Ibid.,* p. 29 ff. and p. 38 ff.

32 For full details see *Ibid.,* p. 33 ff.

33 *Ibid.,* p. 38., For a more detailed account of Soloveitchik's understanding of *halakhah,* see his important essay *"Ish ha-Halakhah"* in *Talpiot* (in Hebrew) (1944), pgs. 651–735.

34 *Ibid.,* p. 40.

35 *Ibid.,* p. 28 and note on p. 28 f.

36 *Ibid.,* p. 49 ff. See also his *"Ish ha-Halakhah"* p. 690 ff.

37 Soloveitchik also discusses the meaning of the Adam narratives in an article entitled "Confrontation" in *Tradition* vol. 6 No. 2 (1961) pgs. 5–29. Here he adds certain elements not found in his longer article "The Lonely Man of Faith."

38 Another figure who holds a heteronomous position is the Israel thinker Yeshayahu Leibowitz.

39 Elie Wiesel's personal and literary expressions belong to a totally different class of responses to the Holocaust, though his view is probably most closely approximated "theologically" by Emil Fackenheim.

40 *After Auschwitz,* "The Making of a Rabbi," p. 223.

41 This came in an interview with a German theologian, Heinrich Grueber, Dean of the Evangelican Church of East and West Berlin, in August 1961. The

whole incident is recorded in *After Auschwitz*, "The Dean and the Chosen People," pgs. 47–58.

42 *After Auschwitz*, p. 46.

43 *After Auschwitz*, p. 46.

44 Hagigah 14b ff.

45 The older, more famous religious existentialism of Rosenzweig and Buber, for example, fiercely protested against the denial of value and the need to create it. See, for example, Buber's sharp criticism of Sartre in *The Eclipse of God*.

46 *After Auschwitz*, p. 68.

47 Rubenstein uses the term "demythologize" regularly to describe the process whereby Jews recognize the "death of God" and their new, post-Holocaust situation. The term "demythologize" Rubenstein borrows from the contemporary German Christian theologian and N.T. scholar, Rudolph Bultmann. For more on what this process implies see Bultmann's *Jesus and Mythology*.

48 *After Auschwitz*, p. 119.

49 *After Auschwitz*, p. 119.

50 *After Auschwitz*, p. 119.

51 For more on Rubenstein's use of psychoanalytic categories to re-interpret Judaism and especially Jewish rituals and symbols see his *After Auschwitz*, *The Religious Imagination*, and *My Brother Paul*. See also "Psychoanalysis and the Origins of Judaism" in the *Reconstructionist*, December 2, 1962.

52 *After Auschwitz*, p. 223 ff., for Rubenstein's entire discussion on Bar Mitzvah.

53 *The Religious Imagination* (Indianapolis: Bobbs Merrill, 1968).

54 *After Auschwitz*, "The symbols of Judaism and the Death of God", p. 240. See especially on this natural paganism Rubenstein's essay, "Atonement and Sacrifice in Contemporary Jewish Liturgy" in *After Auschwitz*, pgs. 93–111.

55 *After Auschwitz*, "The Rebuilding of Israel in Contemporary Theology," especially p. 135 ff.

56 *After Auschwitz*, ibid., p. 135.

57 *After Auschwitz*, "Religion and the Origins of the Death Camp", p. 9.

58 This is a summary of Rubenstein's views in *After Auschwitz*, "Person and Myth in the Judeo-Christian Encounter", pgs. 73–74.

59 He spent a short time in a concentration camp in 1938–39. He has written about this experience with great power in his paper delivered to the Sixth World Congress of Jewish Studies and published in its *Proceedings*, Jerusalem, 1974.

60 Fackenheim scathingly replied to Rubenstein in *God's Presence in History* with the following remark. "What assures him [Rubenstein] of his own capacities to deal with the trauma—or stills his fear that some other mechanism may

cause him to utter words which should never have been spoken ["God is dead"]? We need not go beyond his jarring expression "the facts are in." Will all the facts ever be in? And what, in this case, are the facts apart from the interpretation? The statistics?" (p. 72).

61   *God's Presence in History*, p. 31.

62   The term neo-orthodox is used here to mean a position analogous to Franz Rosenzweig's. This position argues for divine revelation and seeks to find meaning in the Torah so it can become the basis of Jewish life. For a statement of Fackenheim's debt to Rosenzweig (and Buber) see "These Twenty Years" in *Quest for Past and Future* pgs. 3–26. For Rosenzweig's and Buber's views, in detail, see pgs. 184–96 of this work.

63   For more on this see *Quest for Past and Future*, p. 5 ff.

64   For Fackenheim's views see, for example, the various essays relating to the theology of Liberal Judaism in Fackenheim's collection, *Quest for Past and Future.*

65   *Quest for Past and Future*, p. 5.

66   For details of Buber's *I-Thou* philosophy and his view of I-Thou encounter as 'revelation' see the section on Buber in this work.

67   Perhaps the clearest statement of Fackenheim's views on this are found in his essay entitled "Elijah and the Empiricists" which originally appeared in *The Religious Situation* ed. Donald Cutler, 1969 and which was reprinted in a new collection entitled *Encounters Between Judaism and Philosophy*, 1973. For some critical comments see the review of this collection by S. Katz in the *Journal of Jewish Social Studies*, Spring 1974.

68   The Buberian account and its usage by Fackenheim is not without serious philosophical and theological difficulties which may ultimately undermine it. Fackenheim, however, is aware of many of the problems himself and has written an important essay on Buber's doctrine of revelation, see "Buber's Doctrine of Revelation" in *The Philosophy of Martin Buber*, ed. Schilpp & Friedman, 1967.

69   See *Quest for Past and Future*, p. 10.

70   See especially Buber's analysis of the Biblical events surrounding the Exodus-Sinai episode in his book *Moses*, 1946.

71   *God's Presence in History*, "The Structure of Jewish Experience", p. 8 ff.

72   *Ibid.*, p. 9.

73   *Ibid.*, p. 11.

74   *God's Presence in History*, p. 11. Fackenheim here calls attention to how this past event becomes present reality by reminding us of the statement in the Passover Haggadah: "It was not one only who rose against us to annihilate us, but in every generation there are those who rise against us to annihilate us. But the Holy One, blessed be He, saves us from their hand."

[75] *God's Presence in History*, p. 16 ff.

[76] Fackenheim's detailed account of this Rabbinic reaction to the destruction of the 2nd Temple is to be found in *God's Presence in History*, pgs. 25–31.

[77] *God's Presence in History*, p. 20.

[78] *Presence of God in History*, p. 84, repeated from Fackenheim's earlier essay, "Jewish Faith and the Holocaust," *Commentary* 1967.

[79] *Ibid.*, p. 84. Fackenheim spells out the implication of these 'commandments' in some detail. See *ibid.*, pp. 85–92.

[80] Brief critiques of Fackenheim's view can be found in the last section of M. Meyer's article on Fackenheim entitled "Judaism After Auschwitz" in *Commentary*, vol. 53, No. 6, June 1972; and in "The Questions and Answers after Auschwitz" by Seymour Cain in *Judaism*, vol. 20, No. 3, Summer 1971.

[81] I. Maybaum, *The Face of God After Auschwitz*, p. 32.

[82] *Ibid.*, p. 32.

[83] *The Face of God After Auschwitz*, p. 29.

[84] *Ibid.*, p. 31.

[85] *The Face of God After Auschwitz*, p. 35.

[86] *Ibid.*, p. 36.

[87] See *The Face of God After Auschwitz*, pgs. 62–63 for a more detailed view of this.

[88] *Ibid.*, p. 63.

[89] *Face of God After Auschwitz*, p. 67.

[90] *Ibid.*, p. 67.

[91] *Ibid.*, p. 59 ff. for Maybaum's discussion of "The Remnant"; see also p. 87 ff.

[92] This incident is not recorded by Berkovits who gives other equally moving incidents.

[93] This incident is recorded in Menashe Unger, *Sefer Kedoshim* (1967), p. 36.

[94] *Faith After the Holocaust*, p. 88.

[95] *Ibid.*, p. 90.

[96] *Ibid.*, p. 89.

[97] *Ibid.*, p. 89.

[98] Berkovits discusses this in detail, *Ibid.*, p. 94 ff. See also Psalm 44 which Berkovits cites.

[99] *Faith After the Holocaust*, p. 106.

[100] See *Ibid.*, p. 109 ff. for Berkovits' views on "Israel in history."

[101] See Berkovits discussion *Ibid.*, p. 134 ff.

[102] *Ibid.*, 145. See the whole last chapter, "In Zion Again" pgs. 144–169 for full details of how Berkovits views the State of Israel and its relation to a modern Jewish theology. One is forced to note that Berkovits' book was published in 1973, though having been written over several years. It was published however before the *Yom Kippur* War of October 1973.

[103] *Ibid.*, p. 152.

[104] *Ibid.*, p. 156. See the whole of his discussion on p. 156 ff.

[105] See his biographical statement "From Marxism to Judaism" in *Commentary*, (Jan. 1947) and reprinted in A. Cohen, *Doctrines and Arguments* (1970).

[106] Cohen, *Arguments and Doctrines* p. 103.

[107] For some views on Niebuhr's thought as it relates to Judaism see the exchange between Levi Olan and Emil Fackenheim in *Judaism*. Olan's article, "Reinhold Niebuhr and the Hebraic Spirits: A Critical Inquiry" appeared in *Judaism*, Vol. V (1956) pgs. 108–122; Fackenheim's reply is found in *Judaism* vol. V (1956) pgs. 316–324.

[108] *Judaism and Modern Man* (1951): new paperback edition (1970).

[109] *Protestant, Catholic and Jew*, 1955, 1960.

[110] See on these issues also the important work of Nathan Glazer whose findings coincide generally with Herberg's account. Nathan Glazer, *American Judaism*, 1957[1], 1972[2].

[111] See pgs. 196–98.

[112] For example, since 1945, Kaplan has published, among other works, *The Greater Judaism in the Making* (1960): *Judaism Without Supernaturalism* (1958): *The Purpose and Meaning of Jewish Existence* (1964): *The Religion of Ethical Nationhood* (1970).

[113] Jacob Agus had already seen the major weaknesses in Kaplan's position in 1941 in his *Modern Philosophies of Judaism*, pgs. 298–315.

[114] E. Berkovits, "Reconstructionist Theology", *Tradition* (Fall 1959), Vol. 2 no. 1, p. 42.

[115] *Ibid.*, p. 42.

[116] E. Fackenheim, "A Critique of Reconstructionism" in *CCAR Journal*, (June 1960).

[117] I. Eisenstein, "Communication", *CCAR Journal* (Oct. 1960), pgs. 39–43.

[118] Jack J. Cohen, *The Cast for Religious Naturalism*.

[119] "A Critique of a Critique", in *The Reconstructionist* vol. 36, no. 14 (Jan. 15, 1971): Part II, vol. 37 no. 1 (March 5, 1971): Part III, vol. 37 no. 3 (May 7, 1971).

[120] M. Kaplan and A. Cohen, *If not Now, When?* (1973).

[121] See his *Evolution of Jewish Thought* p. 418 among other places.

[122] *The Vision and the Way*, "The Case for the Dialogue", p.17.

[123] *Ibid.*, "The Enduring Tensions in Judaism", p. 521.

[124] *Book of God and Man: A Study of Job* (1965).

[125] *Koheleth: The Man and His World* (1955).

[126] *A Faith for Moderns* (1960).

[127] *The Root and the Branch* (1962).

[128] *Judaism in a Christian World* (1966).

[129] p. 155.

[130] *Ibid.*, p. 156 ff.

[131] See *Ever Since Sinai*, pgs. 78 ff.

[132] *Ever Since Sinai* p. 111. Emphases are in the original text.

[133] See *Ever Since Sinai,* Ch. 5 "Giver of Torah", and especially Petuchowski's conclusion on p. 83.

[134] *The Growth of Reform Judaism* N.Y. 1965.

[135] *A History of Jewish Messianic Speculation* (1927).

[136] R. Gittelsohn, *Man's Best Hope* (N.Y. Random House) 1961 p. 113.

BIOGRAPHICAL INDEX

Aaron ben Elijah (c. 1330–1369)—The major Karaite thinker. Lived mostly in Constantinople.

*Abelard (Abaelard), Peter (1079–1142)—French Christian philosopher and theologian.

Abner of Burgos (1270–1340)—Physician and philosopher. Apostate to Christianity.

Abrabanel, Isaac ben Judah (1437–1508)—statesman, philosopher and biblical exegete. Born in Lisbon.

Abrabanel, Judah (called Leone Ebreo or Leo Hebraeus; c. 1460–after 1523)—Italian poet, physician, and one of the foremost philosophers of the Renaissance.

Abraham bar Ḥiyya (Ḥayya; d. c. 1136)—Spanish philosopher, mathematician, astronomer and translator.

Abraham ben Moses ben Maimon (1186–1237)—leader *(nagid)* of the Egyptian Jewish community and religious philosopher; only son of Maimonides.

Abulafia, Abraham ben Samuel (1240–after 1291)—Spanish mystic.

Abulafia, Meir (1170?–1244)—talmudic commentator, thinker, and poet; the most renowned Spanish rabbi of the first half of the 13th century.

Adret, Solomon ben Abraham (known from his initials as RaShBA; c. 1235–c. 1310)—Spanish rabbi and one of the foremost Jewish scholars of his day.

Agus, Jacob Bernard (1911–)—American rabbi and historian of Jewish philosophy.

Aḥad Ha'am (Asher Hirsch Ginsberg; 1856–1927)—Hebrew essayist, thinker and leader of the Ḥibbat Zion movement; he wrote under the name of Aḥad Ha'am ("One of the People").

Albalag, Isaac (13th century)—translator and philosopher.

Albo, Joseph (d. 1444)—Spanish philosopher and preacher; author of *Sefer*

---

1. One asterik (*) indicates a Christian thinker.
   Two asterisks (**) indicate a Muslim thinker.
   Three asterisks (***) indicate a Greek (non-Christian) thinker.

ha-Ikkarim ("Book of Principles"), a famous treatise on Jewish articles of faith which he completed in Soria (Castile) in 1425.

**Al-Farabi, Abu Nasr Muhammad (c. 870–c. 950)—one of the greatest Islamic philosophers of the medieval Islamic world; had considerable influence on Jewish philosophers, particularly Maimonides.

**Al-Ghazali, Abu Hamid Muhammad Ibn Muhammad Al-Tusi (1058–1111)—Persian Muslim theologian, jurist, mystic and religious reformer; wrote mainly in Arabic.

Altmann, Alexander (1906–   )—rabbi and historian of Jewish philosophy; born in Germany; now holds chair in U.S.

*Anselm of Canterbury (1033–1109)—abbot of Bec (Normandy) and from 1093 archbishop of Canterbury; theologian and philosopher; canonized by the Catholic Church. Originator of the ontological argument for the existence of God.

*Aquinas, Thomas (1225–1274)—most important of the Christian medieval philosophers; the author of the *Summa Theologica;* canonized by the Church.

Arama, Isaac ben Moses (c. 1420–1494)—Spanish rabbi, philosopher, and preacher.

Aristobulus of Paneas (first half of the 2nd century B.C.E.)—Jewish Hellenistic philosopher; one of the earliest allegorical interpreters of the Bible.

***Aristotle (4th century B.C.E.)—greatest Greek philosopher and founder of the peripatetic school; the most influential philosopher in the late medieval period (12th century onward).

Asher ben Jehiel (also known as Asheri and Rosh; c. 1250–1327)—talmudist.

*Augustine (354–430)—bishop of Hippo (North Africa) and most important Church Father of early Western Christianity.

Avempace (Abu Bakr Muhammad ibn Yaḥya ibn Bajja, called **Ibn Al-Sa'igh; d. 1138)—Muslim philosopher, born in Saragossa; lived in Seville, Granada, and Fez. He was a celebrated philosopher, mathematician, musician, poet, and served as vizier.

**Averroes (Abu Al-Walid Muhammad Ibn Rushd; 1126–1198)—one of the greatest Islamic philosophers and a noted physician; primarily known as commentator on Aristotle's works; lived in Spain.

**Avicenna (Abu Ali Al-Hussein ibn Abu Abdallah ibn Sina; 980–1037)—physician, scientist, man of affairs, and one of the greatest Muslim philosophers.

Baal Shem Tov—see Israel ben Eliezer.

Baeck, Leo (1873–1956)—German rabbi and religious thinker; leader of Progressive Judaism.

Bahya (Baḥye) ben Joseph Ibn Paquda (2nd half of the 11th century)—Jewish moral philosopher and author of the most important Jewish ethical work of the medieval period, *Duties of the Hearts.*

Baron, Salo W. (1895–   )—Jewish historian; author of *A Social and Religious History of the Jews.*

Bergman, S. H. (1883–   )—Israel historian of philosophy; Professor at Hebrew University, Jerusalem.

Berkovits, Eliezer (1908–   )—American Orthodox rabbi and theologian.

*Bernard of Clairvaux (1090–1153)—French Cistercian, homilist, and theologian.

Borowitz, Eugene Bernard (1924–   )—American Reform rabbi and existentialist theologian.

Buber, Martin (1878–1965)—philosopher and theologian; Zionist thinker and leader; born in Germany; Professor at Hebrew University, Jerusalem.

*Buridan, Jean (c. 1295–c. 1358)—medieval logician and thinker; taught at the University of Paris.

Caspi, Joseph (1297–1340)—Provençal philosopher, exegete, and grammarian.

Cohen, Arthur A. (1928–   )—American author and theologian.

Cohen, Hermann (1842–1918)—German idealist philosopher and Jewish thinker.

Cohen, Morris Raphael (1880–1947)—American philosopher.

Cordovero, Moses (known as the Remak; 1522–1570)—Kabbalist of the 16th century Safed school; disciple of Joseph Karo.

Crescas, Ḥasdai (d. 1412?)—Spanish philosopher, theologian, and statesman; most important Jewish critic of medieval Aristotelianism.

Da Costa (Acosta), Uriel (1585–1640)—Dutch Jewish philosopher and free thinker; older contemporary of and influence on Spinoza.

Delmedigo, Elijah ben Moses Abba (c. 1460–1497)—philosopher and talmudist; born in Candia (Crete); also known as Elijah Cretensis.

Delmedigo, Joseph Solomon (1591–1655)—rabbi, philosopher, mathematician and astronomer; also known as Joseph Solomon Rofe (acronym YaSHaR) of Candia (Crete).

Dubnow, Simon (1860–1941)—Polish Jewish historian.

*Duns Scotus, John (1266–1308)—Catholic theologian and philosopher; opposed many of the views of Thomas Aquinas.

Duran, Profiat (Profayt; d. c. 1414)—scholar and physician; one of the outstanding anti-Christian polemicists of Spanish Jewry.

Duran, Simeon ben Ẓemaḥ (RaSHBaẒ, Hebrew acronym of Rabbi SHimon Ben Ẓemaḥ; 1361–1444)—rabbinic authority, philosopher, and scientist.

*Eckhart, Meister (c. 1260–c. 1327)—theologian and one of the great Christian mystics.

Efros, Israel Isaac (1891–   )—Hebrew educator, scholar, and historian of Jewish philosophy.

Eleazar of Worms (ben Judah Kalonymous; 1165–1236)—Kabbalist and talmudist; important figure in Ashkenazi Ḥasidism.

Elijah ben Solomon Zalman (the "Vilna Gaon" or "Elijah Gaon"; acronym Ha-GRA = Ha-Gaon Rabbi Eliyahu; 1720–1797)—one of the greatest spiritual and intellectual leaders of Jewry in modern times. He was the leading opponent of Ḥasidism, the followers of which he excommunicated.

Fackenheim, Emil Ludwig (1916–   )—Canadian rabbi and existentialist theologian; born in Halle (Germany).

Falaquera (Ibn Falaquera, Palquera), **Shem Tov ben Joseph** (c. 1225–1295)—medieval Spanish philosophical author and translator.

***Fichte, Johann Gottlieb** (1762–1814)—German idealist philosopher.

Formstecher, Solomon (1808–1889)—German Jewish idealist philosopher and rabbi.

Friedlaender, David (1750–1834)—communal leader and author in Berlin; a pioneer of the practice and ideology of assimilation and a forerunner of Reform Judaism.

****Galen** (Galenus) **Claudius** (131–c. 201 C.E.)—prominent physician in antiquity and author of important works.

Gans, David ben Solomon (1541–1613)—chronicler, astronomer, and mathematician.

Geiger, Abraham (1810–1874)—one of the leaders of the Reform movement in Judaism and an outstanding scholar of the 'Wissenschaft des Judentums' (Science of Judaism).

Gerondi, Jonah ben Abraham (c. 1200–1263)—Spanish rabbi, author, and moralist.

Gordon, Aharon David (1856–1922)—Hebrew writer and spiritual mentor of the Zionist labor movement which emphasized self-realization through settlement on the land *(halutziut);* born in Troyanov (Russia).

Gracian, Zerahiah ben Isaac ben Shealtiel (13th century)—physician, philosopher, and translator.

Graetz, Heinrich (1817–1891)—Jewish historian and Bible scholar; author of the well-known *History of the Jews.*

Guttmann, Julius (Yizhak; 1880–1950)—German philosopher and historian of Jewish philosophy.

***Hegel, Georg Wilhelm Friedrich** (1770–1831)—German idealist philosopher whose work dominated 19th century thought.

Heller, Yom-Tov Lipmann ben Nathan Ha-Levi (Yom-Tov Heller; 1579–1654)—Moravian rabbi; commentator on the Mishnah.

Herberg, Will (1906–   )—American theologian and sociologist.

***Herder, Johann Gottfried** (1744–1803)—German philosopher, author, critic, and translator.

Heschel, Abraham Joshua (1907–1972)—European-born American scholar and philosopher.

Ḥibat Allah, Abu Al-Barakat (11th–12th century)—philosopher, physician, and biblical commentator.

Hillel ben Samuel (c. 1220–c. 1295)—physician, talmudic scholar, and Aristotelian philosopher.

Hirsch, Samson (ben) Raphael (1808–1888)—rabbi and theologian; leader and foremost exponent of Orthodoxy in Germany in the 19th century; critic of the Reform movement.

Ḥiwi Al-Balkhi (2nd half of 9th century)—from Khorasan, Persia (now Afghanistan); freethinker and radical Bible critic.

Husik, Isaac (1876–1939)—American historian of medieval Jewish philosophy.

Ibn Alfakhar, Judah (d. 1235)—physician at the court of Ferdinand III of Castile; opponent of Maimonides.

Ibn Daud, Abraham ben David HaLevi (known as Rabad; c. 1110–1180)—Spanish historian, physician, and astronomer; first Jewish Aristotelian of the medieval period.

Ibn Ezra, Abraham (1089–1164)—poet, grammarian, biblical commentator, philosopher, astronomer, and physician.

Ibn Ezra, Moses ben Jacob (also known as Abu Harun; c. 1055–after 1135)—Spanish Hebrew poet and philosopher.

Ibn Gabirol, Solomon ben Judah (c. 1020–c. 1057)—in Arabic: Abu Ayyub Sulayman ibn Yahya ibn Gabirol; in Latin: Avicebron; Spanish poet and Neoplatonic philosopher; influenced medieval Christian thought.

Ibn Migash, Joseph ben Meir Ha-Levi (1077–1141)—Spanish talmudic scholar.

Ibn Tibbon, Samuel ben Judah (c. 1160–c. 1230)—French philosopher; disciple and translator of Maimonides' *Guide* into Hebrew; a member of the famous Tibbonide family which comprised at least four generations of translators and scholars.

Ibn Ẓaddik, Joseph ben Jacob (d. 1149)—philosopher and poet.

Isaac ben Sheshet Perfet (known as RIBaSH from the initials of Rabbi Isaac Ben SHeshet; 1326–1408)—Spanish rabbi and halakhic authority.

Israel ben Eliezer Ba'al Shem Tov (known by the initials BESHT—Ba'al SHem Tov; c. 1700–1760)—charismatic founder and first leader of the Ḥasidic movement.

Israeli, Isaac ben Solomon (c. 855–c. 955)—physician and Neoplatonic philosopher; North African.

Jabez, Joseph ben Ḥayyim (d. 1507)—Hebrew homilist and exegete.

Jacobs, Louis (1920–　)—English rabbi and theologian; translator of Ḥasidic texts.

Joseph ben Abraham Ha-Basir (11th century)—Persian Karaite philosopher.

Judah ben Barzillai of Barcelona (11th–12th century)—Spanish talmudist and halakhic codifier.

Judah ben Samuel He-Ḥasid (d. 1217)—German author of *Sefer ha-Ḥasid;* mystic and talmudist; leader of German Ashkenazi Ḥasidism.

Judah Halevi (before 1075–1141)—great Spanish Hebrew poet and philosopher; one of the most important figures in the medieval period.

Judah Loew (Liwa, Loeb) **ben Bezalel** (known as Der Hohe Rabbi Loew and MaHaRaL mi-Prag; c. 1525–1609)—rabbi, talmudist, moralist and mathematician.

*****Kant, Immanuel** (1724–1804)—German philosopher; the most important of all modern philosophers who exerted a major influence on Jewish thought in the 19th and 20th centuries.

Kaplan, Mordechai Menahem (1881–   )—U.S. rabbi, theologian, and founder of the Reconstructionist movement.

Karo, Joseph (1488–1575)—great halakhist and codifier of the *Shulḥan Arukh,* one of the most important of all halakhic works.

Kimḥi, David (known as RADAK from the acronym of Rabbi David Kimḥi; Maistre Petit: (1160?–1235?)—grammarian and Bible exegete of Narbonne, Provence.

Kohler, Kaufmann (1843–1926)—American Reform rabbi and president of Hebrew Union College; author of works on Jewish theology.

Kook (Kuk), Abraham Isaac (1865–1935)—rabbinical authority and mystical thinker; first Ashkenazi Chief Rabbi of modern Israel.

Krochmal, Nachman (1785–1840)—philosopher and historian; one of the founders of the "science of Judaism" ("Wissenschaft des Judentums"); a leader of the Haskalah movement in Eastern Europe.

Landauer, Gustav (1870–1919)—German philosopher and writer.

*****Lavater, John Casper** (1741–1801)—Swiss theologian who engaged in a famous debate with Moses Mendelssohn.

Lazarus, Moritz (1824–1903)—German philosopher and psychologist; author of important work on Jewish ethics written from a Kantian perspective.

*****Leibnitz, Gottfried** (1646–1716)—major German rationalist philosopher and mathematician.

*****Lessing, Gotthold Ephraim** (1729–1781)—German dramatist, philosopher and critic; one of the outstanding representatives of the Enlightenment in Germany; devoted to the principles of toleration; a close friend of Moses Mendelssohn.

Levi ben Gershom (acronym: RaLBaG; also called Maestre Leo de Bagnols, Magister Leo Hebraeus, Gersonides; 1288–1344)—mathematician, astronomer, Aristotelian philosopher and biblical commentator; born probably at Bagnols-sur-Creze (France).

Loanz, Elijah ben Moses (1564–1636)—German kabbalist.

*Locke, John (1632–1704)—probably the most important 17th century empiricist philosopher; an important figure in the spread of political toleration and parliamentary democracy.

Luria, Isaac ben Solomon (referred to as Ha-Ari; 1534–1572)—Kabbalist; one of the most important figures in the Jewish mystical tradition; led the mystical community in Safed in Erez Israel.

Luria, Solomon ben Jehiel (known as *Rashal* or *Maharshal*—Morenu Ha-Rav Shelomo Luria. c. 1510–1574). Rabbinic authority and Talmudic commentator.

Luzzatto, Moses Ḥayyim (Ramḥal; 1707–1746)—Italian Kabbalist and moralist.

Luzzatto, Samuel David (SHaDaL or SHeDaL; 1800–1865)—Italian scholar, philosopher, Bible commentator, and translator.

*Magnus, Albertus (c. 1206–1280)—Christian theologian.

Maimonides—see Moses ben Maimon.

Malbim, Meir Loeb (1809–1879)—rabbi, preacher, and biblical exegete.

Meiri, Menahem ben Solomon (1249–1316)—Provençal scholar and commentator on the Talmud.

Mendelssohn, Moses (Moses ben Menahem, acronym RaMbeMaN or Moses of Dessau; 1729–1786)—philosopher of the German Enlightenment in the pre-Kantian period and spiritual leader of German Jewry. First major modern Jewish philosopher.

*Moore, George Foot (1851–1931)—American scholar; expert on Talmudic Judaism.

Moses ben Joshua of Narbonne (Narboni; d. 1362)—French Aristotelian philosopher and physician.

Moses ben Maimon (Maimonides; known in rabbinical literature as "Rambam" from the acronym Rabbi Moses Ben Maimon; 1135–1204)—rabbinic authority, codifier, Aristotelian philosopher, and physician. The greatest single figure in medieval Judaism in both philosophical and halakhic scholarship.

Moses ben Naḥman (Naḥmanides; also known as Naḥamani and RaMBaN—Rabbi Moses Ben Naḥman; 1194–1270)—Spanish rabbi and scholar; philosopher, Kabbalist, biblical exegete, poet, and physician; one of the leading authors of talmudic literature in the Middle Ages.

Naḥman (ben Simḥah) of Bratslav (1772–1811)—grandson of the Baal Shem Tov; ḥasidic *zaddik* in Podolia and the Ukraine and the center of a theological and social storm throughout most of his life.

Nissim of Gerondi (Nissim ben Reuben Gerondi; known from the acronym of Rabbenu Nissim as the RaN; c. 1310–c. 1375)—Spanish talmudist.

Petuchowski, Jacob (1925–   )—American Reform rabbi; Professor of Rabbinics at Hebrew Union College; Reform thinker.

Philo Judaeus (Philo of Alexandria; c. 20 B.C.E.–50 C.E.)—Hellenistic Jewish philosopher; credited with being the founder of the medieval philosophical movement.

*Pico della Mirandola, Giovanni (1463–1494)—one of the most remarkable figures of the Italian Renaissance.

***Plato (427–347 B.C.E.)—major Greek philosopher who exerted enormous influence on all later thinkers, especially in the early medieval period.

***Plotinus (205–270 C.E.)—the most important neo-Platonic philosopher in the Hellenistic period; author of the *Enneads*.

Pollegar, Isaac (early 14th century)—Spanish talmudist and philosopher.

***Proclus (410–485 C.E.)—Neoplatonist thinker; his commentaries on Greek thought were links in the transmission of Greek learning to later ages.

Rashi (Solomon ben Isaac; 1040–1105)—leading commentator on the Bible and Talmud.

Rosenstock-Huessy, Eugen (1888–1973)—German philosopher and theologian; convert from Judaism to Christianity; important influence on Franz Rosenzweig.

Rosenzweig, Franz (1886–1929)—German Jewish theologian; influential modern Jewish thinker.

Rossi, Azariah (Bonaiuto) **ben Moses Dei** (c. 1511–c. 1578)—scholar of Hebrew letters during the Italian Renaissance.

Rotenstreich, Nathan (1914–)—Israeli phenomenologist and philosopher; Professor at Hebrew University, Jerusalem; historian of philosophy.

Roth, Leon (1896–1963)—English philosopher and historian of philosophy.

Rubenstein, Richard Lowell (1924–)—American Conservative rabbi; proponent of a Jewish "death of God" theology.

Saadiah (ben Joseph) Gaon (882–942)—scholar and author of the geonic period: leader of Babylonian Jewry. The first medieval Jewish philosopher.

Samuel ben Hophni (d. 1013)—gaon of Sura (Babylonia); halakhist and translator of the Bible into Arabic.

*Schelling, Friedrich Wilhelm Joseph (1775–1854)—German idealist philosopher.

Scholem, Gershom Gerhard (1897–)—Jewish scholar; pioneer and leading authority in the field of Kabbalah and Jewish mysticism.

Shneur Zalman of Lyady (1745–1813)—founder of Ḥabad Ḥasidism.

Simon, Ernst (1899–)—Israeli thinker; Professor at Hebrew University, Jerusalem.

Solomon ben Abraham of Montpellier (13th century)—French talmudic scholar; initiator of the Maimonidean controversy that took place in the third decade of the 13th century.

Soloveitchik, Joseph Dov (1903–   )—American talmudist and theologian: the leader of American Orthodoxy.

Spinoza, Baruch (Benedict) **de** (1632–1677)—Dutch philosopher; one of the greatest philosophers of all time; critic of normative Judaism and expounder of a pantheistic system.

Steinberg, Milton (1903–1950)—American Conservative rabbi: disciple and popularizer of Mordecai Kaplan's thought.

Steinheim, Salomon Ludwig (1789–1866)—German poet and religious philosopher.

Steinschneider, Moritz (1816–1907)—father of modern Jewish bibliography; one of the founders of modern Jewish scholarship.

**Tabrizi, Mahomet Abu-Bekr-At-Ben Mahomet (probably 2nd half of the 13th century)—Persian Muslim commentator on the 25 propositions appearing at the beginning of the second part of Moses Maimonides' *Guide of the Perplexed.*

Vajda, Georges (1908–   )—French Arabist and Hebraist; historian of medieval Jewish philosophy.

Wiesel, Elie (Eliezer; 1928–   )—novelist and witness to the Holocaust; the author of works on the Holocaust, Soviet Jewry and Ḥasidism.

*William of Ockham (c. 1285–1349)—English medieval logician and philosopher of major significance.

Wolfson, Harry Austryn (1887–1974)—American historian of philosophy, author of works on Philo, the Church Fathers, and Spinoza.

Wyschogrod, Michael (20th cent.)—American philosopher.

Zacuto, Abraham (c. 1450–1510)—Spanish thinker and astronomer.

Zerahiah ben Isaac Ha-Levi (known as Ferrarius Saladi; 14th–15th century)—rabbi of Saragossa and of all the communities of Aragon.

Zunz, Leopold (Yom Tov Lippmann; 1794–1886)—historian; among the founders of the Wissenschaft des Judentums ("Science of Judaism") in Germany in the early 1820s. Subsequently he produced important pioneer studies on the liturgy of the synagogue and on Jewish religious literature and cultural history.

Aggadah—(Heb.) Non-legal parts of the Talmud, i.e., homiletics, ethical teachings, parables, biographical details.

Akedah—(Heb.) Literally "binding"; used most commonly to refer to the 'binding of Isaac' (*Gen.* 22) i.e., the sacrifice of Isaac.

Amoraim—(Heb.) Title given to the Talmudic Sages of the Gemara, i.e., those who appear in the later discussions of the Talmud between the close of the Mishnah (200 C.E. approx.) and the close of the Talmudic canon (500 C.E. approx.).

A Posteriori—(Lat.) Literally, 'after experience', i.e., knowledge gained from experience.

A Priori—(Lat.) Literally, 'prior to experience', i.e., reasoning done deductively or on the basis of innate and intuitive knowledge present in the mind without experience.

Articles of Faith—The basic beliefs of a religion which define its character and essential dogmatic nature.

Ashkenazim—(Heb.) The name given to Jews of Eastern Europe, Germany and Northern Europe and their descendants.

Av Bet Din—(Heb.) Head of the Court, i.e., the chief justice of a Jewish religious court.

Avodat Ha-Elohim—(Heb.) Divine worship.

Bet Din—(Heb.) Literally, "House of Law," i.e., a Jewish court of law.

Bittaḥon—(Heb.) Trust in God.

Cosmogony—A theory which attempts to explain the origin and cause of the universe.

Creatio ex Nihilo—(Lat.) "creation from nothing," i.e., created solely by God without any pre-existent material.

Dat Elohit—(Heb.) Divine Law.

Dat Nimusit—(Heb.) Conventional Law.

Dat Tivit—(Heb.) Natural Law.

Dayyan—(Heb.) Judge.

De'ot—(Heb.) Beliefs.

Devekut—(Heb.) "Clinging or adhesion to God." A term used to express an

275

extreme closeness to God; used especially by Jewish mystics to describe the mystical relation of man and God.

Ein Sof (Eyn Sof)—(Heb.) Literally, "without end." Term used by the Kabbalists for God as He exists in His unknowable and inexpressible self-perfection and transcendence.

Emunah—(Heb.) Trust, belief.

Emunot—(Heb.) Dogmas or beliefs.

Epicurean (Heb. **Apikoros**)—A follower of the Greek philosopher Epicurus, more generally used in Jewish thought as a term of reproach and disapproval for one who denies the existence or Kingship of God; also applied to those who seek pleasure as an end in itself.

Eschatology—The "science" of the four last things: death, judgment, heaven and hell; more generally, speculation about the "end of days."

Eudaemonism—The ethical system which defines morality in terms of happiness and moral action as action that produces happiness.

Galut—(Heb.) Exile; the term applied to Jewish life outside of the land of Israel.

Gaon—(Heb.; plural *Geonim*) Formal title of the heads of the Talmudic academies of Babylonia between the 7th and 11th centuries. The *Geonim* were recognized by the Jews as the highest authority in religious matters and were considered to be the successors of the Talmudic Sages.

Genizah—(Heb.) Literally: "hiding"; more generally: the name given to the synagogue store room for old and unusable Torah Scrolls and sacred books.

Geulah—(Heb.) Redemption.

Gezerah—(Heb.) "A decree," a technical term for a rabbinical prohibition.

Halakhah—(Heb.) A legal enactment; more generally the term applied to the whole biblical-rabbinic legal tradition whose pronouncements on legal matters are considered binding on every Jew.

Ha-Makom—(Heb.) 'The Place'. A rabbinic term for God.

Ha-Olam Ha-Ba—(Heb.) The world to come.

Hasid—(Heb.) "A pious one"; generally used for pious Jews; more technically refers to a follower of the Hasidic (18th century) movement.

Hasidim—(Heb.) Plural of Hasid (pious ones). Specifically used to refer to the followers of the Hasidic movement.

Hasidism—(Heb.) The 18th century religious-mystical movement founded by Israel ben Eliezer (the Baal Shem Tov). It began in southern Poland and the Ukraine and soon spread throughout Eastern European Jewry.

Haskalah—(Heb.) Jewish 'Enlightenment' movement begun in the late 18th century to bring modern culture and secular learning to the Jewish people.

Herem—(Heb.) Ban of excommunication.

Hermeneutics—Rules of interpretation; especially applied to the principles governing interpretation and exegesis of the Bible.

Hermetic Writings—Ancient Greek writings dealing with the occult, magic and alchemy.

Homer—(Heb.) Matter.

Homiletics—The art of preaching; more specifically, a sermon or other discourse preached to a congregation, generally with the aim of moral or spiritual edification.

Hovot Ha-Levavot—(Heb.) "Duties of the hearts"; name of Baḥya ibn Pakuda's famous ethical treatise.

Hypostasis—The essence of something, i.e., its substantial being as compared to its accidental qualities.

Idealism—19th century philosophical movement which stressed the centrality of mental phenomena, especially holding that the objects of perception were in some sense a creation of the mind.

Ikkarim—(Heb.) Principles. It is used to refer to the basic premises of a philosophical or theological system.

Ishurim—(Heb.) Articles (of faith).

Josippon—Historical narrative in Hebrew written in the 10th century in Southern Italy by unknown author. It describes the period of the Second Temple.

Kabbalah—(Heb.) Literally, "tradition"; more generally used to describe the Jewish mystical tradition.

Kalam—(Arabic) Literally, "speech," or "word." More generally: the term for Islamic theology.

Karaites—8th century Jewish sect founded by Anan ben David. This sect rejected the Rabbinic Oral Law, insisting that only the Written Law (Torah) was authoritative. The sect continued to exert considerable influence until the late 12th and early 13th century.

Kiddush Ha-Shem—(Heb.) Literally: "sanctification of the name"; more generally: the doctrine that Jews must act so as not to blemish or discredit their God. The most extreme and well known case is martyrdom in the face of conversionary pressures, i.e., dying rather than discredit Judaism.

Kinot—(Heb.) A religious poem of lament composed for personal or national tragedies.

Ma'amarim—(Heb.) treatises.

Ma'aseh Bereshit—(Heb.) "The mysteries of Creation". This is the name given to the esoteric mystical theories regarding the world's creation.

Ma'aseh Merkavah—(Heb.) "The mysteries of the chariot." This is the name given to the esoteric mystical doctrines connected with Ezekiel's chariot.

Malkhut Shamayim—(Heb.) Kingdom of Heaven.

Masorah—(Heb.) The "authorized" Hebrew version of the Bible used by Jews.

Middot—(Heb. plural; *Middah*=singular). Conduct, ethical behavior or virtue; also used for "quality" or dimension.

Midrash—(Heb.) from the Hebrew root "to inquire." It is the process whereby one claims to discover meanings in biblical texts which are not apparent or based on a literal reading of the text. The Sages drew both legal meanings from the biblical text *(Midrash Halakhah)* and non-legal meanings *(Midrash Aggadah)* in this way.

Minhagim—(Heb.) Customs.

Mitzvot Shimiyyot—(Heb.) *Mitzvot* (religious norms) which do not seem to have their basis in reason, i.e., appear irrational to man.

Mitzvot Sikhliyyot—(Heb.) *Mitzvot* which have their basis in reason, i.e., which appear rational to man.

Musar—(Heb.) Ethical instruction.

Mutazilites—(Arabic) Members of the Islamic theological school of Mutazilah. The most influential early Islamic theological school which was later superseded.

Neoplatonism—Term used to cover a variety of philosophical schools claiming to be dependent on Plato's thought, though with modifications.

Olam Ha-Ba—(Heb.) The world to come.

Ontology—The branch of metaphysics which is concerned to study 'Being', i.e., to discover the true nature of reality and its laws, and more particularly, to decide what can exist and what can not.

Paytan—(Heb.) creator of *piyyutim* (synagogue poetry).

Perishut—(Heb.) ascetism.

Piyyut (pl. **Piyyutim**)—(Heb.) Synagogue poetry which became standard elements of Jewish liturgy.

Razon—(Heb.) Will (as in The 'Divine Will').

Savoraim—(Heb.) 6th century sages who were responsible for the final editing of the Talmud, and thus the first post-Talmudic group of sages.

Sefer (Book) **Bahir**—(Heb.) One of the most ancient Jewish mystical texts. Ascribed by tradition to a 1st. century sage, it was probably produced in the early medieval period (8th to 10th century C.E.).

Sefer Yezirah—(Heb.) 'Book of Creation'. An ancient Jewish mystical text (3rd. to 6th century C.E.) which gives an esoteric account of creation.

Sefirot—(Heb.) Kabbalistic term for God's emanations and manifestations.

Selihot—(Heb.) Literally, 'forgivenesses; more generally prayers asking for forgiveness of sins.

Sephardim (Sefaradim)—(Heb. pl.) sing. **Sefaradi.** The name given to Jews of the Iberian peninsula and their descendants. More generally used to cover the Jews of North Africa and Middle East who were influenced by Spanish Jewry in their religious practices and liturgy.

Shekhinah—(Heb.) Literally "(the) Dwelling," i.e., God's Presence or Radiance. The term was sometimes used interchangeably with the word "God" for Divine activity in the world.

Shema—(Heb.) First word of the prayer: "Hear O Israel, The Lord thy God, The Lord is One." This is the Jewish prayer most often recited, an affirmation most insistently made by the pious from childhood until death.

Sufism—(Suf—garment worn by Muslim ascetics) Islamic mysticism which aimed at mystical union with Allah.

Takkanah (pl. **Takkanot**)—(Heb.) Positive Rabbinic enactments which supplement the written Torah; usually promulgated to aid the public welfare or to strengthen the religious and moral life of the community.

Tannaim—(Heb.) Earliest strata of Talmudic Sages; the title given to the Sages of the Mishnah (approx. 200 B.C.E. to 200 C.E.).

Tautology—A repetition of the same statement, usually in different words. In philosophy generally used to cover arguments where the conclusion is only a restatement of the arguments' premises, i.e., the conclusion adds nothing new. The argument is, in fact, circular.

Teshuvah—(Heb.) Repentance.

Tetragrammaton—The term applied to the most sacred name of God in the Bible and made up of four letters: YHWH. It is incorrectly vocalized as *YAHWEH* or *JEHOVAH*.

Theodicy—The attempt to justify God's goodness and righteousness despite the apparent evil in the world and the suffering of the righteous.

Therapeutae—Ancient Jewish mystical sect centered in Alexandria mentioned by Philo.

Wissenschaft des Judentums—(Ger.) 'Science of Judaism'. Primarily a 19th century movement which attempted to apply modern scientific methods to all branches of Jewish scholarship. Intended to help with the emancipation and integration of the Jew into modern society.

Yesod—(Heb.) Foundation or fundamental element.

Yezer Ha-Ra—(Heb) Evil inclination.

Yihud—(Heb.) Unity of God.

Yissurin shel Ahavah—(Heb.) "Afflictions of love."

Zohar—14th century Jewish mystical work; most important Jewish work in the Kabbalistic tradition, produced in Spain.

BIBLIOGRAPHY TO PARTS ONE, TWO, AND THREE

I. GENERAL, GREEK, CHRISTIAN, AND ISLAMIC THOUGHT.

Readers are advised to consult the bibliography found in F. C. Copleston's *History of Philosophy* (8 volumes; N.Y., 1946, 1950, 1953) for much bibliographic information on every aspect of western philosophical thought; Copleston's *History of Medieval Philosophy* (London, 1972) provides a fine specialized bibliography of the medieval period.

For works on Greek philosophy readers are referred to W. K. C. Guthrie's *History of Greek Philosophy* (in progress, 3 volumes have already appeared; Cambridge University Press). For the Hellenistic and early Christian period *The Cambridge History of Later Greek and Early Medieval Philosophy*, ed. A. H. Armstrong (Cambridge, 1966), is valuable. For all aspects of Islamic thought and bibliographical assistance, the *Cambridge History of Islam* (Cambridge, 1970) is recommended.

II. HISTORIES OF JEWISH PHILOSOPHY.

There are a number of standard histories of Jewish philosophy. Some cover the whole history of the subject while others concentrate on a specific period, i.e., medieval or modern. In order to avoid repetition in the individual bibliographies, these works are listed here. In addition, where there is no individual listing of a particular thinker in this bibliography, readers can consult the relevant bibliographies in the works listed below, especially the English translation of J. Guttmann's *Philosophies of Judaism.*

Agus, J., *The Evolution of Jewish Thought: From Biblical Times to the Opening of the Modern Era* (New York, 1959).

———, *Modern Philosophies of Judaism: A Study of Recent Jewish Philosophies of Religion* (New York, 1941; paperback 1970). A reasonable account of 19th and 20th century Jewish thought.

Bergman, S. H., *Faith and Reason: An Introduction to Modern Jewish Thought.* Translated and edited by Alfred Jospe. (Washington, 1961; New York, paperback 1963). Six excellent introductory essays on 20th century thinkers: Cohen, Kook, Buber, Rosenzweig, Magnes, and A. D. Gordon.

Blau, J. L., *The Story of Jewish Philosophy* (New York, 1962). A light, general treatment for the non-specialist.

Cohen, A. A., *The Natural and the Supernatural Jew: An Historical and Theological Introduction* (New York 1962; paperback 1964). An uneven though helpful study of modern Jewish thought since Mendelssohn.

Guttmann, Julius, *Philosophies of Judaism: The History of Jewish Philosophy from Biblical Times to Franz Rosenzweig.* Translated by David W. Silverman. (New York, 1964; paperback 1966). The classic work in the field, covering the whole of Jewish history until Rosenzweig; for serious students of the subject.

Husik, I., *A History of Medieval Jewish Philosophy* (New York, 1930). The standard history of medieval Jewish thought written in English. An excellent study.

Kaplan, M. M., *The Greater Judaism in the Making: A Study of the Modern Evolution of Judaism* (New York, 1960). Standard work for the medieval and early modern period with a valuable discussion of the modern period.

Rotenstreich, N., *Jewish Philosophy in Modern Times: From Mendelssohn to Rosenzweig.* (New York, 1968; translated from the Hebrew original, Tel Aviv, 1950).

Steinschneider, M., *Die hebraeischen Uebersetzungen des Mittelalters* (Berlin 1893). Standard work on Jewish philosophy for the medieval and early modern period.

Vajda, G., *Introduction à la pensée juive du moyen age* (Paris, 1947). An excellent introduction to medieval Jewish philosophy.

III. INDIVIDUAL PHILOSOPHERS.

Philo

An edition of Philo's writings in the original Greek with English translation has been published in the *Loeb Classical Library Series* (F. H. Colson and G. H. Whitaker, translators), 10 vols. (1929–62), with two supplementary volumes containing English translations of the writings preserved in Armenian (R. Marcus, trans.; 1953). Each volume contains an introduction. An English translation by H. Lewy of selections of Philo's writings is to be found in *Three Jewish Philosophers* (New York, 1960). For literature on Philo prior to 1937 an exhaustive list is given by H. L. Goodhart and E. R. Goodenough, "A general bibliography of Philo" in E. R. Goodenough, *The Politics of Philo Judaeus* (New Haven, 1938). For literature 1937–1962, see L. H. Feldman, *Scholarship on Philo and Josephus* (New York, 1963).

Belkin, S., *Philo and the Oral Law* (Cambridge (Mass.), 1940).

Goodenough, E. R., *Introduction to Philo Judaeus* (2nd edn.; Oxford, 1962).

Sandmel, S., *Philo's Place in Judaism* (New York, 1956).

Wolfson, H. A., *Philo, Foundations of Religious Philosophy in Judaism, Christianity and Islam* (2 vols.; Cambridge (Mass.), 1947).

Saadiah (Ben Joseph) Gaon

Saadiah Gaon, *The Book of Beliefs and Opinions.* Transl. by S. Rosenblatt (New Haven, 1948).

——, *Sifrei R. Saadia Gaon.* Edited by J. Derenbourg and M. Lambert. (5 vols.; Paris, 1849–1893).

Baron, S. W., (Ed.), *Saadiah Anniversary Volume* (New York, 1943). cf. pgs. 9–74. Also includes a bibliography compiled by A. Freimann.

Finkelstein, L., (Ed), *Rab Saadia Gaon, Studies in his Honor* (New York, 1944). Includes a selected bibliography by Boaz Cohen.

Heschel, A. J., "The Quest for Certainty in Saadia's Philosophy", in *JQR*, n.s. XXXIII (1942–43).

——, "Reason and Revelation in Saadiah's Philosophy", in *JQR* n.s. XXXIV (1944) pp. 391–408.

Malter, H., *Saadia Gaon, His Life and Works* (Philadelphia, 1921, 1970).

Neumark, D., "Saadya's Philosophy", in Neumark's *Essays in Jewish Philosophy* (Cincinnati, 1929), pp. 145–218.

Rosenthal, E. I. J., (Ed), *Saadya Studies* (Manchester, 1943). This volume contains a number of important studies by A. Altmann, A. Marmorstein, S. Rawidowicz, and E. Rosenthal, among others.

Isaac Israeli

Isaac Israeli, For the English translation of Israeli's work see A. Altmann and S. Stern, *Isaac Israeli, a neo-Platonic Philosopher* (Oxford, 1958).

Stern, S., in, *Oriens* 13–14 (1961), pgs. 58–120.

Ibn Gabirol

Ibn Gabirol, S., *The Fountain of Life.* A partial translation by H. E. Wedneck with an introduction by E. James (New York, 1962).

——, *The Improvement of the Moral Qualities.* Translated by S. S. Wise, and includes the Hebrew text. (New York, 1902).

——, *Selected Religious Poems.* Translated by I. Zangwill. Edited and with an introduction by I. Davidson (Philadelphia, 1930).

Heschel, A. J., "Der Begriff der Einheit in der Philosophie Gabirols", in *MGWJ*, LXXXII (1938) pgs. 89–111.

——, "Das Wesen der Dinge nach der Lehre Gabirols", in *HUCA*, XIV (1939) pgs. 359–385.

Marx, A., *HUCA*, 4 (1927) pgs. 433–448.

Rosin, D., "The Ethics of Solomon Ibn Gabirol", in *JQR* n.s. (1891) pgs. 159–181.

Bahya Ibn Paquda

Bahya ibn Paquda, *Sefer Torat Ḥovot ha-Levavot*. Edited by A. Zifroni (Jerusalem, 1928).

——, *Duties of the Heart*. English translation of *Ḥovot ha-Levavot*. Text and translation by M. Hyamson (Philadelphia, 1925). New translation by M. Mansoor (London, 1973).

Kaufmann, D., "Die Theologie des Bahja ibn Pakuda", in *Schriften*, 2 (1910) pgs. 1–98.

Vajda, G., *La theologie ascetique de Bahya ibn Paquda* (Paris, 1947).

Abraham Bar Ḥiyya

Bar Ḥiyya, A., *Hegyon ha-Nefesh ha-Aẓuvah*. Edited by Y. I. Freimann (Leipzig, 1860). English translation by G. Wigoder, *Meditation of the Sad Soul* (London, 1969).

Stitskin, L. D., *Judaism as a Philosophy: the Philosophy of Abraham bar Ḥiyya* (New York, 1960).

Judah Halevi

Judah Halevi, *Shirei Rabbi Yehudah Halevi*. Edited by S. Bernstein (New York, 1945). Popular edition with notes and an explanation.

——, *Selected poems of Jehudah Halevi*. Translated by N. Salaman (Philadelphia, 1924).

——, *Judah Halevi's Kitab al Khuzari*. English translation of *Sefer ha-Kuzari* by H. Hirschfeld (1905–6, 1931; repr. 1945; reprinted with an introduction by H. Slonimsky, 1964).

Baron, S., in *JSOS*, 3 (1941) pgs. 243–272.

Druck, D., *Yehuda Halevy: His Life and Works*. Translated by M. Z. R. Frank (New York, 1941).

Neumark, D., "Jehuda Halevi's Philosophy in its Principles", in *Hebrew Union College Catalogue* (Cincinnati, 1908) pgs. 1–91.

Strauss, L., "The Law of Reason in the Kuzari", in *PAAJR*, XIII (1943) pgs. 47–96.

Wolfson, H. A., "Halevi and Maimonides on Design, Chance and Necessity", in *PAAJR*, XI (1941) pgs. 105–163.

Wolfson, H. A., "Halevi and Maimonides on Prophecy", in *JQR* n.s., XXXII (1942) pgs. 345–370; *JQR*, XXXIII (1942) pgs. 49–82.

Ibn Daud

Ibn Daud, A., *Sefer Ha-Qabbalah* ("Book of Tradition"). Edited with English translation by G. D. Cohen (London, 1967).

——, *Sefer ha-Emunah ha-Ramah* ("The Exalted Faith"). Edited with German translation by Samson Weill (Frankfurt a. M., 1852; Hebrew text reprinted 1967).

Moses ben Maimon (Maimonides)

Maimonides, Moses, *The Guide of the Perplexed*. Translated with introduction and notes by S. Pines (Chicago, 1963). Also contains introduction by L. Strauss.

——, *Le Guide des Egares*. Edited by S. Munk (3 vols.: Paris, 1856–1866). Contains the Arabic text and a French translation.

——, *Moreh Nebukhim*, with vowel points and a commentary by Judah Even Shemuel (3 vols.; Tel-Aviv 1935–60).

——, *Iggeret Teman: Epistle to Yemen*. Edited with introduction and notes by Abraham Halkin. English translation by Boaz Cohen. (New York: American Academy for Jewish Research, 1952).

——, *Sefer ha-Mitzvot*. New Hebrew translation from the original Arabic published by Y. Kafaḥ (Jerusalem, 1958). An English version based on this translation was published by C. B. Chavel as *The Commandments: Sefer ha-Mitzvoth of Maimonides*, 2 vols. (London, 1967).

——, *Mishneh Torah, The Code of Maimonides*. An English translation of the entire *Code* started to appear in 1949 in the Yale Judaica Series: by 1973 eleven volumes had appeared.

——, *Shemonah Perakim*. Translated into English by J. L. Gorfinkle under the title, *The Eight Chapters of Maimonides on Ethics* (New York, 1912).

Baron, S. (Ed), *Essays on Maimonides: An Octocentennial Volume* (New York, 1941).

Epstein, I. (Ed), *Moses Maimonides: 1135–1204* (London, 1935). Contains essays by (among others) W. M. Feldman, S. Rawidowicz, E. Rosenthal, and includes a bibliography prepared by J. L. Gorfinkle.

Heschel, A. J., *Maimonides, Eine Biographie* (Berlin, 1935).

Twersky, I., *A Maimonides Reader* (New York, 1972). Contains a helpful introductory bibliography.

The following are important essays by H. A. Wolfson on Maimonides: Wolfson, H. A. in *JQR*, 1 (1911–12) pgs. 297–339; *JQR*, 25 (1934/35) pgs. 441–467; *JQR*, 26 (1935/36) pgs. 369–377; *JQR*, 32 (1941/42) pgs. 345–370; *JQR*, 33 (1942/43) pgs. 40–82; *PAAJR*, 11 (1941) pgs. 105–163; *Mordecai M. Kaplan Jubilee Volume* (New York, 1953) pgs. 515–530; "The Amphibolous Terms in Aristotle, Arabic Philosophy and Maimonides", in *Harvard Theological*

Review, XXXI (1938); "The Aristotelian Predicables and Maimonides' Division of the Attributes" in *Essays and Studies in Memory of Linda R. Miller* (New York, 1938) pgs. 201–234; "Maimonides on Negative Attributes" in *Louis Ginzberg Jubilee Volume* (New York, 1945) pgs. 411–446.

Maimonidean Controversy

Sarachek, I., *Faith and Reason. The Conflict over the Rationalism of Maimonides.* (Williamsport, 1935).

Silver, D. J., *Maimonidean Criticism and the Maimonidean Controversy,* 1180–1240. (Leiden, 1965) Bibliography pgs. 199–210.

Levi ben Gershom (Gersonides)

Levi ben Gershom, *Sefer Milḥamot Adonai* (Leipzig, 1866; reprint of the 1560 edition).

——, *Die Kampfe Gottes von Lewi ben Gerson,* 2 vols. (Berlin, 1914–16). A German translation of Parts 1–4 of *Sefer Milḥamot Adonai* by B. Kellerman, with notes.

Husik, I., "Studies in Gersonides", in *JQR* n.s. 8 (1917–18), pgs. 113–156; 231–268.

Wolfson, H. A., in *M. M. Kaplan Jubilee Volume* (New York, 1953) pgs. 515–530.

Crescas

Crescas, Ḥasdai, *Or Adonai* (Ferrara, 1555; Vienna 1859–60; Johannisburg, 1861). Two sections have been translated, one into English in H. A. Wolfson: *Crescas' Critique of Aristotle* (Cambridge (Mass.), 1929); and the other into German by P. Bloch: *Die Willensfreidheit von Chasdai Crescas* (Munich, 1879).

Waxman, M., *The Philosophy of Don Hasdai Crescas* (New York, 1920).

Wolfson, H. A., *Crescas' Critique of Aristotle* (Cambridge (Mass.), 1929). Includes bibliography.

Joseph Albo

Albo, Joseph, *Sefer ha-Ikkarim.* Edited with an English translation and introduction by I. Husik. (Jewish Publication Society: Philadelphia, 1946).

Isaac Abrabanel

Abrabanel, I., *Perush le-Moreh Nebukhim* (Vilna, 1904).

Netanyahu, B., *Don Isaac Abravanel* (Philadelphia, 1953).

Reines, A., *Maimonides and Abrabanel on Prophecy* (Cincinnati, 1970).

Trend, J. B., and Loewe, H. M., (Eds), *Isaac Abravanel: Six Lectures* (London, 1937). Collection of important articles.

Spinoza

Spinoza, *Opera.* Edited by C. Gebhardt. (4 vols.; Heidelberg, 1924). This is
the standard edition in the original Latin.

——, *The Chief Works of Spinoza.* Translated by R. H. M. Elwes. (2 vols.:
New York, 1955; paperback, New York, 1956).

All Spinoza's works have been translated into English in various editions and
translations although no complete and uniform edition of his works in English
translation exists. For the enormous literature on Spinoza, see Copleston's
History of Philosophy, vol. 4.

Moses Mendelssohn

Mendelssohn, M., *Gesammelte Schriften.* 7 vols. New edition by I. Elbogen,
E. Mittwoch and F. Bamberger (Berlin, 1939–1938). Uncompleted; work
has again begun on this edition by A. Altmann.

——, *Jerusalem and other Jewish Writings.* Translated by A. Jospe. (New
York, 1969).

Altmann, A., *Mendelssohn: A Biographical Study* (Alabama Univ. Press,
1973).

Barzilay, I. E., "Moses Mendelssohn: A Study in Ideas and Attitudes", in
JQR, 52 (1961) pgs. 69–93 and 175–186.

Meyer, M. A., *The Origins of the Modern Jew* (Detroit, 1967), pgs. 11–56.

Nachman Krochmal

Krochmal, Nachman, *Moreh Nevukhei ha-Zeman.* Critical edition by S.
Rawidowicz (Berlin, 1924; revised edition, 1961).

Schechter, S., *Studies in Judaism* (Philadelphia, 1896) pgs. 46–72.

Samson Raphael Hirsch

Hirsch, S. R., *Horeb: A Philosophy of Jewish Laws and Observances.* Translated by Isidor Gruenfeld (London: Soncino, 1962).

——, *Judaism Eternal: Selected Essays from the Writings of Samson Raphael
Hirsch.* Translated by Isidor Gruenfeld (London: Soncino, 1956).

——, *The Nineteen Letters of Ben Uziel: Being a Spiritual Presentation of
the Principles of Judaism.* Translated by Bernard Drachman (New York,
1899; reissued New York, 1969).

Grunfeld, I., *Three Generations: The Influence of Samson Raphael Hirsch
on Jewish Life and Thought* (London, 1958). Includes extensive bibliography.

Heinemann, I., *Ta'amei ha-Mitzvot be-Sifrut Yisrael,* 2 (Jerusalem, 1956)
pgs. 91–161.

Samuel Hirsch

Hirsch, S., *Die Religionsphilosophie der Juden* (Leipzig, 1842).

Fackenheim, Emil, "Samuel Hirsch and Hegel: A Study of Hirsch's *Religions-*

philosophie der Juden (1842)", in A. Altmann (Ed), *Studies in Nineteenth-Century Jewish Intellectual History* (Cambridge (Mass.), 1964) pgs. 171–201.

Samuel David Luzzatto

Luzzatto, S. D., *The Foundations of the Torah.* Printed in English translation in Noah H. Rosenbloom, *Luzzatto's Ethico-Psychological Interpretation of Judaism* (New York, 1965).

Moritz Lazarus

Lazarus, M., *Ethik des Judentums.* Translated into English by Henrietta Szold as *Ethics of Judaism.* (2 vols.; New York, 1900–1901).

Hermann Cohen

Cohen, H., *Judische Schriften* ("Writings on Judaism"). Edited by Bruno Strauss with an introduction by Franz Rosenzweig (3 vols.; Berlin, 1924).
——, *Religion of Reason from the Sources of Judaism.* English translation of *Religion der Vernunft.* (New York, 1971).
Altmann, A., "Hermann Cohens Begriff der Korrelation", in *In zwei Welten: Siegfried Moses zum 75. Geburtstag.,* edited by Hans Tramer. (Tel Aviv, 1962) pgs. 377–399.
Kaplan, M., *The Purpose and Meaning of Jewish Existence* (New York, 1964), pgs. 42–252.
Melber, J., *Hermann Cohen's Philosophy of Judaism* (New York, 1968).

Leo Baeck

Baeck, Leo, *The Essence of Judaism.* English translation by V. Grubenwieser and L. Pearl of *Das Wesen des Judentums,* the primary source for Baeck's view of Judaism. (Revised edition, New York, 1948; paperback, 1961).
——, *Judaism and Christianity.* Translated with an introduction by Walter Kaufmann (Philadelphia, 1964).
——, *This People Israel.* English translation of *Dieses Volk* (New York, 1965).
Friedlander, A. H., *Leo Baeck: Teacher of Theresienstadt* (New York, 1959).

Abraham Isaac Kook

Kook, A. I., *Rabbi Kook's Philosophy of Repentance.* English translation of *Orot ha-Teshuvah* (New York, 1968).
Agus, J. B., *Banner of Jerusalem* (New York, 1948).
Epstein, I., *Abraham Yitzhak Hacohen Kook: His Life and Times* (London, 1951).

Franz Rosenzweig

Rosenzweig, F., *Judaism Despite Christianity.* Edited by E. Rosenstock-Huessy with essays by A. Altmann and D. M. Emmett. Contains Rosenzweig's correspondence with Eugen Rosenstock-Huessy (New York, 1969).

——, *Understanding the Sick and the Healthy: A View of World, Man and God*. Edited and with an introduction by Nahum N. Glatzer. This is the English translation from the manuscript of *Das Buchlein vom gesunden und kranken Menschenverstand* (New York, 1953).

——, *On Jewish Learning*, edited by Nahum N. Glatzer. English translation of the three epistles: "Zeit ists", "Bildung und kein Ende", "Die Bauleute", and additional material (New York, 1955: Schocken paperback edition, 1965).

——, *The Star of Redemption*. English translation of *Der Stern der Erlosung*; translated by William Hallo from the second (1930) edition. (New York, 1971).

Glatzer, N. N., *Franz Rosenzweig, His Life and Thought* (New York, 1953: paperback, 1961). Includes bibliography.

Schwarzschild, S., *Franz Rosenzweig: Guide for Reversioners* (London, 1960).

Martin Buber

Buber, Martin, *At The Turning: Three Addresses on Judaism* (New York, 1952).

——, *Between Man and Man*. Translated by Ronald Gregor Smith (New York, 1948; paperback edition, 1965).

——, *Eclipse of God: Studies in the Relation between Religion and Philosophy* (New York, 1952; paperback edition, 1957).

——, *Hasidism and Modern Man*. Translated and edited by Maurice Friedman (New York, 1958); second volume of set is *Origin and Meaning of Hasidism*.

——, *I and Thou*. Translated by Walter Kaufmann (New York, 1970).

——, *Tales of the Hasidim*. Translated by Olga Marx (2 vols.: New York, 1947–48; paperback edition, 1961).

For a complete bibliography of Buber's writings see the bibliography in the *Philosophy of Martin Buber*, (ed) by P. Schilpp and M. Friedman (details below).

Friedman, M., *Martin Buber: The Life of Dialogue* (Chicago, 1955: New York, 1960).

Schilpp, P. and Friedman, M., (Eds), *The Philosophy of Martin Buber*, The Library of Living Philosophers, Vol. 12 (Illinois, 1967). Contains contributions by thirty authors and Buber's replies.

The volumes listed above are the most important secondary sources on Buber in English. There is, however, a very extensive bibliography of secondary literature on Martin Buber's thought and the reader should consult the Friedman and Schilpp volumes listed above for further details of these studies.

Mordecai Kaplan

Kaplan, M., *The Greater Judaism in the Making: A Study of the Modern Evolution of Judaism* (New York, 1960).

——, *Judaism as a Civilization: Toward a Reconstruction of American-Jewish Life* (New York: Schocken, 1967).

——, *The Meaning of God in Modern Jewish Religion* (New York, 1937).

——, *The Religion of Ethical Nationhood* (New York, 1970).

Berkovits, E., *Reconstructionist Theology: A Critical Evaluation* (New York, 1959). Reprinted from *Tradition,* vol. 2 (1959).

Eisenstein, I. and Kohn, E., (Eds), *Mordecai M. Kaplan: An Evaluation* (New York, 1957).

BIBLIOGRAPHY TO PART FOUR

Agus, Jacob B., *Banner of Jerusalem* (New York: Bloch, 1946).

——, *The Evolution of Jewish Thought: From Biblical Times to the Opening of the Modern Era* (New York: Abelard-Schuman, 1959).

——, *Guideposts in Modern Judaism: An Analysis of Current Trends in Jewish Thought* (NewYork: Bloch, 1954).

——, *The Meaning of Jewish History* (New York: Abelard-Schuman, 1963).

——, *Modern Philosophies of Judaism: A Study of Recent Jewish Philosophies·of Religion* (New York: Behrman House, 1941; paperback, 1970).

——, *The Vision and the Way* (New York: Ungar, 1966).

Belkin, Samuel, *In His Image: The Jewish Philosophy of Man as Expressed in Rabbinic Tradition* (London and New York: Abelard–Schuman, 1960).

——, *The Philosophy of Purpose*, Studies in Torah Judaism series, #1, (third edition, New York: Yeshiva University, 1958).

Bergman, Samuel H., *Faith and Reason: An Introduction to Modern Jewish Thought*, translated and edited by Alfred Jospe (Washington: B'nai B'rith Hillel Foundations, 1961; New York: Schocken, paperback edition, 1963).

Berkovits, Eliezer, "Faith and Law," *Judaism*, 13 (1964), pp. 422–430.

——, *God, Man and History* (New York: Jonathan David, 1959).

——, *A Jewish Critique of the Philosophy of Martin Buber* (New York: Yeshiva University, 1962).

——, *Prayer* (New York: Yeshiva University, 1962).

——, *Reconstructionist Theology: A Critical Evaluation* (New York: Jonathan David, 1959; reprinted from *Tradition*, Vol. 2, Fall 1959).

——, *Faith After the Holocaust* (New York: Ktav, 1973).

Borowitz, Eugene, *A New Jewish Theology in the Making* (Philadelphia: Westminster Press, 1968).

——, *How Can a Jew Speak of Faith Today?* (Philadelphia: Westminster Press, 1968).

——, "The Problem of the Form of a Jewish Theology," Hebrew Union College Annual, Vols. 40/41, Cincinnati, 1969–1970, pp. 391–408.

Cohen, Arthur A., ed., *Arguments and Doctrines: A Reader of Jewish Thinking in the Aftermath of the Holocaust* (Philadelphia: Jewish Publication Society and New York: Harper & Row, 1970).

——, *Martin Buber* (New York: Hillary House, 1957).

——, *The Myth of the Judeo-Christian Tradition* (New York: Harper & Row, 1969).

——, *The Natural and the Supernatural Jew: An Historical and Theological Introduction* (New York: Pantheon Books, 1962; paperback edition, New York: McGraw-Hill, 1964).

Cohon, Samuel S., *Jewish Theology* (New York: Humanities Press, 1971).

Fackenheim, Emil L., *God's Presence in History: Jewish Affirmations and Philosophical Reflections* (New York: New York University Press, 1970).

——, *Quest for Past and Future: Essays in Jewish Theology* (Bloomington: Indiana University Press, 1968).

——, *Encounters Between Judaism and Philosophy* (Philadelphia, Jewish Pub. Society, 1973).

Finkelstein, Louis, *The Beliefs and Practices of Judaism* (New York: Devin-Adair, 1952).

——, *The Jews,* two volumes (third edition, New York: Harper & Row; Philadelphia: Jewish Publication Society, 1960; New York: Schocken, 1970; three-volume paperback edition).

——, *Judaism as a System of Symbols* (New York: Jewish Theological Seminary, n.d.).

Gittelsohn, Roland, *The Meaning of Judaism* (New York: World, 1970).

——, *Man's Best Hope* (New York: Random House, 1961).

Gordis, Robert, *A Faith for Moderns* (New York: Bloch, 1960).

——, *Judaism for the Modern Age* (New York: Farrar, Straus & Cudahy, 1955).

——, *Judaism in a Christian World* (New York: McGraw-Hill, 1966).

——, *The Root and the Branch: Judaism and the Free Society* (Chicago: University of Chicago Press, 1962).

Herberg, Will, *Judaism and Modern Man: An Interpretation of Jewish Religion* (New York: Farrar, Straus and Cudahy, 1951; paperback edition, New York: Atheneum, 1970).

——, "Judaism as Personal Decision," in Alfred Jospe, ed., *Tradition and Contemporary Experience* (New York: Schocken-Hillel Books, 1970), pp. 77–90; also in *Conservative Judaism,* Vol. 22, # 4 (Summer) 1968.

——, *Protestant, Catholic, Jew,* second edition (Garden City: Doubleday Anchor Books, 1960, paperback edition).

Hertzberg, Arthur, *The Zionist Idea* (New York: Atheneum, 1969).

Heschel, Abraham, J., *Between God and Man: An Interpretation of Judaism from the Writings of Abraham J. Heschel,* selected, edited, and introduced by Fritz A. Rothschild (New York: Harper & Bros., 1959; New York: The Free Press-Macmillan, 1965, paperback edition).

——, *The Earth is the Lord's: The Inner Life of the Jew in East Europe* (New York: Henry Schuman, 1950). *The Earth is the Lord's and the Sabbath* (New York: Harper Torchbook, paperback edition).

——, *God in Search of Man: A Philosophy of Judaism* (New York: Farrar, Straus & Cudahy, 1956; Philadelphia: Jewish Publication Society, 1956; New York: Harper Torchbook, paperback edition).

——, *The Insecurity of Freedom: Essays in Applied Religion* (New York: Farrar, Straus & Giroux, 1965; Farrar, Straus, paperback edition).

——, *Israel: An Echo of Eternity* (New York: Farrar, Straus & Giroux, 1969; paperback edition).

——, *Man Is Not Alone: A Philosophy of Religion* (New York: Farrar, Straus, and Young, 1951; and Philadelphia: Jewish Publication Society, 1951; New York: Harper Torchbook, paperback edition).

——, *Man's Quest for God: Studies in Prayer and Symbolism* (New York: Scribners Sons, 1954; paperback edition).

——, "The Mystical Element in Judaism," in *The Jews: Their History, Culture and Religion*, edited by Louis Finkelstein (New York: Harper & Row; Philadelphia: Jewish Publication Society, 1949), pp. 602–623 (in Vol. I of the 2-volume edition, and in Vol. 2 of the 3-volume paper edition).

——, *The Prophets* (New York and Evanston: Harper & Row, 1962; Philadelphia: Jewish Publication Society, 1962; New York: Harper Torchbook in 2 vols., paperback edition).

——, *The Sabbath: Its Meaning for Modern Man* (New York: Farrar, Straus, and Young, 1951).

——, *Theology of Ancient Judaism* (Torah Min Ha-Shamayim Be-Aspaklaryah Shel Ha-Dorot) in Hebrew (London and New York: Soncino, Vol. I, 1962; Vol. II, 1965).

——, *Passion for Truth* (New York: Farrar, Straus & Giroux, 1973).

Jacobs, Louis, *Faith* (London: Vallentine, Mitchell, 1968).

——, *Principles of the Jewish Faith* (New York: Basic Books, 1964).

——, *We Have Reason to Believe*, third edition (London: Vallentine, Mitchell, 1965).

——, *A Jewish Theology* (Behrman House: New York, 1974).

Maybaum, Ignaz, *The Face of God After Auschwitz* (Amsterdam: Polak and Van Gennep, 1965).

——, *Trialogue Between A Jew, Christian and Moslem* (London: Routledge & Kegan Paul, 1973).

Miller, Alan W., *The God of Daniel S.* (New York: Macmillan, 1969).

Olan, Levi, "Rethinking the Liberal Faith", in *Reform Judaism* Cincinnati: Hebrew Union College Press, 1948.

——, "New Resources for a Liberal Faith", in *Yearbook of the Central Con-*

ference of American Rabbis (1962).

Petuchowski, Jakob J., Ever Since Sinai: A Modern View of Torah (New York: Scribe Publications, 1961).

——, Heirs to the Pharisees (New York: Basic Books, 1970).

——, Prayerbook Reform in Europe: The Liturgy of European Liberal and Reform Judaism (New York: World Union for Progressive Judaism, 1968).

Rubenstein, Richard L., After Auschwitz (Indianapolis: Bobbs-Merrill, 1966: also paperback edition).

——, Eros and Morality (New York: McGraw-Hill, 1970).

——, The Religious Imagination (Indianapolis: Bobbs-Merrill, 1968).

——, My Brother Paul (New York: Harper & Row, 1972).

Silver, Abba Hillel, Where Judaism Differed (Philadelphia: Jewish Publication Society, 1957: paperback edition, Schocken, New York, 1973).

Soloveitchik, Joseph B., "The Lonely Man of Faith," Tradition, Vol. 7, #2 (Summer 1965), pp. 5–67.

——, "Confrontation," Tradition, Vol. 6, #2 (Spring-Summer 1964), pp. 5–29.

——, "Ish Ha-Halakhah" in Talpiot (1944), pp. 651–735.

——, "Al Ahavat Ha-Torah v-Geulat Nefesh Ha-Dor" in Ha-Doar (vol. 39, No. 27), pp. 519–22.

Steinberg, Milton, Anatomy of a Faith, edited by Arthur Cohen (New York: Harcourt Brace, 1960).

——, Basic Judaism (New York: Harcourt Brace, 1947).

——, A Partisan Guide to the Jewish Problem (Indianapolis: Bobbs-Merrill, 1945).

Wolf, Arnold J., ed., Rediscovering Judaism: Reflection on a New Theology (Chicago: Quadrangle, 1965).

ILLUSTRATION CREDITS

Jerusalem, Jewish National and University Library, pp. 38, 109, 169
Cecil Roth Collection, p. 70
Photo Zev Radovan, Jerusalem, p. 87
New York, Daniel Friedenberg Collection, p. 161
Jerusalem, Israel Museum Photo Archives, p. 169
Jerusalem, Jewish National and University Library, Schwadron Collection, pp. 172, 183
Cincinnati, Ohio, American Jewish Archives, p. 180
Jerusalem Municipality Historical Archives, Photo Ben Dov, p. 183
Jerusalem, Hebrew University Public Relations Department, Photo W. Braun, p. 196
Photo Lotte Jacobi, Hillsboro, N.H., p. 214
Courtesy Mordecai Hacohen, p. 214
Photo Ashley and Crippen, Toronto, p. 238
Skokie, Ill., Hebrew Theological College, S. & G. Photographers, Inc., Chicago, p. 238

INDEX